THE WALL
DANCERS

THE WALL DANCERS

Searching for Freedom
and Connection on
the Chinese Internet

Yi-Ling Liu

Alfred A. Knopf
New York | 2026

A BORZOI BOOK
FIRST HARDCOVER EDITION
PUBLISHED BY ALFRED A. KNOPF 2026

Published by Alfred A. Knopf, a division of Penguin Random House LLC,
1745 Broadway, New York, NY 10019.

Knopf, Borzoi Books, and the colophon are registered trademarks of
Penguin Random House LLC.

Portions of this work have been previously published,
in different form, in *Guernica*, *The New York Times Magazine*,
The New York Review of Books, *The New Yorker*, *Rest of World*, and *WIRED*.

Library of Congress Cataloging-in-Publication Data
Names: Liu, Yi-Ling author
Title: The wall dancers : searching for freedom and
connection on the Chinese internet / Yi-Ling Liu.
Description: First hardcover edition. |
New York : Alfred A. Knopf, 2026. | Includes index.
Identifiers: LCCN 2025018333 |
ISBN 9780593491850 hardcover | ISBN 9780593491867 ebook
Subjects: LCSH: Internet—Government policy—China | Social media—
Government policy—China | Internet—Censorship—China | Social media—
Censorship—China | Information society—China | Freedom of speech—China |
Freedom of information—China | Firewalls (Computer security)—China
Classification: LCC HN740.Z9 I56784 2025 |
DDC 302.23/10951—dc23/eng/20250731
LC record available at https://lccn.loc.gov/2025018333

penguinrandomhouse.com | aaknopf.com

Printed in the United States of America
1st Printing

The authorized representative in the EU for product safety and compliance is
Penguin Random House Ireland, Morrison Chambers, 32 Nassau Street,
Dublin D02 YH68, Ireland, https://eu-contact.penguin.ie.

to my family

Contents

Part III

THE WALL
DANCERS

Introduction

On January 14, 2025, Chinese internet users awoke to find millions of Americans crossing into their corner of cyberspace. For decades, the Chinese internet had existed as an enclosed ecosystem, sealed off by the Great Firewall, China's vast and complex system of censorship and control. Inside the Firewall, sensitive words vanished, dissenters disappeared, and most global platforms like Google and Facebook were inaccessible. "To go online" in China meant something different than it did anywhere else. It was not only to speak a distinct language—one shaped by coded puns and cryptic memes—and to follow a distinct set of rules, enforced by an opaque web of algorithms and human censors. It was to inhabit a parallel online universe: to communicate on WeChat instead of WhatsApp, to query DeepSeek instead of ChatGPT, to scroll through Douyin instead of its sister app TikTok—two platforms conceived by the same company but split across two cyberspaces like twin siblings raised apart.

Yet on that January day, China's internet users discovered that a portal had opened in the walls of their web. As a TikTok ban loomed in the United States, American users migrated en masse to Xiaohongshu, a Chinese social media app popular among young women, who used the app to exchange tips on fashion and travel. For Chinese users, the irony was hard to miss. Long amused by Western fears of Chinese influence, they jokingly called themselves

"Chinese spies" and welcomed the newcomers with Mandarin lessons, interface tutorials, and tips for bypassing censorship (avoid politics, religion, and drugs). Americans, self-dubbed "TikTok refugees," in turn volunteered English tutoring and paid a "cat tax" (a cute photo of their cat). Chinese and new American users swapped jokes and flirty memes, compared work hours and grocery bills, and shared virtual tours of their hometowns, from Dalian to the Dakotas.

Scrolling through my Xiaohongshu newsfeed that day, I was delighted by the flurry of exchanges across what usually felt like an unbridgeable divide. As a Hong Kong–born journalist covering China for an American readership, I have long straddled these two digital ecosystems, the central fault line between them running deep through my psyche. In my years living in and reporting on the country, I watched this gulf deepen—between two internets, two worldviews, and two ways of thinking. On most days, I opened my Weibo newsfeed to a chorus of patriotic voices glorifying China's rise, only to then turn on my virtual private network, or VPN—the essential tool for Chinese people who wanted to scale the Firewall—and open Twitter to a torrent of angry tweets warning of a dire China threat. At a time when China and the rest of the world seemed further and further apart, it felt almost miraculous to watch these two communities come together. I was under no illusions that this gathering would last; Xiaohongshu had swiftly begun to hire English-language censors to control and cleanse their speech. But for a fleeting moment, the spirit of the early internet—open, exploratory, and filled with promise—was rekindled.

It's easy to forget that the story of the internet began as a romance, and perhaps nowhere else was its promise as great as it was in China. In the 1990s, in the wake of Deng Xiaoping's economic reforms, China was opening up to the world. Private enterprises flourished, state regulations over culture relaxed, and foreign ideas and innovations flowed freely into the country, from Coca-Cola to psychotherapy to rock 'n' roll. Amid all this, China embraced the revolutionary power of the internet: In 1994, researchers at the Chinese Academy of Sciences in Beijing built the first cable connection to the World Wide Web, opening the door to an entirely new realm. Just as the digital pioneers in the United States saw the internet as an "electronic frontier"—a vast and self-governing territory like the American West—early adopters in China saw the web through the image of the *jianghu,* or "Rivers and Lakes," a mythical world from martial arts lore filled with mystery, heroism, and adventure.

At the heart of the Chinese Communist Party plan to modernize China was technology. As Chinese citizens flocked to the web, the leadership realized that the internet served as a source of both innovation and instability, growth and subversion. Deng is widely claimed to have said, "If you open the window for fresh air, you have to expect flies to come in." In 1997, authorities started constructing an online censorship apparatus that became known as the Great Firewall, designed to control the flow of information while keeping some "flies" out.

Still, a bounded cyberspace did not mean a barren one. Within the Firewall, the Chinese internet burgeoned into a space of connection, opportunity, and freedom. By the turn of the millennium, a sleepy university suburb in northwest Beijing had transformed into a bustling hub for tech start-ups known as the Silicon Valley of China. Kai-Fu Lee, the president of Google China at the time, touted the liberatory potential of information technologies, pointing to *Super Girl,* China's version of *American Idol*—a television show where viewers vote for their favorite competitors via text messages—as a nascent form of grassroots democracy.

Growing up in Hong Kong and working as a high school intern in Beijing in 2010, I witnessed the flowering of blogs, message boards, and a vibrant online civil society. I saw how Weibo, a newly launched microblogging site, became a digital town square where millions of Chinese netizens could gather, debate ideas, and speak out. Across the globe, people praised social media as a force for democratic change. After all, Facebook and Twitter fueled grassroots movements from the Arab Spring to Occupy Wall Street, emboldening citizens to bypass censorship, amplify their voices, and mobilize against power. I believed the conventional wisdom of the time, that change was inevitable and that the internet would set

China, and the world, on a path toward liberalization. Any attempt to control its spread was like "trying to nail Jell-O to the wall," as Bill Clinton once said. "We know how much the internet has changed America . . . Imagine how much it could change China."

When I returned to Beijing almost a decade later, after graduating from college in 2017, I found that the internet had indeed changed China. The country was swept up in a mobile internet boom: Shared bikes proliferated on the streets, rural farmers livestreamed their lives to fame and fortune, and WeChat, which I once knew as simply a messaging app, had evolved into a digital Swiss Army knife, combining the functions of Facebook, PayPal, and Yelp into one. With a swipe of my phone, I ordered dinner and paid rent; I could hire a therapist and get my genes sequenced. Alibaba, the e-commerce giant, once run out of a sweaty-sock-filled apartment in Hangzhou, landed the largest initial public offering in global history; its founder, Jack Ma, once a college English lecturer, was now a national idol. Chinese cyberspace had evolved into an entirely separate ecosystem, a walled garden flowering with its own cultures and innovations.

At the same time, the smartphone did not bring emancipation. In 2013, the Party suppressed the burgeoning "Weibo Spring" by silencing the platform's vocal liberal influencers and cleansing the web of "negative energy." New red lines were drawn around permissible expression, prohibiting not only the explicitly political content that I knew from my high school days (like the "Three T's": Tibet, Tiananmen, and Taiwan) but anything deemed "vulgar" (from "unhealthy marital values" to "excessive flaunting of wealth" to tattoos). By the time I arrived in 2017, authorities had indeed found a way to nail Jell-O to the wall. The Great Firewall had expanded into a sprawling system of censorship, from powerful cyberspace regulators to rank-and-file content moderators. Above all, citizens had internalized a kind of psychic self-censorship, wary of crossing a line they could not see.

Today, the Party has reversed the past thirty years of liberalizing changes, reining in China's private sector, curtailing Chinese civil society, and closing the country off from the outside world.

The Covid pandemic accelerated these developments, allowing the state to restrict public gatherings, close China's borders, and deploy surveillance technologies to monitor citizen movement in the name of public health. Even the nation's once-beloved tech entrepreneurs were not spared from the Party's intensifying control: In 2021, the government launched a sweeping crackdown on China's tech companies to curb what they called "the disorderly expansion of capital"—a broad accusation targeting everything from monopolistic practices to video games. In 2023, the Ministry of State Security created its first social media account, urging its citizens to mobilize against espionage, root out spies, and guard against perceived threats to the nation.

Just as the romance of the Chinese internet has waned, so has the fantasy of a free and open World Wide Web. The Arab Spring failed as regimes repurposed the internet into a tool of repression; Edward Snowden's revelations of surveillance by the US National Security Agency exposed governments' capacity for mass surveillance. Once hailed as a harbinger of free speech, Weibo is now derided by the Chinese intellectual Guo Yuhua as a "maggot-infested pile of shit," overrun with illiberal incels and patriotic trolls. Likewise, Twitter— renamed X—has shifted from what American journalist David Carr once praised as a "throbbing networked intelligence" to a widely condemned "hellsite," shaped by its mercurial new owner, who happens to be one of the world's most powerful men. The conventional wisdom had shifted: The internet was a force not of liberalization but of authoritarian control. The expansive frontier and the free-spirited *jianghu* that we once imagined had splintered into competing fiefdoms. The honeymoon was over.

· · ·

Outsiders have long reduced China to simplistic narratives at opposite extremes: China is at once an unstoppable economic juggernaut of boundless opportunity and an omnipotent, techno-authoritarian regime of repression. In English-language media, news on China is increasingly filtered through the lens of US national security interests, where China is often named the "biggest threat" to the

United States. On bookshelves, such titles as *When China Rules the World* sit beside books on *The Coming Collapse of China*. In a scroll through my newsfeed, analyses of "China's Two Paths to Global Domination" follow an article headlined THE "GREAT FALL OF CHINA"? CHINA "HAS NEVER BEEN WEAKER THAN IT IS TODAY." In the first China, anything is possible; in the second, the window of change is closed and locked. It follows, then, that a Chinese person can have only one of two identities: an apologist of the regime or a dissident, its beneficiary or its victim, a patriot or a traitor.

These narratives present an unchanging monolith, stripping individuals of their agency and failing to capture the society that I lived in, in all its dynamism and contradiction. Rich with innovation and yet rigidly constrained, life in China was filled with fear and ennui but also creativity and potential. Hip-hop music went viral there and soared to mainstream popularity within a month, then got banned by authorities the next; a gay dating app was shut down one year, while another went public a couple years later.

Anyone wishing to navigate this shifting terrain needed to remain agile and nimble. Those who tried to do so played with language itself. In my years of reporting in and out of the country, people have introduced me to an array of different metaphors to capture this unstable experience. Artists who tiptoed around the capricious line of the censor described the process as "a game of cat and mouse." Entrepreneurs compared the experience of predicting the state's limits on their actions as akin to divining the weather: hazy, fickle, and shifting without warning. Bloggers who wanted to pen provocative posts used the table tennis term "playing boundary ball"—serving a hit at the edge of the opponent's table while staying safely within bounds.

The metaphor I found most apt and most enduring was that of the "dance in shackles." As far as I could tell, its first use came in the early 2000s by Chinese journalists describing what they could achieve under state constraints on their writing and reporting. Since then, I have seen the phrase used everywhere, by software engineers and musicians alike. "In China, every enterprise and individual has to dance with shackles on," one tech executive wrote in a viral blog post, chastising Google's withdrawal from the Chinese market in 2010. "Every era puts invisible shackles on those who have lived through it," the writer Liu Cixin wrote in the afterword of the English-language edition of his science fiction epic *The Three-Body Problem*. "And I can only dance in my chains." "Dancing in Shackles" was the title of a song by beloved Chinese indie rock band Miserable Faith, a shape-shifter of the Beijing music scene.

My reporting, both for this book and for stories I pursued before undertaking it, affirmed the power of this metaphor. To live in China is to participate in a dance: a dynamic push and pull between state and society. Censor and censored tango to an erratic rhythm of subversion and acquiescence. Artists act as both critics and collaborators of the state. Authorities and entrepreneurs find themselves at times in hostile confrontation and at other times entangled in mutual embrace. Nowhere has the drama of this Chinese dance been more evident than on its internet.

This book is about that dance, which has evolved over the past three decades, a period that encapsulates China's transformation into both the world's largest online user base and one of its longest-running authoritarian states. It begins in 1995, in the heady days of China's opening, when ordinary Chinese people first logged on to the internet, swept up by its liberatory potential. It follows the flowering of China's mobile internet in the 2010s, as Chinese cyberspace transformed into a walled garden—on one hand, blooming with new innovations and subcultures, and on the other, increasingly constrained and segregated from the global web. It ends in the wake of the pandemic, as China tightens control of the public sphere, closes its physical and virtual borders, and turns inward, away from the world.

This shift from liberalization toward retrenchment is not new: For much of modern Chinese history, society has moved in cycles of what scholars have observed as *fang* and *shou*, opening and tightening. The repressive era of Mao's Cultural Revolution preceded a period of pragmatic loosening; the freewheeling reforms of the 1980s were followed by the Tiananmen crackdown. When the system opens up too quickly, destabilizing state power, authorities step in to assert control; when their grip becomes too rigid, calls for reform emerge, provoking a loosening again. But this time, this shift takes place amid a global technological turn—from the early promise of a free and open World Wide Web to one that has become closed, siloed, and commoditized.

Most crucially, this book is told through the stories of people I have come to call dancers: individuals pushing for greater openness and freedom within the state's shifting bounds on the Chinese internet and, more broadly, in Chinese public life. How has China's embrace of the internet both unleashed and also suppressed their dreams and aspirations as entrepreneurial, intellectual, and creative beings? Faced with the encroachment of authority on both their offline and online lives, how have they continued to navigate a dance between confrontation and compromise to challenge the status quo?

Although their backgrounds and worldviews are diverse, their stories are united by their struggles and dreams and disappointments. In spotlighting the book's protagonists, I turned my attention to the margins, the underground, the subaltern, where I believed the most creative, imaginative dances bloomed: queer communities, feminist activist groups, the hip-hop underground, and science fiction writing circles. There is Ma Baoli, once a closeted cop from Northern China running an underground gay website, who transforms into an openly gay tech mogul, steering the largest gay social networking app through precarious political terrain. Kafe Hu, an aspiring rapper from Sichuan, who learns to toe the line of the provocative and permissible to articulate a voice of his own. Lü Pin, a journalist turned activist, who taps into a nationwide feminist awakening and builds a grassroots movement across China and its diaspora. Chen Qiufan, a tech worker turned science fiction writer, who—fascinated by and skeptical of the nation's rapid technological rise—strives to imagine alternative visions of the future.

Although they live and work on the margins, they know how to operate in the mainstream. They are idealistic and pragmatic, wear many hats, speak several tongues. They have come to understand that survival in the system requires adaptability, creativity, and the ability to identify leverage points—situations when a right push with just-so timing and force can open possibilities for change. Having lived through a period of both unprecedented economic opening and tightening political control, each has undergone immense personal transformation and, in that process, has been forced to grapple with questions about success and authenticity, love and solidarity, faith and survival. How will Ma harness the mobile internet to help millions of other queer Chinese love more freely? How will Lü sustain the feminist movement, and what must she sacrifice in the name of her beliefs?

Brought together, their stories show that even in increasingly repressive conditions, within the most sophisticated systems of control, individuals continue to push for dignity and freedom. When headlines warn of a bifurcated internet, these divisions extend down to the intimate and the individual, each crack in cyberspace running deep into flesh and bone. Changing the system, their stories reveal, begins with changing the self.

. . .

I am also a dancer. My dance began when I was fifteen. I grew up in Hong Kong, a haven of free speech at the doorstep of the mainland, on the fault lines of two political systems. I was born just before the handover in 1997, when the city, once a British colony, was returned to China. Under the "One Country, Two Systems" agreement, Hong Kong would become part of China but retain its unique civil liberties: an independent judiciary, the right to assembly, and freedom of expression.

The international school I attended was similarly bicultural: We learned both English and Putonghua, celebrated Christmas and Chinese New Year, studied Dickens and Lu Xun. We studied the history of our own city with a critical detachment afforded to students who belonged everywhere and nowhere. The mid-nineteenth-century Opium Wars were a result of aggressive British expansionism as well as the failures of corrupt Qing dynasty rule. Mao was both a capable leader who unified the peasantry and a ruthless tyrant who enabled the brutal excesses of the Great Leap Forward. I learned about the 1989 Tiananmen Square protests during a documentary screening in English class, watching history unfold before me as a montage projected on the classroom wall: the upheaval of the free-wheeling eighties; the students with their raw, wide-eyed idealism; the row of tanks that drove into the city one night; and the soldiers opening fire.

The summer after that screening, I did an internship at a state-run publication in Beijing. After drafting an article about literary magazines in Hong Kong, I received feedback from my editor asking me to remove all references to the Tiananmen protests, which were forbidden in print. I was not surprised: To write within the system was to subject oneself to censorship. But I was at once indignant and intrigued. It was the first time I'd felt the censor's red pen strike my words, and it sparked questions I've continued to wrestle with ever since: How is it possible to write within the constraints of the Great Firewall? What does it mean to "live within the truth," as Václav Havel once wrote of his life under Soviet rule, within the bounds of an authoritarian state?

Over the next decade, I looked for answers. In high school, I began to learn more about June 4th, struggling to make sense of a history I was too young to bear witness to. I studied the rival student groups and their dance between moderate compromise and radical confrontation. I read about the shaky tango within the Party itself, between reformers like Zhao Ziyang, who wanted to engage in dialogue with the students, and hard-liners like Li Peng, who pushed for martial law and crackdown.

In college in the United States, I studied democracies (what birthed and sustained them?) and autocracies (why did some change while others remained stubbornly in place?). I learned of the fledgling power of the internet to embolden people to speak out, to remember, and to bring communities together. I attended the June 4th vigil in Hong Kong's Victoria Park summer after summer, standing among sweaty strangers, clutching a small wax candle in a paper cone, to mourn the lives that I would never know. After graduating from college, I returned to Beijing to live and write, because I still wanted to know—not just what could've been changed at the square that day but also what could be changed today and who had the power to do the changing.

I pursued the stories of the people I met in reporting this book because I wanted to learn from them and because we shared a set of personal stakes. I approached the hip-hop artists as I was trying to figure out my place as an artist, evading the gaze of authority. I sought out the queer community as I was coming to terms with whether I could love openly in the city I called home. I reached out to the feminist activists at the height of the pandemic because I wanted to understand what solidarity could look like under lockdown and isolation. I followed tech workers and blue-collar workers as we were both rejecting the mythologies of the marketplace.

Woven into their stories is my own; as I followed their paths, I hoped to find my way, too. I have encountered countless dancers over the years, but only a handful have so generously shared their stories with me, from beginning to end, even when the political climate chilled and the risks of speaking out became at once more numerous. When I have wielded a scalpel over my own words, it has only been to preserve their safety and the communities they care for. It pains me to say that, throughout the process of writing this book, I've learned to become my own self-censor. But I'd rather dance in shackles than not dance at all.

·   ·   ·

To understand China today and where it'll go tomorrow, we must learn to read the Chinese internet: what goes viral and what disappears just as swiftly, how it shapes and is shaped by the outside world, and how it is controlled from the top down and mobilized from the bottom up. Social media feeds allow us to gauge public opinion when other forms of polling are inaccessible. Censorship directives often give us a better grasp of the Party's fears and aspirations than any official communiqué. Viral memes reveal sharper diagnoses of popular sentiment than a think tank analysis. There are over twice as many Chinese web users as there are people in the United States; if Chinese netizens formed a sovereign country, it would be the world's third largest. American "TikTok refugees" who migrated to Xiaohongshu were shocked by the dynamism they found on the other side of the Great Firewall. After all, few had ever set foot upon this online terrain; until then, they knew little about the texture of its landscape and the lives of its inhabitants.

As China's influence expands beyond its borders, the boundaries of the Chinese internet have become increasingly blurred. Shenzhen-based Transsion serves as Africa's largest mobile phone supplier, and Shein, now the biggest fashion retailer in the world, influences clothing trends in Los Angeles. Xiaohongshu, popular among the Chinese diaspora, shapes culinary tastes in Düsseldorf and tourism trends in Laos. Sichuanese vlogger Li Ziqi was lauded by *The New York Times* as the global web's "Quarantine Queen"; the viral ethos of "lying flat" is now part of the lexicon of burned-out millennials the world over. Douban dissidents migrate to Reddit; Weibo lingo goes viral on Twitter; Douyin videos travel to TikTok. In 2023, I took on a role as the China editor at *Rest of World,* an international news publication covering technology outside the West. The reach of the Chinese web was so significant that we had to create a separate beat dubbed "China Outside China," encouraging all correspondents to cover the story regardless of whether they were based in Lagos or Mexico City. From Foxconn workers in Chennai to TikTok livestreamers in Jakarta, many more people were learning to navigate the Chinese web, too.

In tracing the evolution of the Chinese internet—from its lexicon to its influencers to its platforms—and its role in real Chinese lives, I hope to equip readers with this crucial lens. What can the rise and fall of a gay dating app reveal about the undulous relationship between the state and its entrepreneurs? What can a bunny emoji tell us about the limits and possibilities of transnational activism? How is Chinese nationalism shaped by the online alt-right as much as it is by a resurgent Maoist left? How did a British pop psychologist come up with the Chinese Communist Party's most powerful tool of online propaganda?

Reading the Chinese internet requires rigor and nuance, empathy and skepticism. And now, more than ever, we need better readers. The number of foreign students studying in China has plummeted:

In 2023, seven hundred Americans studied in Mainland China, down from fifteen thousand a decade earlier. Twitter commentary is a cesspool of pseudo analysts who have never set foot in the country, drowning out voices of true expertise and reason. Even the most reputable newspapers publish sweeping op-eds, a genre of twenty-first-century Orientalism, in an attempt to demystify a nation of one billion. One such article, published in February 2020, during the onset of the pandemic in *The Wall Street Journal,* titled "China Is the Real Sick Man of Asia," sparked a vicious media conflict between the Chinese and US governments that resulted in the expulsion of many foreign correspondents from China. For those who remain, it has become nearly impossible to get anyone to speak openly—not only for fear of government repercussion but also because of the very real likelihood that their words will be misconstrued by an ignorant readership.

We misunderstand China to our own detriment. The questions Chinese netizens have asked themselves for years are becoming questions many more of us must ask today. Just as NBA players equivocate on whether to curb their online speech to reach a Chinese fan base, Hollywood studios debate whether to cut a scene in order to profit from a Chinese viewership. The TikTok ban is this debate writ large: In 2024, as the Biden administration moved to ban TikTok, the Biden campaign avidly used the Beijing-born platform to reach out to young voters. A platform once praised as a divinatory meme machine used by more than half the US population is now also seen as a geopolitical Trojan horse, enabling the Chinese Communist Party to steal data and brainwash children. The irony of American TikTok refugees flooding Xiaohongshu in 2025 underscored a deeper reality: that the US internet had become much more like China's, not the other way around. "In trying to 'protect' Americans from China, our gripped-by-moral-panic political class has made us just like China. The government has decided that the only way to combat China's techno-authoritarian censorship model is to emulate it," wrote the American blogger Mike Masnick. American alarm at Chinese influence has begun sounding like China's own rhetoric: In August 2020, Secretary of State Mike Pompeo urged the United States and its allies to develop a "clean fortress" around its internet—in other words, to build a Great Firewall of its own.

Most crucially, through the stories of China's dancers, we might better understand the shackles within which all of us must dance now in our own lives. The Chinese internet is shaped by forces not unique to China but present in autocracies and democracies alike: the amplification of illiberal voices, the contraction of the public sphere, the erosion of common sense. Today, both autocrats and oligarchic CEOs have taken over the once-open space of the web, monitoring our private lives, ensnaring us in an endless feed, and extracting our attention for influence and profit. As I write, Silicon Valley's attention moguls work alongside the ascendant Trump administration, centralizing power in their hands beyond democratic oversight. We find ourselves fettered by the very technologies that once promised to liberate us; they shape our behavior in ways we ourselves cannot even see, dictating what we choose to click and consume, to pay attention to and ignore, to say and not say. The imperative for us to "live within the truth"—authentically and with greater human agency in the face of manipulative systems—has become more urgent than ever before.

Part I

CHAPTER 1

Coming Out

Qinhuangdao, Hebei, 1995

When Ma Baoli felt that he could no longer contain his secret, he would go to the beach. He'd walk out of the squat police bureau building, where he worked as an officer, across the train tracks that cut through downtown Qinhuangdao, straight down the sandy path to the sea. The police bureau was his home, but the sea was his refuge. Standing alone on the stretch of golden sand, watching the tides come and go in silence, he'd calm down. His secret was safe with the sea.

Ma grew up in Qinhuangdao in the eighties, when the city was just a quiet port town where container ships picked up coal and timber, a passing point between Beijing and China's northern hinterlands. As a child, he was raised in a working-class household with modest means but was happy; his father was a factory worker at the local distillery, and his mother took care of him as a housewife. The three of them shared a courtyard home with two other families and had everything they needed. If it became cold in the winter, they lit the stove under their large wooden *kang;* if they got bored, they passed the time chatting with their neighbors in the courtyard.

The Mas were proud of their son, who enrolled in the all-boys Qinhuangdao police academy when he was sixteen and was training to become a great officer one day. As a student, Ma was hardworking and diligent, quickly commanding the respect of his peers. He kept his hair short and neatly trimmed, spoke with a voice that was gentle but authoritative, and smiled with his brows slightly furrowed. He aced his classes—not only math and physics but specialized police courses like constitutional law and criminal investigations. Outside of class, he managed the school paper and ran the campus radio station, playing cassette tapes of the latest pop hits. He loved the academy, its rules and routines, and the students' easy camaraderie. Every morning before sunrise, they gathered by the courtyard and jogged to the beach to complete their daily sprints and wrestling exercises by the sea. Every evening, they slept together in dorms, eight to a room, huddled together for warmth in winter. The world was simple. His ideals were clear: Learn how to be a good cop, enforce the law, keep the city in order.

When he turned seventeen, a secret began to take root and bloom inside him, quietly and unannounced. While his classmates boasted about girls they wanted to date, he nursed crushes on boys. He became infatuated with his best friend—a playful, mischievous student from the Hebei countryside. The two spent all their time together—during their morning exercises, at meals, after class—and, sometimes at night, shared the same bed. "We'll issue you two a marriage certificate after we graduate," their classmates joked. During the holidays, they exchanged long letters. Few households had their own phone then, so if Ma was desperate, he used the convenience store phone booth and called the number of his friend's neighborhood committee, the only phone in his village. That feeling of anticipation—receiver pressed to his ear, lightheaded with pleasure, waiting to hear his friend's voice—was delicious and disorienting, like tasting ice cream for the first time.

"What's going on between us? What do you think our relationship is?" Ma blurted out anxiously during one of their conversations.

"Do you think we're homosexual?" his friend responded.

"No, we're not," Ma said. "Of course not."

The first time Ma encountered the word "homosexual," or *tongxinglian*, was in one of his school textbooks, entitled *Criminal Psychology*. The book dedicated an entire page to "sexual deviancy" and explained how men who desired other men were more likely to commit crimes. At the time, homosexuality was still prosecuted as "hooliganism," a vague descriptor that encompassed crimes like "humiliating women" and "stirring up a crowd to create brawls." As a small-town boy, Ma did not know this, but in larger cities, police routinely raided cruising spots; in Beijing, one man—dubbed "Lady Paris" for his dalliances with a Parisian chef at the French embassy—was arrested at a popular spot on the east side of Tiananmen Square and sent to a labor camp for two years.

Homosexuality was then also officially classified as a mental disorder. Across the country, clinics offered pills, injections, and electroshock treatments as forms of "conversion therapy." Desperate parents sent their gay sons and daughters to psychiatric institutions in hopes that their "illness" might be cured. Doctors told their gay patients that if they did not change, they would get sick and bring shame to their families. Deep-seated Confucian values—an unshakable emphasis on having a respectable marriage, giving birth to sons, and honoring one's elders—meant that the family was one of the most intense places of discrimination. To not bear offspring, a popular proverb declared, was the greatest act of disrespect toward one's ancestors.

Ma was terrified of being found out. As far as he understood, the textbooks were right, and his feelings were deviant and perverted. The secret grew like a tumor in his chest, threatening to overtake the order of his life. After graduation, he would go to the hospital to fix himself, he thought. For now, he would keep his secret to himself and the sea.

· · ·

One night in 1998, Ma stopped by a new internet café that had opened next to the police bureau. He had graduated two years before and started working as a police officer, first in the investigations department, then writing speeches, strategy documents, and public announcements for the police chief.

The first internet cafés had recently arrived in Qinhuangdao, and everyone was flocking to these cramped, computer-filled establishments to get a taste of the online realm. In 1995, after China's first private internet service provider, China Infohighway Communications, gave ordinary users access to the web, China was swept up by an internet fever. Computer companies sold hardware from street stalls and department stores; roadside billboards advertised Acer and Microsoft. Internet start-ups proliferated, launching China's first search engine, instant-messaging platform, and popular email service, 163.net. The number of internet users doubled every six months. People waited in line to visit China's first internet café, Sparkice, in Beijing's Haidian district, paying 20 yuan per hour—to spend a whole day would cost nearly the average monthly income at the time—to surf the web. As these cafés sprouted across the country, news reports insisted that the traditional greeting of "Have you eaten?" was being replaced with "Have you logged on?" Ma wanted to see what all the hype was about.

The café was a small, dim room, sandwiched into an alleyway, lit by two rows of desktops with buzzing screens. Ma picked a computer and searched *tongxinglian*—homosexual. First, he scrolled through what he expected to find: a messy jumble of advertisements promoting electroshock therapy clinics and conversion medication. Then he stumbled upon a discussion forum entitled "Chinese Men's and Boy's Paradise," which featured a link to an online novel called *Beijing Story.* The novel was penned by an author who went by the pseudonym Beijing Comrade. Ma clicked on the link.

The story's protagonist, Lan Yu, a poor architecture student, moves from China's far-flung west to Beijing in 1988. Enter Han Dong, spoiled princeling and rakish businessman, who squanders his money on houses and lovers. They meet for the first time and have sex. Han Dong tries to pay Lan Yu off with 3,000 yuan, Lan Yu rejects his money, and their first encounter evolves into a tumultuous romance.

Ma devoured the passages, heart racing. He'd never read anything like this before—so cruel and tragic and yet so brazenly sensual, another man's body described with the language of appetite and desire. The novel reached its emotional climax at a moment of tragedy and reckoning; after Lan Yu narrowly survives the crackdown at Tiananmen Square, he finally accepts his love for Han Dong:

"Having just escaped death, we began to feel each other. We tried to confirm with our bodies that we were still alive. I caressed his skin with my face: it was warm; it was alive; he was still in my *life*."

By the time Ma finished reading, the sun had risen. Hunched in front of the computer, he broke down in tears, crying so intensely that a young woman in the seat next to him checked in on him.

"All good, brother?" she asked. "What are you reading that's such a downer? Can I read it, too?"

He shook his head, switched off his screen, and hurried out of the café, face shiny with tears. It was a revelation, a catharsis, knowing that there were people who shared his secret, who felt the way he did. "It felt like I'd opened up a new world," he would later say, "a world where such a beautiful love between two men could exist."

The internet café became Ma's new refuge. Online, he stumbled upon a world where he belonged. He joined gay chat rooms, befriending other gay men seeking kinship and connection. He found gay film and television shows, such as *Dosokai,* a Japanese series about a gay man trapped in a marriage to a woman, and *East Palace, West Palace,* a Chinese film about a gay man arrested in a popular cruising spot in Beijing. Eventually, Ma bought his own computer and a clunky dial-up modem to access the internet. During his lunch breaks, he would lock the door of his office and watch every gay film he could get his hands on, sobbing over his takeout noodles. The Chinese films almost always ended in tragedy—gay men being disowned by their families, detained by authorities, dying in car crashes—but he still saw hope in their love. He was no longer alone.

. . .

Drive twenty minutes from Ma's seaside refuge down the length of the Qinhuangdao coast, and you will arrive at Beidaihe Beach. Everything about this place, a popular summer vacation spot for local and foreign visitors alike, feels incongruous: A dumpling shack serves lunch next to an Austrian bakery; buildings feature kitschy Tudor gables and Habsburg-style domes; rental bikes pedal past black Audis with tinted windows. *The New York Times* once described Beidaihe as "a Chinese combination of Jersey Shore and Martha's Vineyard, with a pinch of red fervor." On the public beaches, shirtless tourists eat garlic prawns off paper plates; in the private enclaves of luxury villas, tucked among the evergreens, the Communist Party elite gather each summer to decide on the future of the nation.

Nicknamed the "Summer Capital," Beidaihe has long been the retreat for the Party's top echelons. In 1958, it was at Beidaihe that Mao, an avid swimmer who spent his spare time in black trunks wading in the sea, dictated the blueprint for the Great Leap Forward, a social experiment that instead led to the deaths of tens of millions of people by famine. After Mao died, in 1976, leaving China impoverished and rudderless, Beidaihe became the forum to discuss conflicting views on the nation's path ahead.

Under the leadership of Deng Xiaoping, in 1978, China introduced the Reform and Opening policy: loosening the planned economy from state control and opening China's doors to the world. While Party members agreed on the country's urgent need to modernize, they disagreed on how far and how fast. Opening the door to foreign technology, such as Boeing aircraft and IBM computers, enabled the country to catch up with the West but also let in other forms of unwelcome Western influences—"spiritual pollution," as the Party liked to call it, which included everything from pornography to detective thrillers. Without a clear road map to reform, Deng followed an improvisational philosophy he often referred to as "crossing the river by feeling the stones."

But after the brutal Tiananmen Square crackdown in 1989, thousands of protesters who took to the square demanding democratic reform were shot to death, arrested, or driven underground. Reforms came to a sudden, tragic halt. Reeling from the crisis, the Party faced a dilemma: Meet the growing demands of the Chinese people, emboldened by reform and desiring more freedom, or appease the unyielding grip of Party hard-liners, who believed that tightened control was crucial to preserving order. The Party's sense of crisis was compounded by the fall of the Soviet Union in 1991.

They had to do whatever was necessary to avoid repeating the missteps of what they believed to be Mikhail Gorbachev's failed and chaotic perestroika.

Deng's solution was to play it both ways: Hold tight to the reins of political authority but accelerate market reforms. In 1992, he traveled south by train, starting in Wuhan and stopping by Shenzhen and Shanghai, in a monthlong journey that would be immortalized as the "Southern Tour." He visited technology companies and stock exchanges, encouraging local officials to push for growth and attract foreign investment and calling upon ordinary Chinese people to engage in private business. He championed the "East Asian Tigers"—the booming economies of Hong Kong, Singapore, South Korea, and Taiwan—as models of prosperous governance. The government, Deng said, "must not act like women with bound feet" but, rather, "should dare to experiment and break a new path." His message was clear: The Party would stay firmly in control, but China's doors would remain open.

By the time Ma Baoli was nursing schoolboy crushes at the police academy two years later, market reforms were in full gear—overnight, it seemed to many, like a nation of communes and Mao jackets transformed into a land of Gucci-wearing, Pepsi-drinking businessmen.

As the economy liberalized, so did attitudes toward everything else—not only education and business and enterprise but also sex and love. Economic revolution fertilized a sexual renaissance; the nation's libido, bottled up for decades, burst loose. Prostitution skyrocketed, trashy romances flooded bookstore shelves, and porn—once seen as a symbol of a depraved capitalist way of life—proliferated. The percentage of Chinese people having premarital sex soared from 15 percent in 1989 to 70 percent more than a decade later, according to the surveys of Li Yinhe, a prominent Chinese sociologist. A call-in sex education radio show called *Midnight Whispers* taught young people the secrets to lust and love; a wildly popular soap opera called *Yearnings* told a melodramatic tale of loves found and lost, devoid of Mao-era political dogma. In 1993, China's first legal sex shop, Adam & Eve Health-Care Center, opened in Beijing.

Free from the bonds of Maoist prudishness, young people began to embrace desires they'd never before imagined: extramarital affairs, premarital sex, passionate love over familial obligation, and, of course, queer desire. If they couldn't choose their leaders, the people realized, at least they could choose their lovers.

. . .

Historically, Chinese society neither recognized nor shunned same-sex intimacy. Chinese religious traditions, such as Buddhism and Confucianism, did not overtly condemn homosexuality, which meant that cultural attitudes were more malleable than in other Asian countries, such as Indonesia or the Philippines. Nor was queerness considered by authorities to be a decadent Western import; on the contrary, it was widespread in Chinese history and culture. One of China's literary masterpieces, *Dream of the Red Chamber,* an eighteenth-century novel, is filled with same-sex relationships. A term still used today to refer to gay relationships—*duan xiu,* or "cut sleeve"—comes from a story in *The Book of Han,* from the second century, in which the emperor wakes from his nap to find his male lover still asleep on the sleeve of his robe, and cuts off his sleeve to avoid waking him. Another term once used to describe lesbian sex— *mojingzi,* or "rubbing mirrors"—christened the nineteenth-century Shanghai lesbian association Mojing Dang, or "Rubbing Mirrors Party."

It was only when China began to turn toward Western science and technology in the late nineteenth century, after its humiliating defeat in the Opium Wars, that it also absorbed the West's pathological view of homosexuality as an illness. After the Communist victory in 1949, arguably the most sexually repressive period in Chinese history, homosexual behavior became grounds for persecution, with punishment ranging from forced labor to imprisonment.

After the enactment of Deng's Reform and Opening agenda, China's adopted negative attitude regarding homosexuality began to reverse. During the United Nations' Fourth World Conference on Women, in Beijing in 1995, British queer activist Susie Jolly and Chinese queer activist Wu Chunsheng organized raucous lesbian dance parties out of Jolly's apartment in the Sanlitun Diplomatic Compound, which became the hub of Beijing's burgeoning queer scene. (To persuade the compound's security guards to let guests in, they gave them a DVD of Ang Lee's film *The Wedding Banquet*, a romantic comedy about a gay Taiwanese immigrant in America.) In 1997, the crime of "hooliganism," which encompassed offenses ranging from sexual assault to indecent conduct with minors, was abolished. Consequently, homosexuality, categorized under this crime, was effectively decriminalized. Deng Xiaoping died that year, at the old age of ninety-three, and Jolly remembered hanging out at a gay bar shortly after. "I was sort of being a bit flippant about [his death]," she said. "A gay guy . . . said to me: don't knock Deng Xiaoping. If it wasn't for him, we wouldn't be here." Capital and desire, in other words, were inextricably entwined, ushering China toward its place in the modern world.

Whereas gay men previously met in secret, at cruising spots like Dongdan Park or the public toilets in parks near the Forbidden City, they now met at gay bars like Half and Half, a narrow spot nestled in a backstreet of the hip Sanlitun neighborhood. Half and Half evolved from bar to community space where queer activists organized meetups, celebrated the anniversary of the Stonewall Riots, and set up China's first gay-and-lesbian hotline. In 1998, the first Chinese gay-and-lesbian conference convened in Beijing, and one of China's first lesbian groups, Beijing Sisters, formed. The lesbian community adopted the name Lala, taken from Lazi, the name of the lesbian protagonist in the queer Taiwanese novel *Notes of a Crocodile*, by Qiu Miaojin.

As a whole, the new queer communities no longer referred to themselves as *tongxinglian*, or "homosexual," which carried a repressive and clinical tone. Instead, they referred to themselves as *tongzhi*—"comrade." Whereas the gay and lesbian movements in the United States repurposed the word "queer" to celebrate the uniqueness of their identity, those in China wryly adopted the most official, sacred words in the Party's vocabulary—the characters *tong* ("the same") and *zhi* ("ideal")—to assert themselves as equals.

. . .

Ma Baoli had never really been alone. All over the country, queer people were logging on for the first time, finding their people, and coming to terms with their sexuality. For gay men growing up at the turn of the millennium, that process followed a remarkably similar trajectory: a secret crush on a handsome classmate; a keyword search at the local internet café; and almost inevitably, a stumbling upon the web novel *Beijing Story*, by Beijing Comrade. Its pseudonymous author remained a mystery. In the postscript of the Taiwanese version, published three years later, the author revealed themselves only to be a young Chinese person living in New York City who was disappointed with the Chinese-language erotica available at the time and decided to write their own:

> I immersed myself in the world of the Internet: playing chess, chatting online, surfing porn sites. After reading all the pornographic stories that were out there, I cursed: FXXX! . . . I knew I could write something better. And so I threw myself furiously into writing, then posted my writing online . . . Had I created a story, or stepped into one? Was this a dream or was it the real world?

The world that Beijing Comrade created became a touchstone for a generation of queer men, who saw their lives reflected in a story for the first time. Eventually, it was adapted by the Hong Kong director Stanley Kwan into the 2001 cult classic *Lan Yu*. Set against the backdrop of the Tiananmen demonstrations, the film only gestured quietly to the tragedy of that spring: a scene of Lan Yu holding his lover on the morning of June 4th and the sound of his ragged, wordless sobs. At a moment when hope had been so brutally crushed, the very least he could do was to hold on to the man he loved. China was filled with "the cries of a hundred Lan Yus," as the queer

Chinese poet Mu Cao named a book of his short stories. They just needed someone to bring them together.

In 2000, Ma decided to create his own website. With the help of a secondhand coding book called *The Oriental King of Web-Making*, he put together a bare-bones browser page, featuring a blue background and photos of handsome men at the beach. A soundtrack of waves played, followed by melancholic love songs that he updated every month. He shared earnest, vulnerable posts—about unrequited love, smoking a cigarette alone, and waning youth—and invited other gay men to exchange their personal stories and share information on everything from safe sex to gay literature. He ran the site under the pseudonym Geng Le, after a handsome actor he saw on television, and named the site Danlansedehuiyi, or "Light Blue Memories," after the color of the Qinhuangdao coast. Like the sea—vast, faraway, yet full of possibility—Danlan would be a sanctuary for gay men to share their hopes and dreams.

By day, Ma Baoli was a respected police officer, rising through the ranks of the bureau. By night, he became Geng Le, leader of a website for gay men and keeper of their secrets. So began his double life.

CHAPTER 2

Speaking Out

In her early twenties, Lü Pin, a master's student at Shandong University, started suffering from insomnia. She spent nights lying awake in bed as her roommates slept, her dormitory walls awash in moonlight. At the time, she couldn't understand why. When she had first arrived as a wide-eyed undergraduate, in 1987, college campuses across the country had been stirring with a raw new energy that would explode into action one fateful spring two years later. But nobody talked about that spring anymore. Its memory was now taboo, a ghost, buried in the past. So what, then, was this feeling inside her that kept her awake and denied her the solace of sleep?

Lü grew up in the outskirts of a city in Shandong Province in the 1970s, in the factory where her parents worked as technicians. During the Cultural Revolution, they were sent from the city to live in the countryside. As the only college-educated couple in their neighborhood, her parents read voraciously, a habit she picked up, too. Her mother loved detective novels. Her father devoured the news and subscribed to many periodicals. He read nightly from at least ten subscriptions—*People's Daily, Reference News, Youth Digest, Shenzhen Youth News*—and Lü read alongside him.

She didn't know it at the time, but China was changing. Through the news, she caught a glimpse of the intellectual awakening about to sweep through the country. She remembered when, one day in December 1978, the headlines in *Chinese Teenagers News* were printed in celebratory green to mark the commencement of the Third Plenum of the Eleventh Central Committee of the Chinese Communist Party—a pivotal meeting of the Party's leadership. Deng Xiaoping had just announced a grand new vision for China's future, calling on the Chinese people to "emancipate the mind."

Just like that, Deng's words unleashed a decade of intellectual opening and ferment. Writers broke away from the didactic propaganda mandated by Mao and penned everything from subversive poetry to "scar literature." Artists ditched their staid Socialist Realist paintings, experimented with radical new forms, and showcased their work on the streets for the public to critique. Universities, closed during the Cultural Revolution, became hotbeds of discussion, where scholars devoured new ideas indiscriminately—not just Marxist thought but also Freudian psychoanalysis and Sartre's existentialism—and debated those ideas in public.

Lü read the words of Liu Xiaobo, a PhD student at Beijing Normal University, in *Shenzhen Youth News*. Liu, bold and unapologetic, had gained a reputation as the enfant terrible of the Chinese literary intelligentsia, offending peers and establishment figures alike. "I can sum up what's wrong with Chinese writers in one sentence," Liu said in an interview in 1986. "They can't create themselves, they simply don't have the ability, because their lives don't belong to them."

In 1989, the ferment reached a boiling point. Lü was then a second-year student in the Chinese Literature Department of Shandong University. In Beijing, students protested at Tiananmen Square throughout the spring, and their fervor spread across the country, including onto Lü's campus. There, students stopped going to class in order to join marches. On the windowsill of one dormitory, a classmate set up a massive radio, which blasted nonstop news coverage of the protests from Voice of America. Since Tiananmen Square was the center of the action, Lü and her classmates took a train to Beijing in April. When they arrived, they found the square chaotic, covered with trash. Everyone looked exhausted and directionless after weeks without proper food or sleep. Where were the protests going? By then, the state-run newspaper *People's Daily* published a front-page editorial accusing a "small handful of people with ulterior motives" of plotting to overthrow the Chinese Communist Party. Looking back, Lü saw the publishing of the editorial—later known as the "April 26 editorial"—as a turning point. When Lü went back to school, the mood had shifted. Rumors spread that military trucks were crossing the Yellow River, headed for Beijing.

After the June 4th crackdown, a dark lull fell across campus. The university launched investigations, calling on students to confess their involvement in the protests, identify culprits, and write confessions. One classmate, unable to process her trauma, was sent to a psychiatric ward. When she returned months later, nobody talked about what happened anymore. Classes resumed, and the grass that had grown tall and unruly over the spring was trodden back to the ground.

Lü enrolled in a graduate program, remaining at the university for three more years and many sleepless nights. Only later in life did she name the feeling that kept her awake: disillusionment. She was disillusioned by her country. She no longer trusted her government. Many of China's once-loquacious intellectuals—if they had not already been arrested or gone into exile or hiding—simply stopped speaking, shell-shocked by the massacre. What was the point of speaking out if all it resulted in was crackdown? She was a nobody, Lü realized—a nobody with no voice.

· · ·

After Deng's Southern Tour, in 1992, as China pushed ahead with economic reforms, the chill of Tiananmen began to thaw. Those Chinese intellectuals began to stir again—albeit cautiously and quietly—searching for less confrontational paths to reform. In China, demands for democracy had been met with violent suppression. In an even greater shock, in the Soviet Union—for decades known as the ideological "big brother" to China—similar demands led to the crumbling of a great power, imploding overnight. Just as the Chinese intellectuals had observed how their country moved between cycles of opening and closing, the Soviet sociologist Yuri Levada described how Soviet society moved like a pendulum, swinging back and forth between liberalization and repression.

Gorbachev's perestroika seemed to begin as another temporary loosening of the reins, but then the pendulum swung too fast and too far, bringing the entire edifice down. To avoid implosion, the Chinese needed to find another way. China's edifice had to hold.

Within the walls of the academic establishment, several competing schools of thought emerged—most notably, the liberals and the New Left. The liberals broadly believed in greater individual freedoms, economic reform, and cultural openness to the West. Some emphasized the importance of the rule of law and constitutional reforms; others prioritized free markets and property rights. They believed that Gorbachev was not wrong to push for opening but mismanaged the process and started too late. Intellectuals of the New Left, such as the scholar Wang Hui, condemned Deng's call to let some Chinese "get rich first" and believed that the state needed to intervene to address issues of wealth distribution and social justice.

Unlike the most vocal intellectuals of the 1980s, who paraded their thoughts before the public, the establishment intellectuals were "theologians speaking to the clergy," in the words of the modern-China historian Timothy Cheek. The different camps engaged in heated arguments among themselves, nicknamed "Spittle Wars," that played out in the popular academic journals of the day, such as *Dushu* ("Reading") and *Strategy and Management*. Although they vehemently disagreed with one another, they sought answers to the same question: What did it mean to be both modern and Chinese?

An ideological framework that would allow China to modernize without challenging its one-party leadership was crucial for holding the edifice together. One young professor warned that the Party needed to urgently consider how its "software"—its cultures, values, attitudes—was just as important as its "hardware"—its economics, systems, institutions—in shaping its future. "There are no core values in China's most recent structure," he wrote, and without values, the system could not hold.

Wang Huning, the young professor, was a rising star of the International Relations Department at Shanghai's elite Fudan University. Fluent in French and a specialist in Western philosophy, he read and wrote prodigiously, drawing inspiration from thinkers ranging from Socrates to Montesquieu to Marx. In 1991, Wang published a book titled *America Against America,* recounting his observations from a six-month trip to the United States as a visiting scholar in 1988, when he traveled across the country interviewing congressmen and farmhands and visiting everywhere from the Coca-Cola headquarters in Atlanta to homeless encampments to Washington, DC.

Wang was impressed by many aspects of American society, such as the peaceful transfer of presidential power from Reagan to Bush, and in particular, he was astounded by the nation's technological prowess: cars speeding across its highways, telephones ringing in every home, and computers glowing in every office. America's spirit of innovation and embrace of the future allowed its people to produce a dazzling array of novel technologies—from its work on particle colliders to B-2 bombers to water mattresses. Everything was "computerized": schools, libraries, banks, factories, military operations. American society was a "system of information extending in all directions" that enabled the movement of people, objects, ideas, and energy, Wang observed in *America Against America.* "If Americans are to be overtaken," he concluded, "one thing must be done: surpass them in science and technology."

But for all he admired about American technological might, he described the country as a "nation in crisis." Although its hardware gleamed, its software was decaying. Where his more starry-eyed peers might have seen wealth and opportunity, Wang observed industrial decay, racial strife, ignorant youth, the commodification of sex, and, most crucially, what he believed to be a nihilistic individualism unraveling the fabric of American society. He cited the conservative philosopher Allan Bloom's bestseller *The Closing of the American Mind,* which criticized American youth for losing touch with "traditional values," as a key influence on his thinking. "If the value system collapses, how can the social system be sustained?" Wang wrote.

He returned home with stronger convictions: To become rich and modern, China had to embrace the technologies of the future while remaining firmly held together by a strong centralized state, bound by its own values and traditions. The question of "how to manage China" consumed him, a former student on his debate team recalled to *The Wall Street Journal.* "He spent every night in his office and didn't do anything else."

In 1995, Wang's intellect caught the attention of the new Party general secretary, Jiang Zemin, who was tapped as Deng Xiaoping's successor. So impressed was Jiang with Wang's rhetoric that he recruited him to lead the politics department of the Party's in-house think tank, the Central Policy Research Office, as the rare academic joining a leadership of mostly engineers and apparatchiks. The Party was searching for a narrative to sustain its power; Wang provided a vocabulary. He left his post at the university, stopped publishing his own work, and dedicated his voice to the state.

. . .

In 1994, Lü Pin completed her graduate degree in Chinese literature and landed her first job: as a journalist at the state-run paper *China Women's News.* She had no particular interest in women's issues, but it was a solid offer; she took what she could get. Founded by the All-China Women's Federation, a Party-backed organization, *China Women's News* was established in the eighties with the goal to "make society known to women, make women known to society, advocate gender equality, and promote women's progress and development." It published articles ranging from explainers of government policies to reports on challenges women faced in the job market to features celebrating women who excelled in different fields, from science to factory work.

Lü Pin's first assignment was to cover the preparations for the United Nations' Fourth World Conference on Women, in Beijing in September 1995, the first such conference hosted in China. The Party hoped that the conference would revamp its international image, still tainted by Tiananmen, help break through diplomatic barriers, and "link up tracks with the world." They believed the conference to be an easy win. After all, since its founding, the Party had proudly touted its commitment to gender equality. Under Mao, who famously proclaimed that "women hold up half the sky," the Party permitted divorce, mandated equal employment, and enshrined equal rights for men and women into the constitution. But they were concerned about exposing the city to a sudden influx of foreign visitors—along with their crucial views on human rights and the Chinese government—and took precautions beforehand. The NGO Forum on Women was relocated at the last minute from the Workers' Stadium, in the city center, to a middle school campus on the outskirts of Huairou, more than an hour's drive away.

Nevertheless, the NGO Forum remained the most exciting part of the conference, featuring a ten-day smorgasbord of five thousand events. Lü hopped from one to the next. There were discussion panels on women's rights from Algeria to Norway, on public health, on unpaid labor. Amnesty International held a moment of collective silence to grieve victims of domestic violence; Hillary Clinton delivered an impassioned speech in front of a packed audience at the Huairou auditorium, declaring that "women's rights are human rights, once and for all." Soda machines, a novelty in China at the time, spouted free Coca-Cola—a conference sponsor that had just entered the Chinese market.

Just as cities like Shenzhen were designated special economic zones—with tax incentives for foreign investors, free-trade areas, and high-tech development parks—participants dubbed the NGO Forum on Women a "special ideological zone." Attendees freely and publicly discussed issues that would have been taboo anywhere else in China. A group of Tibetan women organized a demonstration against government suppression, walking single file through the campus with their mouths covered in silk scarves as the surrounding crowd spontaneously broke out into song, singing "We Shall Overcome."

In the courtyard, a cluster of open-air "diversity tents" encouraged more informal discussion—from the reproductive-health tent to the (most popular) lesbian tent. For He Xiaopei, at the time a government economist and perhaps the only out Chinese lesbian at the conference, the tent hosted the most lesbians she'd seen in her lifetime. One day, they marched through Huairou's main street with banners reading LIBERTÉ, EGALITÉ, HOMOSEXUALITÉ. Trailing behind them were a group of married police officers, deployed to the scene in response to rumors of a naked parade, clutching white bedsheets to wrap around anyone who tried to strip.

For many Chinese participants, the conference, dubbed by Chinese feminist scholar Song Shaopeng as China's "first handshake with the world since 1989," was a revelation. For Lü, too. With her introduction to the concept of the NGO, she saw for the first time that it was possible to be "nongovernmental." "The forum showed us that grassroots organizations could engage in dialogue with the government on equal footing," said Feng Yuan, Lü's mentor and fellow journalist at *China Women's News*. Most crucially, they learned the concept of "women's empowerment," which they now used instead of the Party's phrase, "women's entitlement." "Entitlement" implied that rights were granted externally by a higher power. "Empowerment," on the other hand, implied that women already had a voice—not given to them but originating from within.

The conference inspired and incubated China's first wave of women's NGOs—including the Anti–Domestic Violence Network, the Beijing Sisters, the East Meets West Feminist Translation Group, and the Media Monitor for Women Network, founded by Feng Yuan, Lü Pin, and their colleagues at the newspaper—to promote gender equality in the media. As part of the network, they wrote a regular column in *China Women's News,* critiquing how news stories romanticized domestic violence or ran advertisements that fetishized women. They conducted training in gender awareness for other journalists, including for those who launched the television show *Half the Sky,* a popular talk show dedicated to women's issues, on the state broadcasting network, CCTV.

In 1998, on International Women's Day, during a workshop with a group of female journalists, Feng Yuan asked everyone the question "Who are you?"

"A journalist," Lü replied.

Then Feng shared her answer: "Female journalist."

The difference between their two answers astonished Lü. Gender was not simply a question of semantics, she realized, but something that could shape her life and her worldview. Once disempowered, she'd been looking for a "weapon with which to confront the world and a place to anchor my soul," she wrote. Once voiceless, Lü Pin had found the language of feminism.

. . .

Outside university campuses, more subversive intellectual voices emerged. After the state loosened its grip on the private sector in 1992, Chinese intellectuals outside the establishment were no longer tethered to their state work units—universities or state media—and could now also moonlight as independent lawyers, journalists, and documentary filmmakers. Unlike the intellectuals of the eighties, they sought a different language of reform—not grand narratives of democracy and saving the country but discourse rooted in the concrete issues of ordinary people in their everyday lives.

Just as China's queer communities had come out of the closet, a whole generation of grassroots intellectuals began to come out of silence. They spoke from the margins and for the voiceless. The filmmaker Jia Zhangke shot realist, low-budget films with amateur camera equipment to capture stories about pickpockets and disaffected youth in small-town Shanxi. Novelists such as Yan Lianke and Liao Yiwu wrote from the perspectives of the rural poor and those living on the fringes of Chinese society: a leper, a human trafficker, a public restroom manager. The novelist Wang Xiaobo and his wife, sociologist Li Yinhe, coauthored the first groundbreaking study on China's gay community, which in turn inspired Wang to write the screenplay for *East Palace, West Palace*—a film about a cop attracted to a gay man he arrests at a cruising park, which Ma Baoli would watch behind his closed office doors. Collectively, the new grassroots intellectuals formed a nascent civil society, organizing independently of the state and speaking for themselves.

Most crucially, by the turn of the millennium, they chose to speak out through the internet—on email chains, online message boards, and personal blogs—which had burst forth as a new and vibrant space of public discourse.

In March 2003, Sun Zhigang, a twenty-seven-year-old migrant worker in Guangzhou, was detained by police for not carrying the correct identity papers—routine practice, part of China's notorious repatriation system. Three days later, he was beaten to death in police custody. His story, picked up by journalists at *Southern Metropolis Daily*, a Guangzhou-based paper renowned for its fearless muckraking, soon became viral on the Chinese web, igniting outrage over the conditions of migrant workers living in cities. Three professors who would go on to found an influential legal reform movement—Teng Biao, Xu Zhiyong, and Yu Jiang—drafted an appeal to the National People's Congress, calling for the state to investigate Sun's death. Three months later, responding to public pressure, the government abolished the entire custody system the police used to detain migrant workers. A court convicted the officials responsible for Sun's death.

Chinese media outlets dubbed 2003 "The Year of Online Public Opinion." The Chinese people had logged on to the internet and carved out a space of public debate—not as subservient but as equals to the state.

. . .

When the internet arrived in China, it placed the Party leadership in a conundrum: How could they reap its benefits without allowing it to destabilize their authority? They knew they were dealing with a technology of not only immense potential but also disruptive power. How could they allow useful information to enter the country via the web while filtering out the most subversive ideas?

In 1996, Premier Li Peng, one of the chief orchestrators of the Tiananmen crackdown, signed a State Council Order giving the state full control of all internet networks. In 1997, the Ministry of Public Security issued its first set of rules governing the web, forbidding use of the internet to harm national security or disclose state secrets. In 1998, to enforce these rules, the ministry began constructing an extensive internet censorship and surveillance system. They called it the Golden Shield Project.

The controls operated on two levels. At the international level, there was a piece of software that blocked forbidden domain names and IP addresses as traffic passed from the global web into the country. The technology was straightforward, much like the firewalls installed at schools around the world preventing students from accessing violent content or porn. Click on the banned site; an error page appears. At the domestic level, the Golden Shield included mandatory surveillance software in internet cafés and ID verification for internet service providers to track users who shared politically sensitive content. The entirety of these web controls and regulations became known by a term first coined in a 1997 *WIRED* article by the Australian sinologist Geremie Barmé and the Chinese scholar Sang Ye: "The Great Firewall of China."

To build the system, the government hired and collaborated with both domestic and international technology companies. Motorola provided wireless communication to China's traffic police; Sun Microsystems linked provincial police departments through computer networks; and Cisco, the Silicon Valley–based network vendor, supplied filtering and surveillance equipment. Cisco viewed the Golden Shield Project as a lucrative business opportunity. The company already produced technology that American corporations used to restrict employee internet access, such as blocking sites like ESPN or playboy.com. This same technology could easily be adapted to censor content for Chinese internet users. According to an internal Cisco presentation from 2002, leaked to *WIRED* reporters several years later, one controversial slide noted how their products could "Combat Falun Gong evil religion and other hostilities." (In 2011, a group of Chinese plaintiffs in the United States would file a lawsuit against Cisco for providing surveillance technology to the Chinese government to persecute members of a religious group.) As the internet historians Tim Wu and Jack Goldsmith wrote, the Great Firewall was originally built with "American bricks."

By the end of 2003—the Year of Online Public Opinion—the Golden Shield Project was fully operational. All of China's internet cafés were required to install its surveillance software, which would collect the personal data of users and alert authorities when they viewed unlawful content. Internet news providers signed a pledge agreeing to "obey government administration" and "resist firmly the internet transmission of harmful information." That year, the number of people detained or sentenced for internet-related offenses increased by 60 percent over the previous year.

Still, the Party's chief concern was not to silence all forms of criticism but to target content aimed at undermining China's sovereignty: calls for Taiwan independence, attempts to propagate new religions, and posts about pro-democracy dissident publications. As the Party took steps to control the internet, so the Chinese people increasingly logged on to speak their minds about everything else possible, from the mistreatment of migrant workers to the government cover-up of the 2003 SARS crisis. To banish every piece of unwanted speech from the web, regardless of how sophisticated the software, seemed like an impossible task.

"As every Chinese school kid knows, the original Great Wall failed in its basic mission," Barmé and Sang wrote in *WIRED*. "Will its digital successor fare any better?"

.　.　.

In March 2003, shortly after the Sun Zhigang incident, Lü Pin took a leave of absence from her job at *China Women's News* to serve as deputy county mayor in a county in Gansu, one of China's poorest provinces, on the edge of the Qinghai–Tibet Plateau, working on poverty development and teaching literacy skills to rural women. She had grown disillusioned with her job at the newspaper. Writing about Chinese women through the rhetoric of the Communist Party felt toothless. She had to fill her articles with meaningless Party-speak, temper her language to fit its values, and scrub her sentences of words that carried any real power. At thirty years old, she had worked her way up the masthead, a step away from being promoted to deputy editor. But the higher her seniority, the more she felt constrained by the system. To become the editor in chief one day, she would have to join the Party. When her boss offered to help her join, Lü replied that she was of the 1989 generation. As long as the Party did not redress June 4th, she would not join.

She had also met suitors her age from similar backgrounds and professions. She imagined her future with them: marriage, government jobs, a comfortable life. But she didn't want that. While living in Gansu, one moment in particular left a lasting impression on her. She was walking in the bitter cold to where she was about to teach a class in a ramshackle room without heat or electricity. As she stepped into the classroom, the women began to sing—spontaneously, joyously, in chorus. She came to a revelation: Power would come from women themselves, not from inside the system.

When she returned to Beijing in 2004, she announced her decision to resign. Her friends didn't understand. One of her colleagues broke down into tears, believing that Lü's departure would be a loss for the paper and a loss for Lü herself. Lü had received a good education, a city resident permit, and a respectable job with stable pay; to her friends and colleagues, giving all this up amounted to failure. But that's not how Lü saw it. She would lose all that, but she would obtain something they didn't have: freedom. As long as she remained shackled to the state paper, Lü realized, she would be absorbed by the system, unable to express herself freely and enact real change. So she handed in her resignation letter to become a freelance writer.

"I gained the ability to write and think freely," she later wrote. "My words and my thoughts would never again be censored—and this was precious." It was time to speak for herself.

CHAPTER 3

Plunging into the Sea

I n June 2005, Ma Baoli traveled from Qinhuangdao to Beijing to attend China's second Gay Website Conference. In the five years since he'd single-handedly created his website, Danlan, the number of Chinese internet users had grown tenfold and thousands of gay web pages and blogs had sprouted across the country. The conference—organized by well-known HIV/AIDS activist and former public health official Wan Yanhai and the founders of Aibai.cn, an LGBT website started in 1999—aimed to bring the creators of those pages and blogs together from all corners of China, from Xi'an Sunny Days to Yunnan Comrades to Danlan. Over one weekend, thirty or so gay website leaders gathered in a small, unassuming guesthouse in southwest Beijing to discuss topics ranging from website server maintenance to HIV/AIDS prevention. It was a gathering of gay minds, an exchange of queer ideas, like "a hundred flowers blooming," said Shen Wenjie, the founder of Night Cat Stories, a gay website named after a popular gay bar in Changsha, Hunan. "It was like a pilgrimage."

Shen was smitten with Ma. Unlike the other participants, mostly scrappy college students and recent graduates, Ma Baoli, dressed in a short-sleeved navy polo, was a handsome policeman, intense and charismatic. And Ma admired Shen, a programming instructor, for his technical prowess—he was the only person at the conference with coding skills. After the conference, they exchanged contact details on QQ, the popular messaging app at the time, and stayed in touch. Sporadic texts evolved into nightly calls. When Ma invited Shen to join him in Qinhuangdao to work at Danlan, Shen accepted without hesitation. He quit his job, told his parents he'd found a new opportunity at an internet start-up up north, and took a thirty-hour hard-seater train from Changsha to Qinhuangdao, giddy with anticipation. The first Danlan team was born.

Soon after, Ma recruited another conference participant, named Jiajia, a graphic designer from Shenzhen. A year later, he brought in three more members: Zhaozhao, a friend of Jiajia's; Teng, a college student in Qinhuangdao; and Yan, a music student from Beijing, who joined after seeing a job posting on the Danlan website. Ma ran the office out of a two-bedroom apartment where they all lived, worked, ate, and slept, single-mindedly pursuing one goal: to become the best gay website in China. They looked like boys living out of a university dorm: hair unkempt, dressed in oversized T-shirts, baggy cargo shorts, and slippers. They redesigned the web page, streamlined the chat room, and responded to endless user requests. They each earned a monthly salary of 1,500 yuan ($200), funded by advertisements, merchandise sales (T-shirts and DVDs of gay films), user donations of 50–500 yuan, and Ma's own savings. After Google entered China in 2005, they paid the site a couple hundred dollars a month to host ads.

Every now and then, they splurged, going for a beer or a seafood barbecue meal on the weekends, but otherwise, the website consumed every waking hour of their lives. Sleep was an afterthought, a luxury. One time, they stayed up all night to rebuild the site so that it would be ready for users when they woke up in the morning. They finished just in time for sunrise and left the office together in a euphoric daze to get a classic Qinhuangdao breakfast: rice buns with salty bean curd. It was the first time Shen, from China's South, tasted the northern delicacy. From that day on, salty bean curd always tasted like joy.

Still, they faced the threat of shutdown. Although homosexuality had been decriminalized, censorship regulations still prohibited depictions of same-sex intimacy, and authorities frequently closed the site for "violating public morality." Server providers blamed Ma for putting their product at risk. "Because it has so many pictures of male bodies," an internet security officer told Ma once when he called to inquire about a shutdown. "It makes people uncomfortable." They installed a peephole on their office door in case one of his colleagues at the police bureau came knocking. As a cop, he was on good terms with the head of the internet security department and often went over to his office to chat. But Ma wasn't there just to chat—he wanted to snoop for policy documents on his desk that mentioned whether gay websites were problematic.

Online regulations were enforced haphazardly, at the whim of a server provider or a local public security bureau, some strict, others more lenient. Servers were the lifeblood of the website; if one went down, users lost access and Danlan lost trust and revenue. Keeping the website alive meant playing an endless game of "server guerrilla warfare." After each shutdown, the team moved fast, physically shuttling the server machinery from one city to another by mail, train, or bus from Qinhuangdao to Shanghai to Zhenjiang, then back to Qinhuangdao. Starting over from scratch, over and over again.

They believed deeply in their work. And yet they ran their business like a contraband operation, always bracing for the next shutdown. Each closure was a rejection, a reminder of their illegitimacy in the public eye. No one understood them—not their families, their neighbors, their country. So they turned to each other. "We had no one else," Ma said.

All were closeted and planned to stay so indefinitely. But when Ma turned twenty-eight, prime marriage age, this got harder. His parents nagged him to settle down. Colleagues at the police bureau kept introducing him to potential girlfriends; each time, he found an excuse to turn them down. But he couldn't stall forever. So he arranged a *xinghun*, or "cooperative marriage," with a friend of one of his colleagues. A perfect arrangement—on paper, at least. They would marry, hold a public ceremony, satisfy their families. But they would then live separately, each with their own partner.

The wedding felt like a surreal piece of theater. Nobody but Ma's closest friends were aware they were just actors performing. His parents beamed. His police academy friends showered him with gifts and good wishes. His boss at the bureau delivered an effusive speech about Ma's professional promise. How lucky straight people are, he thought, to have the whole world celebrate their love so openly. Only his boyfriend at the time and his wife's partner sat in the crowd teary-eyed. They understood—this blissful future was nothing but a carefully staged lie. As long as Ma wanted to build a life in small-town Qinhuangdao and keep his respectable government job at the police bureau, that future would never be his.

. . .

Beyond the beaches of Qinhuangdao, the Chinese people were not resigning themselves to their fates but seizing control of their fortunes. After Deng Xiaoping introduced market reforms in the 1980s, many began leaving behind their government jobs and their "iron rice bowls"—the guaranteed job security and welfare provided by the state—to test the waters of the booming private sector. This process became known as *xia hai,* or "plunging into the sea." The phrase, which once referred to women who decided to engage in prostitution, now described people who decided to pursue the risky and daring life of an entrepreneur. Party officials transformed into restaurateurs; professors moonlighted as corporate consultants. Everybody knew the success stories: The soldier turned real estate mogul. The journalist turned bottled-water magnate. The army technician turned telecommunications CEO.

The most famous story of them all was elevated to national myth: that of Ma Yun, the English teacher who created one of the largest online supermarkets in the world. He had timed his steps impeccably. In 1978, when Deng Xiaoping opened China to the world, fourteen-year-old Ma rode his bike to the Hangzhou Hotel in his hometown, offering free guide service to the city's new influx of foreign tourists to practice his English. He adopted the English name Jack, gifted by a foreign pen pal who had difficulty pronouncing his Chinese name. In 1992, after Deng embarked on the Southern

Tour and the number of registered companies in China jumped by 88 percent, Jack quit his $12-a-month gig teaching English to start a translation company. In English, he named it Hope, and in Chinese, Haibo, meaning "vast like the sea."

But Jack's real breakthrough came after China joined the World Wide Web. He became part of the cohort of internet entrepreneurs who rose to success in the nineties by plunging into the commercialized web. Some came directly from state jobs, such as Ren Zhengfei, from the People's Liberation Army before he established Huawei, the telecommunications giant. Others came from reputable graduate degree programs abroad, such as Charles Zhang, who earned a PhD in experimental physics at MIT before returning to China to found Sohu, one of China's leading internet portals. Many aspired to create Chinese versions of innovations they saw abroad: Pony Ma, the founder of the tech company Tencent, stumbled upon the Israeli-originated online chat system ICQ and started his own chat service, which later became QQ.

In 1995, a translation gig brought Jack to Seattle, where he first used an internet search engine. When he typed in the word "beer," it yielded results for German beer and American beer but nothing Chinese. In fact, there were no web pages from China at all. So he created China's first internet company: China Pages, an online Yellow Pages for the world to discover Chinese businesses. Four years later, Jack gathered seventeen of his colleagues in a cramped Hangzhou apartment to present his vision: an internet platform that connected buyers and sellers. This time, he set his sights higher: Their competitors would not be in China but in America's Silicon Valley. They would beat them through sheer hustle and entrepreneurial spirit. He christened his company Alibaba, after the famous Arabian myth in which an unlikely hero discovers a cave and stumbles into a box of treasure. The company would last eighty years, the length of a human lifespan, he declared. Just as everybody knew the legend of Ali Baba, everybody would come to know Jack Ma.

Months later, Jack's enthusiasm caught the attention of Joe Tsai, a Taiwanese-Canadian investor and Yale graduate, who flew to Hangzhou to meet him. After his visit, Joe quit his $700,000-a-year job as an investor to join Alibaba as its new CFO, making a monthly salary of $50. By the end of the year, Goldman Sachs, equally enamored with Jack's vision, invested $3.3 million in the company. Masayoshi Son, the founder and CEO of the Japanese investment firm SoftBank, topped that in 2000 with $20 million—a decision he made five minutes into Jack's pitch. In 2003, Alibaba launched an online shopping platform called Taobao and announced that it would take on American e-commerce giant eBay to battle for the Chinese market. What began as a David-and-Goliath showdown (eBay dominated about 80 percent of the market share) ended in Alibaba's unrivaled victory (after eBay's market share dropped to around 8 percent, it exited China completely). In 2005, wanting to jump on the bandwagon, Yahoo invested $1 billion in Alibaba.

Yahoo tested Jack's convictions. A month before the investment, news broke that Yahoo had handed private user information over to Chinese state security, which led to the arrest of a Chinese journalist. The journalist was quickly sentenced to ten years in prison for leaking a Communist Party document to an overseas democracy site through his Yahoo email account. The news sparked an international uproar. Human rights groups condemned Yahoo for abetting the suppression of free speech; the US Congress launched an investigation into the company's complicity. Yahoo stumbled upon the dilemma that would entangle more global tech companies in the years to come: Comply with China's rules or lose access to its burgeoning online user base.

"If you were running Yahoo, would you have done the same thing?" a CNN anchorwoman asked Jack in an interview after the incident.

"Yes, I would," he replied without hesitation. "Whenever you do business, you have to follow the local rules and laws. Either you can change the law [or] if you cannot change the law, then follow the law."

. . .

Even though the two could not have been more different, Ma Baoli idolized Jack Ma. Ma Baoli was reserved, cautious, soft-spoken, modestly handsome, and inclined to play by the rules; Jack Ma was charismatic, larger-than-life, and garrulous, earning the nickname "Crazy Jack" in the media for his outsize ambitions and antics. Ma Baoli was unknown outside China's queer community; Jack Ma was "kind of like Bill Gates, the Queen, and Beyoncé rolled into one," Michael Smith, a China correspondent for the *Australian Financial Review*, observed. To celebrate Alibaba's ten-year anniversary, Jack performed an off-key rendition of Elton John's "Can You Feel the Love Tonight," dressed like a metalhead—leather jacket, mohawk, black lipstick—to a stadium of sixteen thousand fawning spectators.

But in other ways, Ma resembled Jack. He, too, believed in the possibility of pushing for change while following the law. He, too, started out in a different profession with nothing but a wild idea, leading a ragtag team in a two-bedroom apartment. He, too, saw the connective power of a technology that few had yet to truly grasp. As a gay man, Ma saw himself as an underdog; Jack was China's most beloved underdog, the catalog of his failures rehashed as badges of honor: two failed college entrance exams, two failed start-up ideas, over a dozen rejected job applications, including one for a role as a server at Kentucky Fried Chicken.

Jack wore his shortcomings on his sleeve and wielded his ignorance like a weapon. He claimed that his role model was Forrest Gump, because "people think he's dumb, but he knows what he's doing." Just as Forrest Gump got rich fishing for shrimp after a storm, Jack made his fortune on what he called "shrimps"—small to medium-size businesses. He was the small guy who placed his bet on the small guys and won. The China that Jack was dreaming into being was consumer-driven, middle-class China, the China where the small guys matter. When the American journalist Charlie Rose asked Jack if he was an "apostle for small business," he replied, "It's my religion."

Jack never stopped being a teacher—CEO stood for "Chief Education Officer," he often quipped. He was a swords master, and his employees were his apprentices, each one required to adopt their own fictional martial arts alias. His teachings took the form of aphorisms—a blend of *Chicken Soup for the Soul*, Aesop's fables, and martial arts strategy—which were quoted, anthologized, and memorized by young admirers like scripture.

Ma Baoli believed in Jack's story: that with enough hustle, ambition, and optimism, anyone, regardless of his or her disadvantages in life—poor, short, ugly, uneducated, gay—could change the world. After all, Jack's story was the myth of Chinese entrepreneurship personified, the myth that propelled his country forward. Embrace the outside world and catch up with the West. Ma took his motivational mantra from Jack, which he repeated endlessly to himself and his team: "Today is hard, tomorrow will be worse, but the day after tomorrow will be sunshine."

. . .

In the summer of 2008, as Ma Baoli and Jack Ma were carefully nurturing their growing businesses, China appeared to be undergoing a reinvention. In the lead-up to the Beijing Summer Olympics, the whole country prepared for its moment to shine on the global stage. New metro lines opened, coal-burning plants halted to ease pollution, and 40 million potted flowers were placed around the streets to beautify Beijing's landscape. The Games' official slogan, One World, One Dream, blasted from speakers and television screens all across the country, boasting China's entrance into the global community. When I spent that summer in Beijing, visiting my grandparents, I bounced from one event to the next, in awe of the city's transformation. I hummed the Games' theme song constantly under my breath like a catchy jingle: "Beijing Welcomes You."

The opening ceremony kicked off in Beijing's "Bird's Nest"—a sprawling, lattice-shelled structure built as the city's new National Stadium. Ninety thousand spectators gathered to watch Li Ning—the Chinese gymnast who won three gold medals in the 1984 Olympics—suspended in air to light the Olympic torch, soundtracked by British singer Sarah Brightman's operatic soprano. "We must bid farewell to autocracy," declared Ai Weiwei, one of the artists who designed the stadium, in the hopes of spurring China to change. "Today, China and the world will meet again." International media dubbed the ceremony China's "coming-out party" to the world.

Ma Baoli saw the Games as a signal—that the weather was shifting, China was liberalizing, fortunes were in his favor. That summer, the English website of the state-run paper *People's Daily* even published an article headlined BEIJING'S GAY SCENE COMES OUT OF THE CLOSET. The article extolled Destination as the capital's "hottest gay club," where "long lines of young hip men wait for entry . . . a place to see and be seen." It praised Danlan as an online community "for young gay men to enjoy a freer environment." On the web page, a "Beijing 2008 Olympics Games" advertisement flashed against a rainbow backdrop.

Ma was delighted. A gay club dubbed by state apparatchiks as the "place to see and be seen"? The official Party mouthpiece rarely acknowledged the existence of China's queer community, let alone did so in a positive light.

Others in the community felt optimistic, too. In 2008 alone, several major LGBTQ organizations were founded, including the Beijing LGBT Center; the Chinese Lala Alliance, a network established to support the rights of Chinese lesbians; and Parents, Families, and Friends of Lesbians and Gays (PFLAG China). "The year 2008 was a really open moment," Ah Qiang, the cofounder of PFLAG, told me. "The roads were getting wider, the buildings taller, the spaces for public discourse more open and tolerant. There was a sense that China would only keep moving in this direction."

On Valentine's Day the following year, Common Language, the queer NGO, staged a same-sex wedding. A gay couple and a lesbian couple dressed up in wedding clothes and posed for NGO volunteers filming them kissing in public in front of a small crowd on Qianmen Street, next to Tiananmen Square. Security guards were present but did not intervene. Volunteers also interviewed spectators on their attitudes toward homosexuality. Some expressed disagreement and disgust, but others showed support and sympathy. The goal was to raise public awareness for LGBTQ rights, and it worked: Discussion of the event mushroomed online and was even covered by the state-run paper *China Daily* and Guangzhou-based *Southern Weekly,* the latter with the headline SAME-SEX WEDDING IN BEIJING: FROM UNDERGROUND TO THE STREET. Footage from the event was compiled into a documentary entitled *New Beijing, New Marriage,* a riff on the 2008 Beijing Olympics slogan, New Beijing, New Olympics.

At that point, Ma had decided it was time to leave Qinhuang-dao for Beijing. If Danlan moved, it could connect with major tech industry players, attract open-minded investors, recruit from larger queer communities, and meet more potential partners. The company would have more room to dance, a bigger stage for its growing ambitions.

Ma believed that if China had come out to the world, Danlan was ready to come out, too. He'd worked for almost a decade in the police bureau's Information and Research Department—mostly a desk job, which involved drafting speeches, briefing reports, and proposals for bureau leaders. In April 2009, he applied for an extended sick leave from the bureau, packed all Danlan's belong-ings into two large trucks and a van, and moved the team to Beijing. He left Qinhuangdao behind to become an internet entrepreneur and plunged into the sea.

. . .

On May 10, 2009, Deng Yujiao, a twenty-one-year-old waitress in Badong County, Hubei, was washing her clothes in the restroom of Dream Fantasy City, a karaoke and entertainment club where she worked, when two local officials walked in demanding "special services"—a euphemism for sex. Deng refused.

"Aren't you all the same? You're a prostitute and you still want to have a good reputation?" one of the officials taunted. He slapped her face with a wad of banknotes. "Don't you want money? Would you believe if I am going to beat you to death with money today?"

When Deng tried to leave the room, he dragged her back, push-ing her onto the sofa. Unable to struggle out of his grip, she pulled out a fruit knife and stabbed the three-inch blade into his neck. As he lay dying, she called the police and turned herself in. After her arrest, she faced homicide charges.

In the pre-internet era, Deng's case might have disappeared and she would have been locked up for good. But this time, a blogger posted news of Deng's arrest online. Her case went viral, erupting into a groundswell of public furor. Netizens condemned the officials and demanded a fair trial for Deng, upholding her as an ordinary citizen resisting unchecked power. They called out the wad of cash that the director used to slap Deng's face. "How do officials get so much money?" one blogger probed. "Was he using public funds or embezzled money?" In response to the uproar, the prosecutor dropped the murder charges and the Hubei court granted Deng bail, ruling that she had acted in self-defense.

Lü Pin, who followed the case closely, was inspired to speak out. Other commentators, she wrote, by focusing their attention on official corruption, had missed the crucial point. At the heart of Deng's case was the problem not of corruption but of patriarchy—a systemic culture of sexual violence that enabled powerful men to oppress marginalized women. But her articles on the subject, published in a handful of magazines and newspapers, brought in a limited readership—a small circle of middle-aged scholars and academics already familiar with her ideas.

In the years since Lü had left her government job for a career as a freelancer, she had grown frustrated with the reach of her voice. She didn't want to preach to the same flock of academics; she wanted to engage with and galvanize a broader, younger audience. But these readers no longer read the periodicals she wrote for; instead, they gathered information from the commercial websites Sina.com and NetEase, as well as a new crop of Twitter-like social media sites called *weibo*s, or microblogs. A third of the Chinese population used the internet, up from close to 0 percent when she first started working as a journalist more than a decade earlier. To join the conversation, she needed a new strategy.

In September 2009, Lü founded *Women's Voices,* a digital magazine dedicated to covering women's rights issues, sent out as an email newsletter distributed weekly as a Word doc to her friends and peers. The magazine's purpose, she wrote in the first issue's introduction, was to "popularize China's feminist movement."

She didn't want to create a closed circle of elite experts. She wanted to create a collective movement of grassroots feminists. A reader suggested a name change: *Feminist Voices* instead of *Women's Voices*. At first, she hesitated. The word "feminism," *nüquanzhuyi* in Chinese—literally, "women-powerism"—conjured up images of aggressive man haters. Would it scare readers away?

It didn't. Readership soared. Lü grew emboldened. If she could find her voice as a feminist, perhaps she could help other women find their voices, too. Propelled forward by the internet, *Feminist Voices* was on its way to becoming the nation's most influential feminist publication, and Lü, its most influential feminist activist.

CHAPTER 4

American Dreams

Like many aspiring Chinese rappers, Kafe Hu first got hooked on Eminem. One day, on the streets outside of a local shopping center, some of his middle school friends who were into break-dancing blasted "My Name Is" from *The Slim Shady LP.* He was unimpressed by the dance moves, but the music was electric. He'd never heard anything like it before—the brash vocals, heavy bass line, in-your-face lyrics ("My English teacher wanted to flunk me in junior high . . . / I smacked him in his face with an eraser, chased him with a stapler"). Eminem was nothing like the rosy-cheeked Mandopop (Mandarin pop) stars who choked the airwaves. The American rapper—swaggering, foulmouthed, strutting around in his snapbacks—sounded alive, angry, and urgent all at once.

Kafe started spending afternoons at Mirage, his local internet café. In a small, smoke-filled room, he sat in a row alongside other pubescent patrons. They paid two kuai an hour to stare at blocky old computers, playing video games, and when the café manager wasn't looking, watching porn. The internet of the early 2000s was still chaotic and unruly—a teenage boy's dream. But Kafe wasn't there for first-person shooters and risqué nudes. He spent his two kuai an hour pursuing his newest obsession: hip-hop.

Kafe wanted his life to go faster. He wanted to bike faster, fall in love faster, get out of his hometown faster. Life in Jiangyou, the county-level city in Sichuan Province where he grew up, was slow and lethargic. Kafe's father owned a hot pot restaurant and a teahouse, and his stepmother took care of him and his stepbrother. They lived together in a low-rise home next to a string of funeral-rites shops that Kafe described as "super old and ghetto." Tall, skinny, and dark-skinned, with hooded eyes and spiky hair he'd later shave down to a buzz cut, he did not look like his father. Instead, he resembled his birth mother, whom he'd met only a handful of times in his life. She'd become a heroin addict, so his father had kept her away from him; she'd passed away when he was a child.

School was stifling, too. Kafe felt suffocated by the conveyor belt future ahead of him: Get good grades, ace the Gaokao (China's notoriously grueling college entrance exams), land a desk job, buy an apartment, and find a respectable spouse, all within a thousand square miles of where he lived. Most of the boys at his school played soccer and worshipped European soccer stars. Why would anyone think running around chasing a ball was cool? "The abide-by-authority DNA just wasn't in me," he said. "I didn't want to wear what they wanted me to wear, to learn what they wanted me to learn, to feel like I was a machine, meeting a certain standard." He dropped out of school and wandered around his hometown with nothing to do but pick fights. His father once told him in a burst of frustration that he had only three paths in life: Join the criminal underworld and get killed, end up in jail, or become a beggar.

Kafe discovered hip-hop just as he was looking for a way out. He immersed himself in Jay-Z and 50 Cent and trawled through BBS (bulletin board) rap forums, where he met other Chinese rap aficionados from across the country, from the Northeast to Guang-zhou. He started writing his own verses and stole 25 yuan from his dad to buy a mic and record his own tracks. While he was trying to come up with a rapper name, a friend jokingly suggested Kafe Hu, meaning "Coffee Pot," because his surname, Hu, was a homonym for the Chinese word for "pot" and Kafe sounded sophisticated and French. His first tracks were thrown together—freestyle riffs plugged into illegally downloaded beats, which he uploaded onto the music-sharing website 163888.net for feedback—but people seemed to enjoy them. In fact, one of his songs—his lyrics set to the beat of Eminem's hit song "Stan"—impressed a singer and music producer in Chengdu, Sichuan's capital, named K-Bo, who was known at the time as the big sister of China's rap scene. She connected him to a breakdance group in the city, and they reached out to recruit him. They liked his song, they said. Did he want to join the group as their MC?

He heard that Chengdu was the place to be, where artists gathered to make a living from their music. If he stayed in Jiangyou, his future would be bleak: destined to become a nobody in an unknown town. "I wanted to go places. I wanted to move to a bigger city, wanted to become a big-city guy," Kafe said. "It was like my American dream, you know? Like how everybody in America wants to go to New York." So, in 2005, at seventeen years old, he packed his bags and, with 500 yuan (about USD 70) in his pocket, hopped on a bus and moved to Chengdu.

.   .   .

Hip-hop was one of the last genres of music to establish itself in China's soundscape after the country opened its doors to the outside world. Its adoption in China was kickstarted in 1979, when Deng Xiaoping went on a weeklong US tour to strengthen diplomatic relations between the United States and China. He visited a Ford Motor Company factory in Georgia and attended a Texas rodeo, smiling under a ten-gallon hat, signaling to the world and his people that China was engaging with the West. America, in particular, loomed large in the Chinese public imagination. Young people, believing the Chinese proverb that "the moon was rounder abroad," became obsessed with studying in the United States, cramming for TOEFL tests and applying for coveted American visas in hopes of landing a spot at a foreign university. When KFC opened its flagship store in China, in Beijing in 1987—three stories tall and decked out in red and white banners—hundreds of customers lined up for a first taste.

The reforms of the 1980s opened China's doors not only to Western capital but also to Western culture—its film, literature, food, and music. Once reared on straightlaced revolutionary anthems,

Chinese listeners now indulged in the sentimental love songs of Taiwanese chanteuse Teresa Teng, the energetic rock hits of British pop duo Wham!, and the country tunes of John Denver. Rock 'n' roll, in particular, captured the adulation of the nation's youth. University students began sporting John Lennon haircuts and belting the throaty rock songs of Cui Jian, the musician who would go on to be known as the godfather of Chinese rock. During the 1989 Tiananmen demonstrations, Cui's most famous track, "Nothing to My Name," became a protest anthem chanted by students at the square.

After the crackdown, Western music was once again more tightly controlled. Cui Jian's concerts were heavily monitored, and in 1990, he was forced to cancel a national tour midway. Students chopped off their long locks and swapped their bandannas for business suits, John Denver for Dale Carnegie. As the eighties gave way to the nineties, the commercial displaced the political, and China's sonic landscape again shifted. Mandopop and Cantopop (Cantonese pop) from Taiwan and Hong Kong began to dominate the sound waves. The soundtrack of the era switched to the sweeter, more conflicted soft rock ballads of the Hong Kong band Beyond, sung not on open streets but within the confines of the nation's sparkling new karaoke bars. In one of its most popular hits, "Boundless Oceans, Vast Skies," the band croons: "Forgive me for loving freedom all my life / But I'm afraid of falling down one day."

Despite controls, the sounds of the outside world eventually found their way to Chinese ears as contraband. Literally translated as "cut hole" tapes, *dakou* were surplus records from the United States, the United Kingdom, and Japan, imported as waste after large-scale foreign trade took off in China in 1992. A *dakou* CD might have a small drilled hole through its outer rim, and a *dakou* tape might have an inch-long cut at the edge of its plastic case—so that, despite the minor damage, most of its tracks remained playable. Discarded at customs as "foreign plastic trash," the tapes were recovered by enterprising salesmen, stocked in warehouses, then resold in black markets across the country.

Dakou found a hole through the Party's cultural wall, enabling Chinese listeners access to centuries' worth of contemporary music—from Celine Dion hits to Finnish metal to Wagner operas—all in one go. Listeners were ravenous for new sounds. A shipment of three hundred thousand Madonna *dakou* albums sold out on the black market in a month. After Kurt Cobain committed suicide, the cost of Nirvana *dakou* tapes inflated from 5 to 80 yuan. "*Dakou* CDs were our first exposure to everything—rock, electronic, jazz, hip-hop," said J-Fever, one of Beijing's earliest and most respected rappers. "We fell in love with everything we could get our hands on."

By the late 2000s, mainstream pop flourished after the internet's arrival gave Chinese listeners access to the full buffet of contemporary music, from Britney Spears to the Backstreet Boys. In 2004, the Culture Ministry approved Britney Spears's first tour of the country, so long as she "didn't reveal too much." (Spears ended up scrapping plans for the tours, citing exhaustion.)

But while the internet rendered *dakou* obsolete, its scrappy, rebellious, and DIY spirit continued to thrive, evolving into a vibrant underground scene of punk rockers, metalheads, and hip-hop artists. In the underground bars of Shanghai and Beijing, rap battles and Iron Mic battles, the first of which was organized by Detroit native MC Showtyme, became popular. After the release of *8 Mile,* the biographical film about Eminem, many young Chinese rap aficionados fell in love with the sound of Slim Shady. "I didn't understand English, but I loved the way he was talking. It was so fresh," said Rita Fan, a hip-hop critic. "I could feel his anger, and I realized that music could be a channel to express these feelings."

The young people who trawled *dakou* stores in search of forbidden melodies copied and remixed those sounds in novel ways, creating sounds of their own. They became known as "*dakou* youth": an entire generation of listeners and artists proudly named after recycled foreign trash.

· · ·

After arriving in Chengdu, Kafe Hu lived on his own terms, without constraint. He got by on a few hundred dollars from each break-dance MC gig, just enough for food and a skimpy mattress on the balcony of an apartment. He frequented the *dakou* stores, too, getting the popular albums that everyone else was listening to at the time, such as 50 Cent, Jay-Z, and Linkin Park. He spent his days getting stoned and his evenings performing on sidewalks for anybody who would listen. After dark, his friends would often shake him awake in the middle of the night, double-fisting Red Bulls, yelling, "Get up, Kafe! It's time to make music!"

He loved Chengdu—the throngs of young people, their creative energy, and their willingness to live in the moment. Insulated from the political authority of the nation's east coast, the city historically served as a refuge for misfits, radicals, and exiled intellectuals. The eighth-century poets Li Bai and Du Fu, two of China's greatest, spent chunks of their careers in Chengdu, composing couplets while getting roaring drunk. (Later, Kafe would often weave Li Bai's poetry into his lyrics, continuing Li's legacy of "making a living out of verse.") The city's history of suffering—from the wars of the Ming dynasty, which wiped out a third of the population, to Mao's man-made famine in the 1960s—only strengthened its residents' resolve to enjoy the present. A distinct identity has flourished in the fertile Sichuanese basin: a laid-back, epicurean approach to life, paired with a stubborn resilience. The phrase that best encapsulates the Chengdu vibe translates into English as "take it easy," or more directly as "easy, breezy, flopping around!" The "flop" character could refer to jitters of excitement or a dead fish flailing on a woodblock. It is a phrase rooted in both joy and suffering, yelled by old grandmothers and young rappers alike.

Kafe soon left the breakdance crew to work at Hemp House, a dimly lit and perpetually smoky reggae bar that sold cheap Tsingtao beers and celebrated Bob Marley's birthday. He continued writing songs, filling notebook after notebook with lyrics. He taught himself how to use Photoshop to design Hemp House's posters and started a side hustle as a graphic designer. The bar hosted a diverse lineup of musicians from around the world, from jazz guitarists to grunge rock bands to Charlie Moseley, an American DJ from Washington, DC, who would become Kafe's best friend and roommate.

Charlie admired Kafe's cool baritone and effortless swagger; Kafe was impressed by Charlie's encyclopedic knowledge of the hip-hop genre. He introduced Kafe to more alternative hip-hop, like Mos Def and Flying Lotus, and taught him how to sample old jazz records. Kafe was in awe. "I was, like, wow," he told me. "Hip-hop can sound like this?" He fell in love with Charlie's American ethos of freedom and authenticity; of charting your own path and keeping it real. His Chinese peers often copied their Western counterparts, producing corny, second-rate imitations. "Walk into a hip-hop concert, and everyone would be wearing jean shorts sagged to their ankles and massive Mets jerseys, because the big act at the time was 50 Cent," said Charlie. "But Kafe understood that you didn't need a hip-hop starter pack to be an artist. You could stay in your own lane."

By 2008, Kafe had found other like-minded rappers in the city, where a nascent hip-hop scene had formed. Young people crowded into Chengdu Little Bar to watch the rappers roll through from their day jobs to engage in rap battles, still dressed in their office clothes. He hung out with a group of Chengdu-based rappers, such as Fat Shady, Mow, Lil Bai, Sleepy Cat, and Ansr J, many of whom would go on to found the rap collective CDC Rap House. In contrast to the Beijing hip-hop scene, which took on a grungier sound and a punk ethos, the Chengdu rappers adopted a more playful style, took on a trap beat, and held fast to the city's irreverent spirit without taking themselves too seriously.

It wasn't just Chengdu. Thanks to the internet, hip-hop germinated everywhere, shared and reinterpreted by different communities across the country. Fans quickly became *wangyou,* or "net friends," with one another through hiphop.cn, one of the most popular rap forums at the time, and Douban, the social media platform beloved by indie musicians and aficionados alike. Created as a film and music review site, Douban gave users a space to find communities to discuss their niche obsessions and interests. Artists posted new music on their pages to share with fans; listeners scoured for new music, live events, and like-minded friends. Online encounters felt both intimate and serendipitous, often turning into offline collaborations. Once, while traveling in Kunming, Yunnan, Kafe saw on social media that J-Fever was also in the city performing a show with the Guangzhou-based rap crew Essence, Energy & Spirit. Kafe messaged him. Within hours, they were sharing a meal together at a local noodle joint. That night, J-Fever called on Kafe to join him onstage, and eventually he invited him to join the crew.

New rap crews formed like this in all corners of China. There was C-Block from Changsha, No Fear from Wuhan, CHAOS from Xi'an, Uranu$ from Guangzhou, GO$h from Chongqing. They were hyperlocal, each shaped by their region's distinct dialect, slang, and culture. Having absorbed the music of the outside world, from Beijing to Brooklyn, they now wanted to cultivate sounds of their own.

.   .   .

In the lead-up to the 2008 Summer Olympic Games, the dominant belief in Beijing was that China and the world were coming together. President Bush visited the capital city that summer, captured on camera, a beaming smile on his face, shaking hands with Vice President Xi Jinping. China welcomed the United States' continued pursuit of a policy of engagement, rooted in the latter's belief that by deepening cultural and economic ties with China, Chinese society would also become more politically liberalized. As part of China's efforts to project a more open and welcoming image of itself to the world, the government lifted some blocks on the Great Firewall, allowing people in different parts of Beijing to access such banned sites as Amnesty International and BBC.

In their musical tastes, China and the world were coming together. Chinese audiences were not only hungry for American music; they were willing to pay to consume it. Rock bands like Linkin Park and the Yeah Yeah Yeahs now played in China to sold-out stadiums. Beijing opened its National Center for the Performing Arts, a titanium dome (known colloquially as "The Egg") west of Tiananmen Square, hosting performances of Puccini operas and Berlioz's

Symphonie Fantastique to packed audiences. "China is on the tip of everybody's tongue," Peter Grosslight, the head of music at the William Morris Agency at the time, told *The New York Times.* "There are 1.3 billion people there. It's becoming a much wealthier place. How can we ignore that?"

Although authorities were wary of the city's more unruly musical elements, they allowed the underground scene to flourish, possibly to showcase China's cultural diversity to the international community. D-22, a hole-in-the-wall punk nightclub inspired by New York punk hotspot CBGB, became the center of China's rock and punk explosion, showcasing the most creative and boisterous acts of Beijing's experimental music scene. Founded in 2006 by American Michael Pettis, a finance professor by day and club owner by night, D-22 nurtured an entire cohort of Chinese bands, from post-punk The Gar to the indie rock trio Carsick Cars. "We were the first generation to hear so much different music via the internet and to be influenced so much by Western music," Zhang Shouwang, the front man of Carsick Cars, told NPR. "All these Chinese bands started coming out and doing what they liked, and a primal sort of energy just exploded."

Yugong Yishan, a live-music venue then located in the parking lot across from Workers' Stadium, featured everything from French rock to Taiwanese aboriginal folk to the monthly hip-hop rager Section 6. The crowd favorite at Section 6 was Yin Ts'ang, perhaps the most notable rap group of Beijing's hip-hop scene. Founded in 2000 by the native Beijinger MC Webber, along with a Canadian-born Chinese rapper and two Americans, Yin Ts'ang presented itself as a Chinese band that aspired to stay true to the roots of the American genre, adopting hip-hop's countercultural ethos to, in the words of one of the band's members, Josh Heffernan, "resist McDonaldization."

Another popular hip-hop group that burst onto the scene at the time was In3, a Beijing-based hip-hop group known for its gritty lyrics and antiestablishment ethos. Seen as the voice of Beijing's hip-hop underground, In3 was angry and jaded. Its most famous track, "Beijing Evening News," released in 2008, was a scathing critique of state media and its disconnect from real life in Beijing.

The band condemned the city's culture of cutthroat hypocrisy: over-priced pharmacies and idiotic professors, "corrupt cops," "north-eastern pimps," "officials rolling up to the bar," and "butchers who hang up a goat's head but actually sell dog meat." It bought into the American dream of consumerism but also adopted America's counterculture and cynicism. "Who's the new leader?" the band snarled in a thick Beijing accent. "Who gives a shit."

. . .

In April 2008, shortly before the Olympics, a rap song with a starkly different ethos went viral on the Chinese internet. Like In3's hit, the track was a vicious tirade against hypocrisy in the media. But unlike "Beijing Evening News," which criticized Chinese state media's failure to capture the country's reality, this song attacked Western media outlets, such as CNN, for their false portrayal of China. Titled "Don't Be Like CNN" and set against the beat of Britney Spears's ". . . Baby One More Time," its lyrics went:

> *Don't be like CNN.*
> *Western media like bullshitting.*
> *. . .*
> *You are fucking idiots compared to us.*

The song appeared on anti-cnn.com, a website launched by twenty-three-year-old Tsinghua University graduate Rao Jin in response to Western media coverage of protests in Tibet, which Rao accused of using fake photos and biased reporting. The website accused CNN, for example, of cropping a photo to exclude Tibetan protesters throwing stones at Chinese trucks, making it appear as if only the Chinese police were attacking. (CNN defended its reporting, stating that any cropping done was for layout purposes rather than manipulation.) It didn't help when, a month later, CNN anchor Jake Cafferty called China "the same bunch of goons and thugs they've been for the last fifty years," a quote that fanned the flames and gave anti-cnn.com even more traction. "We were so angry to see full-page coverage about the Tibetan riots with fake pictures from

Western newspapers," Rao told *China Daily*. He founded the site to collect evidence of biased reporting and "break the perception that the West is all good and China is all bad."

Rao belonged to a group of young nationalists known as *fenqing*, or "angry youths," who lashed out at perceived slights to their nation's honor. Many were educated and tech-savvy and grew up in the nineties, too young to have experienced the chaos of the Mao era or the brutality of the Tiananmen massacre. Instead, they grew up in a more prosperous and stable China, after the Party had launched a "patriotic education campaign" to instill a sense of national pride in its youth. Most crucially, the rise of the internet provided a powerful new channel for forming their opinions and venting their anger. Their first and primary source of Western news was not newspapers or television but the internet, through websites like CNN and BBC. They gathered online—on internet forums and Reddit-like threads like Tianya Club, Baidu Tieba, and university electronic bulletin boards—to draft lengthy essays, spar with like-minded thinkers, and analyze and expose what they perceived to be Western media distortions.

For all the goodwill that the 2008 Beijing Olympics cultivated, it also unleashed a more aggressive strain of patriotism. Lifting blocks on the Great Firewall had an unintended consequence: Many young Chinese at home, who were able to freely access the less-filtered internet for the first time, as well as those overseas in the diaspora, were incensed to discover what the world had to say about their motherland at its moment to shine. Human rights groups called for a boycott of the ceremony. Celebrities like Richard Gere and Sharon Stone condemned China's rights violations. Free Tibet activists disrupted the Olympics torch relay in Paris, where a Chinese paralympics athlete was carrying the torch on its way to Beijing. Infuriated Chinese netizens mobilized an anti-French boycott, with thousands demonstrating in front of Chinese outlets of the French supermarket chain Carrefour.

A more pluralistic internet did not necessarily incubate a more liberal online populace. Opening a crack in the firewall allowed for more varied discourse—but that meant allowing more illiberal, nationalist voices to bloom, too. Nationalist voices surged in September, a month after the Olympics, when the US stock market crashed, thrusting the world into the most severe global financial crisis since the Great Depression. China announced a 4 trillion-yuan stimulus package, triple the size of the US effort that year. In Washington, China was reluctantly seen as the savior of the US economy; in Beijing, the crisis further emboldened Chinese confidence in its own system of governance. In a 2009 bestselling book titled *Unhappy China,* written by a group of Chinese academics, its authors argued that the financial crisis "showed that Chinese people shouldn't copy the West" and that China should stand up to the West to claim its rightful place as a global power.

Although *Unhappy China* was widely criticized as a work of arrogant jingoism, its central argument—that China had stood up and needed to assert its own way forward, independent of the West—had begun to resonate with Chinese people and leadership alike. The chaos of the financial crisis, set against the meticulously executed Beijing Olympics, tainted the United States' reputation as a global leader and the American dream of unfettered liberalization. "You were my teacher, but look at your system, Hank," said Wang Qishan, then a Chinese vice premier, to his longtime friend and advisor Hank Paulson, the US Secretary of the Treasury, as global markets crumbled. "We aren't sure we should be learning from you anymore."

Out west, in Chengdu, far from the political center, Kafe Hu remained insulated from the growing friction. When Olympics ads flooded the streets and Games footage aired nonstop in packed clubs and bars, Kafe didn't pay much attention. He didn't see how the Olympics had anything to do with him. "I didn't care much about the Games," Kafe would tell me more than a decade later. "All I cared about was how I would become a famous rapper."

So Kafe's learning continued. He absorbed new sounds, from A Tribe Called Quest to the Beastie Boys; expanded his musical repertoire to include electronic music, jazz, and reggae; and learned how to beatbox. His friendship with Charlie Moseley bloomed: They moved into a cramped apartment near the US Consulate, where they played *Call of Duty* until dawn, raised a cat called Green

Bean, and smoked weed from a two-foot-tall glass bong. They lived together harmoniously; the only argument Charlie could remember having was about who hogged the shower in the morning. They collaborated on silly songs, like one number called "Have Money Daddy," produced by a musician from San Francisco and featuring a mutual expat friend from Atlanta. They vacationed in Dali, in Yunnan, driving rented mopeds around Erhai Lake while tripping on acid, and frequented boisterous rap battles at Hemp House back in Chengdu. One summer night, the bar got so hot, and the stage so packed with young people cheering on and dancing to a heated freestyle rap battle, that all the light bulbs exploded.

CHAPTER 5

I'm Feeling Lucky

The first time Chen Qiufan watched *2001: A Space Odyssey,* he fell asleep, lulled to slumber by the film's famous star gate sequence. Only nine years old at the time, he didn't understand what was happening. But he was captivated by the portal of pulsating lights and kaleidoscopic colors and the long takes of spaceships gliding through the vast cosmos. He would rewatch the film countless times well into his adulthood, each time noticing something new. Kubrick's epic filled him with a sense of wonder that would drive him to ask the same questions for the rest of his life: Who are we? Where are we from? Where are we going? Chen admired Kubrick so much that, several years later, he even adopted the director's first name: Stanley.

Growing up in reform-era Shantou, a port city in the southern province of Guangdong, Stanley Chan (for his English name, he preferred to use the Cantonese romanization of Chen) came of age as an only child with all the comforts of middle-class life: financial stability and a stable education. His father worked as an engineer at a research institute, his mother as a bank clerk. From an early age, they encouraged young Stanley's voracious reading habits. His father would bring home popular science magazines from work; his mother talked her way into getting him a library card, even though he was too young, so he could spend his afternoons at the local library poring over fantasy novels. He grew into an unusually handsome young man, with the lithe frame, delicate features, and high cheekbones of a Hong Kong movie star and an intense gaze that gave little away but seemed to absorb the world around him.

As he matured, Shantou underwent its own growth spurt. When Stanley was ten years old, Deng Xiaoping set out on his Southern Tour. Shantou, a special economic zone at the doorstep of free-wheeling Hong Kong, prospered from an influx of foreign trade and investment. The city served as one of the first stops for foreign goods flowing into China—a hub of electronic appliances, pirated tapes, and the country's first *dakou* warehouses. Stanley devoured it all. He listened to *dakou* Chemical Brothers and Oasis and played Japanese video games on the newest imported Nintendo consoles. When his family moved from their small low-rise home in an alleyway into a brand-new high-rise apartment, he stuck manga posters all over the walls of his bedroom. In middle school, he encountered his first computer and started learning basic programming languages, like C and Basic.

But if China's opening to the world gave Lü Pin the language of feminism and Kafe Hu the sound of hip-hop, the greatest gift it gave to Chen Qiufan was science fiction. He raced through Jules Verne's *Journey to the Center of the Earth,* devoured the golden age classics of Arthur C. Clarke and Isaac Asimov, and watched a film a day, hunting down bootleg copies of *Blade Runner* and *Star Wars* like contraband treasures from a foreign land. Each encounter was a thrill—like discovering a private portal into an alternate universe. "I was a young boy who liked to ask why, so I turned to science for answers," he said. "But when science couldn't explain everything, I turned to science fiction."

Science fiction provided Stanley a lens through which to understand the world and a vantage point from which to see a panoply of possible futures at a time when the whole country was looking ahead. Everyone around him seemed to be obsessed with questions of growth: how much money they would make, what car model they should buy next, how many square meters their new apartment was. Stanley was different. His love of science fiction gave him a more ambivalent and discerning way of looking at the changes taking place around him. The very reforms that gave him the intergalactic epics of *Star Wars* also ushered in the myth of growth, which brought with it dazzling progress but also all its ills: soaring inequality, cutthroat competition, spiritual malaise.

In high school, when Stanley was sixteen, he channeled this ambivalence into his first short story, "The Bait," which won a science fiction prize for young writers and was published in China's most popular sci-fi fanzine, *Science Fiction World*. In the story, aliens arrive on Earth and gift humans with an invaluable new technology. Then the aliens enslave them with it.

. . .

As a student, Stanley rose up the rungs of conventional success, excelling at his studies, acing his college entrance exams, and landing a coveted spot at Peking University, where he enrolled in 2000. Beijing's elite universities were the first to offer students use of the internet, through an exclusive FTP (file transfer protocol) network on campus. Stanley and six of his dorm mates pooled their cash to buy a computer they could play games on. He surfed new websites, like the online news portals Sina and Sohu, and read popular online novels like *The First Intimate Contact*, by a Taiwanese writer, whose protagonist falls in love with a girl called Flyingdance through a bulletin board. He joined the university's science fiction club and met other sci-fi fans through bulletin boards, the most popular being Shima BBS, where they shared critiques, organized meetups, and published fan fiction. He joined the university start-up club, where members tried and failed to create a campus e-commerce platform, a kind of university-wide eBay.

As graduation approached, in 2004, he had no idea what to do next. He had majored in Chinese literature but had no interest in going into academia. Writing science fiction was a niche hobby, not a viable vocation. Most of his classmates wanted to make money. They sought high-earning white-collar opportunities at large multinationals, the most coveted being "The Big Four"—KPMG, Ernst & Young, Deloitte, and PricewaterhouseCoopers. They prioritized stability over excitement, placing their faith in well-known

Western brand names. One classmate took a job at Walmart after turning down an offer from a fledgling internet start-up, founded by two Peking University alumni, called Baidu.

Stanley jumped at the first opportunity that came his way: marketing real estate in the southern city of Shenzhen. At the time, Shenzhen was growing so fast, from a small fishing village to a metropolis of high-rises, that its pace was called "Shenzhen speed." One local office building was constructed at a rate of one floor every three days. But accelerated growth turned the city into a pressure cooker. Stanley spent his days toiling in front of a computer screen in a zombielike daze, lumbar spine sinking into his desk chair, advertising fancy condos he could never afford. He hated every minute of it.

By then, China stood on the edge of the internet boom, and the Chinese people had bought into a new myth, one that was much more compelling to Stanley: that information technologies had the power to change the world for the better. Pioneers of this myth, a new wave of bold tech entrepreneurs, had gathered in a thirty-eight-square-mile block of tech companies and start-ups in northwest Beijing: a neighborhood called Zhongguancun. Only a few kilometers away from Peking University, Zhongguancun start-ups recruited heavily from neighboring campuses, exerting a gravitational pull on the nation's best and brightest. In 2005, Baidu, the start-up his friend had turned down for Walmart only a year before, went public on NASDAQ. Within a year, it would be worth $3 billion and become the fourth most trafficked website in the world.

Stanley didn't want to be a small cog in a churning system, selling apartments to people so they could build and buy more. He wanted to be working alongside other idealistic, purpose-driven young people who had an active hand in shaping the nation's future. In December 2006, Stanley quit his job in real estate. A month later, he landed an advertising job at Baidu and moved to Zhongguancun.

. . .

In 1978, a decade before Stanley was fantasizing about intergalactic space travel, a physicist named Chen Chunxian toured Silicon Valley as part of a visiting Chinese delegation. He was inspired by what he saw: the fusion of cutting-edge science with the private sector, the brainpower of Stanford and Berkeley merged with the manufacturing might of Hewlett-Packard and Cisco. Why couldn't China create something similar? When Chen returned, he did what no other Chinese scientist had ever done—he set up China's first private company, an electronics consultancy, in the neighborhood where he worked, Zhongguancun, then known as the home of the nation's elite research institutes, secluded but filled with untapped talent.

Others quickly followed suit. Students started tech companies out of cramped dorms and empty classrooms. Entrepreneurs gathered around an area dubbed "Electronics Street" to sell hardware and computer parts. A group of engineers at the Chinese Academy of Sciences founded a company called Legend, later renamed Lenovo.

The government soon took notice, designating the region a high-tech experimental zone and offering free rent and tax subsidies to new enterprises. Technology was crucial to Deng Xiaoping's vision of China's path to modernization. The Party absorbed many of the ideas of futurist Alvin Toffler, who characterized human progress as three "waves" of change: the agricultural, industrial, and upcoming information revolutions. China arrived late to the last wave; in order to catch up with the West, it needed to seize the next.

When Stanley arrived at Peking University at the turn of the millennium, Zhongguancun had earned itself a new nickname: "China's Silicon Valley." A quiet suburb in northwest Beijing transformed into the "most frenetic neighborhood in Beijing, perhaps in all of China," according to a breathless *Newsweek* report, that would "lead the world's most populous nation into the Information Age and beyond." Scruffy students coded in internet cafés, tech executives conference-called in sleek high-rises, and salesmen hawked knockoff Nokia phones all in one neighborhood. Overseas Chinese returned home from abroad with dreams of founding the world's next Intels and Apples, bringing their Silicon Valley money and connections with them. The valley's own giants, from Intel to IBM, flocked to Zhongguancun to set up China offices. In 2001, foreign firms moved in at a rate of one per day.

By the time Stanley graduated, Google wanted a stake in China's future, too. In September 2006, the company set up shop in Zhongguancun. To accommodate China's censorship laws, Google announced that it would introduce a censored version of its search engine for the Chinese market—Google.cn—removing from its search results mentions of the Tiananmen massacre or websites that promoted Falun Gong, a spiritual movement banned by the Chinese government in 1999. But unlike Chinese websites like Baidu, Google's search engine would tell users if they had searched for censored information—even if the information itself was missing.

Google's decision to offer a censored search engine was controversial outside China, criticized as a compromise of the company's values. But the company's leaders were idealistic. They came to China hoping to realize their own dream—the dream of a free and open internet. By offering their search engine, albeit a censored one, to the Chinese market, they believed they could connect Chinese users to the outside world and push the Chinese internet toward greater openness and freedom.

To lead Google China's operations, they tapped Kai-Fu Lee, a Taiwanese-born computer scientist, trained at Columbia and Carnegie Mellon, who had risen through the ranks of Apple and Microsoft before joining Google. Lee embodied how many young, cosmopolitan Chinese envisioned the internet: borderless, fluent in multiple cultures, a paragon of an open and globalized world. In an open letter posted to his personal website, Lee summed up his vision with a simple equation:

youth + freedom + equality + bottom-up innovation +
user focus + don't be evil = The Miracle of Google

. . .

In 2008, after a year at Baidu, Stanley joined the online partnerships team at Google. He loved his new job. The office was vibrant and energetic, filled with idealistic young people who believed in doing good. They were enchanted by the Silicon Valley dream, the so-called Miracle of Google, and the allure of its central ethos: A product, if scaled and optimized, could transform the lives of billions. That year, China's internet user base surpassed that of the United States, becoming the world's largest market. If hundreds of millions of young Chinese now spent their days online—absorbing new cultures, learning new information, meeting new people, at a faster and vaster scale than ever before—freedom must be an inevitable outcome of all this connectivity.

Stanley's own creative career took a promising turn that year when he stumbled upon an online short story and emailed its author, a Chinese American writer named Ken Liu, to express his admiration. Over email, Stan and Ken became fast friends, exchanging ideas and giving each other feedback. Although they lived on opposite sides of the world, both had majored in literature at elite universities (Ken had studied at Harvard) and worked in the tech industry (Ken at Microsoft) while moonlighting as writers. They shared a fascination with humanity's uneasy relationship with technology and its impact on the most intimate matters of the human heart. They even shared the same birthday—November 30. "I felt like I'd found a kindred soul," Ken would later say.

After Stanley asked for translation advice, Ken offered to translate one of his short stories into English. That small, serendipitous idea would kickstart Ken's role as the preeminent English translator of Chinese sci-fi after Stanley recommended him as a translator for a friend, the science fiction writer Liu Cixin. Once a computer engineer at a state power plant, Liu had garnered an enthusiastic fan base among university students and internet entrepreneurs in Zhongguancun. He'd just published the first novel of a three-part epic about an alien invasion of Earth and wanted to have it translated into English. Ken was blown away by the story, which spanned from the Cultural Revolution to the end of the universe, and signed a contract to bring *The Three-Body Problem* to a global readership.

Stanley's fiction remained riven with ambivalence. His stories read like warped alternative visions of our technological future, of the Silicon Valley dream veering into nightmare. In "The Year of the Rat," a genetically engineered rat escapes a Chinese lab, setting off a global rat pandemic. In "The Smog Society," a retired man navigates a near-future China choked by pollution and unknowingly volunteers for a corporation that profits from the toxic smog.

Still, his imaginary dystopias were a far stretch from the optimism of the day. His own future looked promising. As a young professional, he'd joined the tech industry as China was integrating itself more deeply into the global internet. As an aspiring sci-fi writer, he'd connected with readers across the world when they were keen to hear new Chinese voices.

"I'm feeling lucky," Stanley liked to say, quoting Google's new search function—a playful shortcut that took users directly to the most relevant web page—to describe his own life. By connecting with the world online, the Chinese people seemed to have found their own shortcut—a fast track to freedom, equality, and all the inevitable benefits of modernization. But Google's luck in China would soon run out.

. . .

One chilly winter morning, on January 12, 2010, Stanley woke up to a cryptic text message from a colleague: Come to the office now. When he arrived at Google China's headquarters, in Tsinghua Science Park in Zhongguancun, he found the ten-story building completely surrounded. A gaggle of camera-toting reporters crouched by the entrance, filming Stanley and his colleagues as they walked in. They were part of a news story unfolding in real time.

On the first floor, their bosses delivered the bad news: Google's leaders had decided they were no longer going to censor their Chinese search engine. In recent weeks, they had learned of a cyberattack, originating in China, that targeted everything from Google's software source code to the email accounts of Chinese dissidents. They would spend the next few weeks discussing with the Chinese government whether they could "operate an unfiltered search engine within the law, if at all." This could mean shutting down Google.cn and their offices in China.

As the news spread, Chinese Google supporters, self-described "g-fans," flocked to the headquarters. They placed flower bouquets and candles in paper cups at the building's entrance, as if mourning the company's departure. Some supporters sang "The Internationale." They covered the Google logo statue with cards inscribed with poems and well-wishes:

Google Bai Bai

Thank you for holding values over profits!

Spirit of independence, freedom of thought

When Stanley got off work, he saw that security guards patrolling the area had started to clear the supporters out. One guard informed them they would need to "apply for permits at the relevant department"; otherwise, they were conducting an "illegal flower tribute." When Stanley went out for dinner and drinks with his friends that night, the mood was somber, like a post-funeral meal. Google's announcement came as a complete shock. Nobody on the Google China team had been consulted beforehand. It felt as if they had been abandoned overnight. "I realized that I was just a tiny cog in the system," Stanley told me years later. "One decision from up top and all of us had to be sacrificed."

Google's troubles had actually begun over a year earlier. Censors were already on high alert; 2009 was a sensitive year, both the twentieth anniversary of the Tiananmen massacre and the sixtieth of the founding of the People's Republic of China. Tensions rose in May, when China's propaganda chief demanded that Google.cn remove an unflattering link of him and Google refused. That summer, riots broke out in Xinjiang, the result of conflict between its Han and Uyghur populations. The government cut off all internet connections in the region, leading to a year-long internet blackout for over 20 million people. In the rest of the country, foreign sites like YouTube, Facebook, and Twitter were permanently banned. Google remained, but its status was uncertain. When the company uncovered a Chinese hacking attack targeting dissidents' email accounts later that year, it was the last straw. Google cofounder Sergey Brin, who fled the Soviet Union with his family when he was a child, in the seventies, found the hacks "deeply troubling." "In some aspects to their policy . . . I see the same earmarks of totalitarianism," he told *The Wall Street Journal.*

In China, Google's decision sparked intense debate. Some praised Google for standing by its convictions. Others criticized the company for leaving the country under the false pretense of supporting free speech; they believed Google left because it was losing—it controlled only a third of the market, behind Baidu's 60 percent. "Google claims it is withdrawing from China, which proves that it is exactly now what all the so-called 'g-fans' claimed: a human rights warrior. In fact, it is the opposite: nothing but a crafty businessman," wrote Sun Yunfeng, Baidu's chief product designer, in a viral post. "In China, every enterprise and individual has to dance with shackles on . . . Trying your best to do your part, within a limited environment, is a sincere way to conduct yourself as a company and a person."

Days later, Hillary Clinton delivered a speech on internet freedom in Washington, DC, that further inflamed Google's Chinese critics. Referring to Google's case in China, she compared its "virtual walls" to the Berlin Wall. State media outlets retaliated quickly, denouncing the United States for its "information imperialism" and for using the free internet as a scheme to preserve its hegemony. Twenty years later, the specter of the Soviet collapse still loomed large. "Gorbachev was once widely praised in the West . . . but it was Gorbachev who finally ruined the Soviet Union," wrote one author of a *People's Daily* editorial. "Therefore, China must not follow the Western world's practice on crucial issues such as internet control and supervision."

Clinton's speech killed any shred of possibility that the Chinese government would accommodate Google's demands. In March, the company officially dropped Google.cn. Google would keep its advertising and research teams in the country but redirected its Chinese-language website to Hong Kong. Many of Stanley's colleagues relocated to Tokyo, Singapore, Palo Alto. Google's American leadership continued to believe that the departure was a small hiccup in an inevitable path toward global internet freedom. "I personally believe that you cannot build a modern knowledge society with that kind of censorship," Google chairman Eric Schmidt later said. "In a long enough time period, do I think that this kind of regime approach will end? I think absolutely."

By letting Google go, the Party placed a wager: that China did not need Silicon Valley in order to succeed. Even without the valley's giants, Zhongguancun continued to flourish, with homegrown innovations of its own. Before long, Google's departure seemed to many Chinese like no big deal. After all, people had plenty of other options. eBay had left, but now they had Alibaba. They couldn't access Twitter, but they could use a new roster of microblogs, like Sina Weibo. They didn't need Google, because they had Baidu. Two years later, Stanley would quit Google to return to Baidu, too.

But in the moment, all Stanley could feel was a sense of vertigo, as if he were living through a turning point in history. He knew that this event would have profound effects on his life and on his country—but how? He no longer knew where the world was going. It was as if everyone had been hurtling along the same highway until the ground cracked and China swerved off onto a path of its own.

CHAPTER 6

Weibo Spring

In the summer of 2010, shortly after Google left China for good, I took an internship at *China Daily,* the nation's largest state-run English-language newspaper, in Beijing. Every morning, I showed up to the *Daily's* headquarters, a pale white rectangle of a building in the leafy part of the city's Chaoyang district; flashed my ID card at the glum security guard standing at the entrance; and walked to the newsroom, a brightly lit office laid out with rows of cubicles. I sat in a cluster of interns, high school and college students the *Daily* brought on as part of its internship program for English speakers to bring native-language expertise to the newsroom. We socialized in the cafeteria, gathering during lunchtime to exchange story ideas, share plans for the night, and gossip about our colleagues over Styrofoam containers of stir-fried eggplant and spicy, cold *liangpi* noodles.

Established in 1981, *China Daily* was founded as a Western-style paper—not only in language but also in content, style, and organizational structure. Its target readership was diplomats, foreign expats, tourists, and English-speaking locals. This meant that the paper's editorial policies were more liberal and paid lip service to the values of the International Federation of Journalists, espousing "fairness" and "honesty" in its coverage. *China Daily's* reporting on the 2003 SARS crisis, for example, was much more critical and fact-driven than that of its Chinese-language counterparts, such as *People's Daily.* But as a state-owned paper, its coverage was still ultimately shaped and constrained by the government. One foreign journalist who worked for the paper compared his experience there to "working at a public relations firm"—an instrument of public diplomacy, dispatched in major cities around the globe to "make the Chinese government look good."

Nobody told me what I could or couldn't write, and I never gave it much thought. I wrote miscellanea for the culture and features desk—food reviews, humor columns, press-release write-ups—eager to take on any task that a friendly editor was willing to assign me. I'd fully expected to be pouring coffee and photocopying transcripts, so I was thrilled to instead be roaming Beijing, accompanying the culture reporter to an Italian opera at the National Center for the Performing Arts, tagging along with the food critic to review a Peking duck restaurant. I began contributing to the humor-and-lifestyle "Hotpot Column," penned mostly by other interns and Beijing expats who covered such subjects as the challenges of dating in the city or how to drink *baijiu,* the infamously noxious sorghum liquor present at every Chinese banquet. In one of my first columns, titled "Oh, to Be Mistaken for a Beijing'er" (I did not come up with the titles), I wrote about my ambiguous accent and my attempts to assimilate as a Beijing local.

At the end of my internship, I pitched my editor on a subject in which I had a personal interest: the rise of English-language literary magazines in Hong Kong and their ties to the mainland. He was keen on the idea, so I went ahead and interviewed a new Hong Kong–based English literary journal, *Cha,* about the publication of its "China issue," which featured translations of Chinese poets and was slated to be released the following June.

"This project was fueled by a sense of confidence about English writing in Asia," *Cha*'s founder told me. "Our idea of publishing the China issue in June 2011 is, of course, a deliberate choice. We wanted the issue to coincide with the twenty-second anniversary of the Tiananmen massacre. We cannot think of a more appropriate time of the year for us to reflect on the state of our nation."

Then, without much thought, I sent my interview transcripts to my editor and asked for a deadline for the piece.

The reply came promptly. My editor gave me a go-ahead for the article, a tentative publication date, then added, at the end of the email:

> *Also, pls be very careful about the China Issue to be published in June 2011. We strictly forbid any use about the Tiananmen event. It's totally unnecessary to put that political element in such a literary story.*
>
> *Cheers.*

I shouldn't have been surprised. I knew the paper was state-run, tightly bound to the unspoken rules of what could or could not be said. I had a general sense of what that entailed—the "Three T's" of Tibet, Taiwan, and Tiananmen, for example, were considered taboo. Discussion of secession, dissidents, any kind of independence was forbidden. Cheers.

But no one had ever explicitly articulated these rules to me in writing. There was no handbook of forbidden terms—you simply learned the red lines through intuition, through trial and error. For those who grew up on the mainland, this sixth sense was cultivated much earlier in life, for much longer, external bounds gradually internalized as a meticulous self-censor. But growing up in Hong Kong, a haven of free speech at the doorstep of the mainland at the time, it was different. I took these privileges for granted, like running water or clean air.

No one had taught me how to respond to the hand of a state censor—a character I associated with history, not my present day. Now, for the first time, I'd felt the censor's hand press over my lips, redact my words. I read the email again, unsure how to react. One loud voice told me to be indignant. I was a writer! I believed in freedom of expression, admired Salman Rushdie and Vladimir Nabokov for their refusal to be silent. But I didn't wear indignation well, couldn't muster a holler of protest. After all, I was a high school intern writing lifestyle puff pieces that few people would ever read, not a world-class journalist drafting an investigative magnum opus. What good would my indignation do?

But were there only those two options? Loud or soft, active or passive, challenge the system or go with the flow? Follow the paths of those writers, activists, journalists who protested, boycotted, spoke out, and now sit alone behind bars, slowly forgotten by an amnesiac world, writing somber letters to their loved ones? Or follow those who went in the opposite direction—editors who have compiled glossaries of sensitive words, artists who have mastered the art of filtering, writers who self-censor their work? "In this world, there are some things that can be written about and some that cannot; some things that can be said, yet other things can only be thought," wrote the novelist Murong Xuecun in a speech he prepared for (but was forbidden to deliver at) the People's Literature Prize ceremony in 2010. "I am a proactive eunuch. I have already castrated myself before the surgeon raises his scalpel."

.   .   .

In 2010, I sensed that the possibilities of free expression were expanding—not in traditional media outlets but on the internet. Instead of reading newspapers like *China Daily* or watching CCTV, people were increasingly turning to the web to gather news, share information, and gauge public opinion. In particular, a new form of social media had proliferated: *weibos,* or "microblogs." Twitter's arrival in China in the mid-2000s had spawned an array of Chinese clones, most notably Sina Weibo, launched in 2009. The word *weibo* soon became synonymous with Sina Weibo, the largest microblogging site in China.

By the time I arrived in Beijing, Weibo had become a vibrant space for public discourse: a hub for intellectuals and ordinary people to share and debate their ideas. On the platform, free from the regulations that bound traditional media, writers like Murong Xuecun no longer felt pressure to wield the scalpel on their own words. Unlike in the publishing industry, which required many rounds of vetting and filtering through the Party's propaganda apparatus, on Weibo, a netizen could compose a few lines on her computer and share it instantaneously with the world. Famous users—from the A-list actress Yao Chen to the human rights lawyer Teng Biao, designated by the platform as "Big Vs" (V for verified)—could reach millions of followers. At the end of October 2010, Weibo reported 50 million users, doubling by the following January.

Most crucially, Weibo served not only as a megaphone but as a town square—a site of contestation and protest for an increasingly wired public. Offline, mass gathering was prohibited; online, Chinese citizens participated in what was called the act of *weiguan*—the mass gathering of a crowd for a public spectacle. They could communicate on a scale and at a speed never before possible, for example, protesting factory pollution and outing corrupt officials. In October 2010, a drunk driver in a black Volkswagen hit two students, killing one and injuring the other. When he was stopped by campus police trying to flee the scene, he yelled, "Go ahead, sue me if you dare. My father is Li Gang!" Li Gang was the deputy chief of the local public security bureau. Efforts to suppress the incident backfired. Within days, "My father is Li Gang" became a catchphrase on Weibo, condemning the powerful who shirked responsibility with impunity. The driver was sentenced to six years in prison for drunk driving and manslaughter.

When I first learned of the phrase, I felt like I was being let into a big inside joke, inducted into an alternative society where netizens were dreaming up new possibilities, writing new rules, creating new languages. The promise of Weibo resembled that of Twitter and Facebook, heralded as revolutionary new tools that brought people together, amplified marginalized voices, and dismantled power structures. Weibo's promise was even greater, since in China, there was so much more room to grow. In democratic societies, citizens could participate in the public sphere through a range of legitimate forums—through the ballot box, labor unions, an independent press. In China, they did so primarily through the internet—a third space unshackled by the rules that bound the rest of the nation's institutions. Chinese internet users were referred to not simply as "users" but more commonly as *wangmin,* or "netizens." After all, the internet had become a primary venue for civic engagement.

Boundaries, of course, persisted; websites remained inaccessible, and sensitive posts routinely disappeared. But boundary ball now became a more exciting and ubiquitous sport, played not only by a small group of grassroots intellectuals and activists but by anybody who had a social media account and wanted to challenge the status quo. To evade censors, they invented a compendium of playful memes: CCTV (China Central Television), which they mockingly dubbed CCAV (China Central Adult Video) to suggest that its news was as fake and restricted as porn; *Global Times,* the Party mouthpiece, which they nicknamed "Global Turd." The term *caonima* literally translates as "grass-mud-horse," but when you switch the tones of the Chinese characters around, it sounds like "fuck your mother." A meme of a dopey-eyed alpaca known as the "Grass-Mud-Horse" became a mascot for Chinese netizens fighting for free expression. "River crab," or *hexie,* a homophone for "harmonization," became a euphemism for censorship.

. . .

In 2011, the year after I had my first encounter with a censor, Liu Lipeng, whom I would come to know later by his English name, Eric Liu, started training to be one. Every morning at five o'clock, he rolled out of bed and caught the company bus to work. He slept straight through his commute—which took more than an hour from Tianjin's city center to the Haitai industrial park, a barren plot in the city's southwestern suburb—waking up just as they pulled up in front of his office. After the morning briefing, where his boss delivered the day's directives, he sat at his cubicle and logged on to Weibo's backend, the behind-the-scenes system responsible for managing the user interface. The system had already flagged posts with sensitive keywords. Highly sensitive phrases like "Tiananmen massacre" were highlighted in red and automatically blocked; milder words like "government" appeared in orange. His job was to read each flagged post, decide whether it crossed lines, and if so, delete it. Then on to the next post. Read and delete.

When people think of the Great Firewall, the image that comes to mind is typically its most tangible layer: the piece of software that filters traffic passing through the global web, blocking IP addresses deemed forbidden. This feature had been in place since the early days of the Ministry of State Security's Golden Shield Project. Most netizens adapted to it as nothing more than an annoying inconvenience, like traffic or air pollution. In 2010, the Berkman Center for Internet & Society at Harvard University estimated that less than 3 percent of the population used circumvention tools, such as virtual private networks, to "jump the wall" and access the unfiltered web in countries that censor their cyberspace, like China. Most people couldn't be bothered. They switched to homegrown alternatives—Baidu, QQ, and Weibo—which met their needs as well as, if not better than, foreign platforms like Google, Facebook, and Twitter.

Since its advent, the Great Firewall evolved from a list of blocked websites into a complex, multifaceted system of online censorship and control. At the top of the chain of command, an overlapping set of state organs known by a mouthful of initialisms—among them, the State Internet Information Office (SIIO), the State Council Information Office (SCIO), the State Administration of Press, Publication, Radio, Film, and Television (SAPPRFT), and the Ministry of State Security (MSS). All had the power to lay out broad rules of what could and could not be said. Collectively, they were dubbed by internet activists in China "the Ministry of Truth," a name borrowed from George Orwell's novel *1984*.

At the very bottom of the chain of command was Eric, a recent college graduate with spiky black hair, who spent so much time in front of a computer that he started wearing glasses—gold-rimmed, Harry Potter–style round frames that he would wear well into his thirties. As part of a team of 120 Weibo editors, Eric worked as one of China's many rank-and-file censors, hired by social media companies to maintain the bricks of the Great Firewall according to the shifting whims of the Party's various ministries. Weibo's censorship department was based in Tianjin because it was cost-effective and convenient. Located next to several universities, the industrial park guaranteed low rent and a supply of cheap, college-educated labor. Only a half-hour bullet train away from Beijing, the city was accessible to the company's upper-level management and internet security officials. Several other internet companies—including Douban, Tencent, and ByteDance—followed in Weibo's footsteps and set up their censorship operations in Tianjin, giving it its unofficial nickname: Shandu, or "Censorship City."

The various state organs from the Ministry of Truth passed orders to social media companies in the form of censorship directives: instructions on new sensitive keywords to remove from posts, or on how to silence negative news events—accidents, natural disasters, protests—that might spark social instability. For example, when a deadly flash flood hit Beijing, they issued the following directive:

> Reduce the volume of reporting on the Beijing flood. Insist on positive reporting. Do not make critical reports or commentary.

They issued directives to extinguish scandals, in particular, those involving government officials. When nude photographs surfaced of men who appeared to be local officials in Lujiang County, Anhui, engaging in a lively, four-person hotel room orgy, authorities instructed:

> All websites must stop following and hyping the so-called "Lujiang Indecent Photos Incident." Interactive platforms must quickly remove all related photos.

But the Party's greatest fear was of calls to gather. A Harvard study analyzing hundreds of thousands of censored posts found that the primary goal of Chinese internet controls was not to suppress criticism of the state but to silence comments that spurred collective action. This explained why calls for patriotic action were censored, while some critiques of government policies remained untouched. When angry nationalists called to boycott French retailer Carrefour after the Olympics torch relay was disrupted in Paris, authorities urged websites to monitor posts closely. Unchecked nationalist fervor risked sparking social unrest, diplomatic tensions, and criticisms against China's leadership for perceived weakness against outsiders.

The Party viewed collective action as the greatest threat to its rule and grew alarmed in early 2011 over its potential spread. On February 21, the State Council Information Office ordered:

> Immediately delete the phrase "A nice bunch of jasmine" and related information.

Authorities issued the directive after anonymous posts on Chinese social media called for a "Jasmine Revolution," inspired by the revolt in Tunisia and the unfolding Arab Spring. The words "Jasmine," "Egypt," and "Tunisia" were blocked from social media sites. Offline, domestic security officials fanned out across the country. Videos of President Hu Jintao singing "Mo Lihua," a Qing dynasty ode to the flower, were scrubbed from the web. In Beijing, police issued a jasmine ban at flower markets around the city.

Aside from these directives, there existed no official, centralized blacklist of keywords. Companies were wholly responsible for censoring their own content, creating their own keyword databases, and updating them to accommodate new directives. Failure to follow the changing rules resulted in companies' being fined, suspended, or shut down entirely. In 2009, Sina Weibo beat out its competitors, such as Fanfou, Jiwai, and Digu, to become the largest microblogging platform, because it was better at following the rules. During the riots in Xinjiang that summer, many providers failed to censor information quickly enough and were shut down, while Weibo posted information provided only by official media outlets and emerged as victor. As a method of control, the directives always reminded me of the vague "educational decrees" issued by the tyrannical High Inquisitor of Hogwarts, Dolores Umbridge, in the Harry Potter series, which students blindly scrambled to interpret. (Educational Decree Number Forty-One, for example, forbade students from discussing "the upsetting events of last year.")

In fear of falling foul of regulators, platforms therefore often preemptively censored their content to avoid stepping over an ambiguous red line. They were constantly on the lookout for "upsetting events," hot spots of netizen solidarity, new blasphemous euphemisms. Human ingenuity was just as crucial to the growing power of Chinese netizens as it was to the Great Firewall's continued survival. Eric Liu learned that he could not only delete a post but *hide a post* (in such a way that it cannot be searched), *make a post private* (so it is visible only to the author), and *ban a user* (kick them off the platform altogether). As netizens honed their skill at evading censorship, Eric learned to become a better censor.

. . .

Eric joined Weibo because he had no better options. Before joining, he'd never used or even heard of Weibo. He'd just graduated from Tianjin Agricultural University—a "mediocre student" at an "obviously mediocre university," he told me, with a degree in human resources management (a "useless field of study"). He wanted to find a job that would let him stay in Tianjin, where he was born and raised and three generations of his family lived together. His parents worked at state-owned enterprises—his father, as an electrician at a railway company; his mother, as an administrator at a construction firm—and enjoyed steady salaries, good health care, and solid pensions. His paternal grandfather, a veteran who fought for the Chinese People's Volunteers during the Korean War, secured a good reputation for his family. Growing up, Eric was neither ambitious nor rebellious. He was an introverted boy who spent most of his free time watching Japanese cartoons and playing video games with his cousins. He jumped the Firewall for the first time in college, with a free VPN called GoAgent, to watch banned Hong Kong and Hollywood films, going through IMDb's Top 500 movies one by one.

His first year out of college, he took a job that his aunt found him, working for his *juweihui,* or "neighborhood committee." Since Mao's era, such committees functioned as the lowest rung of governance, taking charge of miscellaneous civil affairs, such as sorting household garbage and mediating conflicts between neighbors. Eric spent his days doing whatever the committee leader ordered him to: cleaning windows, shuffling papers, conducting meaningless inspections. The work was stultifying. Realizing that he would rather die than continue working there, he started looking for a new job. So when he saw a listing for a new internet company on a recruitment site, he jumped at it.

Job Title: Weibo Editor

Job Location: Tianjin

Educational Experience: College Degree

Job Requirements:
1. College Degree, Can Read English, Male
2. Familiar with using the Computer and the Internet
3. Can work with a team, innovative

Job Responsibilities:
1. Ensure the company's informational security
2. Thoroughly check all of Sina's blogs, posts, and discussion forums for harmful information
3. Communicate with the technology department to correct these problems every day

After submitting his application, he was invited to the office for an interview, alongside a dozen other applicants. He filled out a quiz of basic questions, identifying the name of China's president, the premier, key cities and geographical regions. One question required a longer response: "What are your thoughts on Weibo users discussing Sino-Japanese relations?" It was a controversial topic, he wrote, but as long as it created traffic and did not violate any rules, online discussion was fine. A few days later, he got the job.

It soon became clear that his job, despite being at an exciting new internet company, was excruciating. The labor of censorship was at once crucial and tedious. On average, each editor processed three thousand posts per hour. A forty-person team processed 3 million posts every twenty-four hours; divided into four teams, they alternated shifts, completing a ten-hour day shift and a fourteen-hour night shift every four days. Like Eric, most team members were recent college graduates, willing to put in long hours for low pay: a monthly salary of 3,000 yuan ($490), roughly the same wage as a local carpenter. His entire team was made up of men. According to his managers, women did not have the stamina to handle night shifts.

At the office, there wasn't any chatter; employees rarely socialized. All day, all he heard was the whirring of mouse wheels scrolling, scrolling, scrolling, and every now and then, a pause, followed by a definitive *click*—the sound of a post being deleted, disappeared. The office was unremarkable: cramped cubicles separated by yellow dividers, identical laptops. A banner across the ceiling read THE BIG EYES OF CHINESE PEOPLE AROUND THE WORLD. The only anomaly was the lights—bright fluorescent tubes switched on twenty-four hours a day to keep employees productive. Sometimes, when Eric got sleepy during a night shift, he'd sneak in a quick nap on the floor next to an empty cubicle. A myth circulated among Weibo users that posts made between 3:00 and 4:00 a.m. would remain untouched.

He grew apathetic toward his work, but it was a stable source of income, just enough to make a living. Most of his colleagues did not use Weibo, did not have Weibo accounts, and did not care who posted what, where, and when. They just went through the motions with a clinical detachment: commute to work, commute home. Day shift, day shift, day shift, night shift. Read and delete. He spent his days slumped in front of his computer, face numb with fatigue—until one evening at around eight thirty, on July 23, 2011. Hundreds of miles south, in the city of Wenzhou, two bullet trains heading south collided, and Eric Liu was jolted from his stupor.

. . .

Earlier that evening, a lightning storm struck. The *Harmony Express* was then the world's largest and fastest high-speed railway, but it still had teething issues. Lightning hit a metal box beside the tracks, damaging the signaling system and leaving the signal stuck on the color green. Railway staff failed to notice the error in time and adjust. After experiencing a signal failure, Train D3115, carrying over 1,000 passengers, stopped for seven minutes, then moved at a slow speed on the tracks as a safety precaution. Behind it, train D301, carrying 558 passengers, continued at full speed, unaware of the train ahead of it, and collided into its rear. Four coaches fell off the viaduct they were traveling over. The crash killed 40 people and injured nearly 200. It was the third-deadliest high-speed rail accident in human history.

One of the first Weibo posts went up several minutes after the crash, posted by a university student on her journey home from Beijing:

> 20:47 p.m.: Help! High Speed Train D301 derailed near Wenzhou South Station! Children are crying in the car! We can't find any crew members! Help us please!

Over the next ten hours, the student's post was reposted more than a hundred thousand times. Millions of users across the country logged on to Weibo to survey the scene. At 21:35, the first eyewitness report was posted, by a fashion photographer who lived near the crash, and she included a photo of the wreckage. By midnight, citizen journalists were flocking to the site, gathering information about the missing and the dead and coordinating blood donations for the injured.

> Li Jianzhong, Male, on Hangzhou–Fuzhou Train Car 15. His family is extremely worried. Please contact over QQ.
>   Mrs. Chen is looking for her husband, Mr. Zhuo Huang. During last night's incident, he was on the first car of D301. Her son and niece have been found. Please dial.
>   Mrs. Zhang Binglian has not found her daughter since the accident. Her daughter's name is Huang Yuchun. 12 years old, white T-shirt and jeans, 1.50 meters tall, short hair, big front teeth, fair-skinned. She was sitting in Car 3, Seat 11. Please get in touch with this number.

The next day, the Party's Central Propaganda Department immediately attempted to quell public anger and cover up the incident, issuing directives to all media organizations: "Do not question. Do not elaborate. Do not associate."

Weibo users clamored for answers. Why was the train behind not aware that there was a train in front? Why was the rescue effort halted so soon? Why had a list of victims not been made public? Why were there photos emerging on Weibo of government workers burying the wreckage near the crash site? Infuriated, someone posted a public poll on Weibo with the question:

For what reasons do you believe that the train was buried?

POLL RESULTS:

To fill the pond (yesterday's news report): 607 (1%)

Better rescue (QQ morning news pop-up): 506 (1%)

Prevent leakage of technology (city newsflash report): 429 (1%)

Destruction of evidence! ! ! ! ! ! ! !: 61,382 (98%)

Some newspapers parroted the party line. But the boldly independent *Southern Metropolis Daily* trampled all over official rhetoric, publishing a scathing article titled "What Friggin' Miracle?" "In the face of such a terrible event and its incompetent handling by the Ministry of Railways," the piece began, "we can only express our views by asking—what the fuck?"

.   .   .

In Weibo's Tianjin office, all employees had to work overtime. As new posts continued to pour into their backends, so did new censorship directives. They were meticulous and precise.

Regarding the 7.23 Wenzhou high-speed train incident. 1. Release death toll only according to figures from authorities. 2. Do not report on a frequent basis. 3. More heartwarming stories are to be reported instead, i.e., blood donation, free taxi services, etc. 4. Do not investigate the causes of the accident; use information released from authorities as standard. 5. Do not reflect or comment.

Eric was overwhelmed by the volume of posts, scrambling to delete them. Their team was much too small and ill-equipped to manage the onslaught of grievances flooding their servers by the thousands, then the millions.

So powerful was the wave of public anger that it pushed the leadership to act. A week after the crash, Premier Wen Jiabao visited the site, vowing to investigate the root cause of the accident. "If corruption was found behind this, we must handle it according to law, and we will not be lenient," he said. The government admitted to "serious design flaws" and a "neglect of safety management," punished officials for corruption, and in 2015 sentenced former Railway Minister Liu Zhijun to life imprisonment for bribery.

For a government that rarely atoned for its errors, the Wenzhou train crash was a watershed moment. Both domestically and abroad, people applauded Weibo's emancipatory potential, predicting the arrival of a free-speech revolution. IN BARING FACTS OF TRAIN CRASH, BLOGS ERODE CHINA CENSORSHIP, read the *New York Times* headline that summer. They called it the Weibo Spring, a moment of civic awakening similar to the Beijing Spring, which had taken place more than two decades before, but even more so, to the Twitter-fueled Arab Spring then unfolding, toppling governments across the Middle East.

China faced many of the issues that were plaguing Middle Eastern countries in upheaval—deepening inequality, rampant corruption, a lack of political transparency—and its people were now equipped with the digital tools that enabled them to speak truth to power. New users continued to flood Weibo, its user base swelling to the size of the United States' population in 2012. Stemming the flow seemed impossible. The Great Firewall could not hold back the deluge of the people's voices.

Something had shifted in Eric, too. When he got the job, he saw himself as just an editor at a social media company, nothing more—just making sure users stayed safe, protecting them from dangerous content. But now? Now it was clear he was deleting far more than he'd expected: news of disasters, evidence of corruption, voices demanding truth and justice. He hadn't signed up for this. He wasn't sure how he was supposed to feel about it anymore.

As a child, Eric always admired his grandfather—for his sharp tongue, his refusal to hold back. Grandpa Liu spoke his mind. Sometimes, when the mood struck him, he'd even rail against Chairman Mao, calling him a slaughterer, until Eric's grandmother would panic, hissing at him to shut up before he got them all in trouble. To her, Grandpa's loquaciousness was a vice. But Eric loved listening to him rehash stories from the past.

There was one story, from when Eric's grandfather was fighting in North Korea, during the war, when he spotted a dead soldier sprawled on the road—someone from his hometown. It was the body of a former Nationalist, incorporated into the army, not a Communist. "Leave him," his superior ordered. But Grandpa refused—everyone deserved a proper burial. In another story, during the Cultural Revolution, he saw a mob of Red Guards beating up a child—a boy no older than eight. "Leave him alone!" he shouted, giving the boy just enough time to slip away before jumping on his bike to flee.

Maybe Eric wasn't as bold as Grandpa Liu. But like him, he just wanted to be a good person, to follow his conscience and do the right thing. As he sat at his desk listening to the whir of scrolls and clicks, to the insidious tune of erasure, something shifted. Even as the uproar of the news cycle cooled and work returned to normal, he felt uneasy. Sometimes, the act of deleting a post made him so uncomfortable that he would read it and, even knowing that a post had crossed a red line, let it go through.

CHAPTER 7

Unbound

On the morning of Valentine's Day 2012, three young women tried on wedding dresses in a small apartment in central Beijing. They each slipped on identical long-sleeved gowns, bought off the e-commerce platform Taobao for 200 yuan apiece. They applied one another's makeup, smearing crimson lipstick across the bodices of their dresses like streaks of blood and brushing dark-blue eyeshadow on their cheekbones like bruises. Then they set out for Qianmen, a busy commercial district just south of Tiananmen Square.

They marched down Qianmen Street hand in hand, wedding gowns blowing in the wind. "Yes to love, no to violence!" they chanted as they marched. "Violence is not intimacy!" Before long, a crowd had gathered, shocked by the sight of three blood-spattered brides gliding through downtown Beijing. "What are you doing? Why are you all bruised?" one passerby asked the women anxiously.

They marched to raise awareness for domestic violence against women, the brides said. Along with other volunteers, they handed out flyers explaining their cause. One woman who received a flyer even shared her own situation—that she herself had suffered from abuse. Reporters flocked to the scene, toting cameras and recording sound bites. Perplexed security guards, unsure what to make of this performance, watched from the sidelines before calling the police. They told the three women that they had to apply for permission from Beijing's Public Security Bureau to assemble publicly, and the police escorted them to the subway station.

Helping coordinate their efforts was Lü Pin. At first sight, with her slight frame and her thin face hidden behind a pair of square-rimmed glasses, she easily slipped into the background. While the younger feminists took center stage, she assumed the role of producer, helping from behind the scenes. She carried herself with a quiet poise and dressed in practical, unassuming clothes—simple blouses, cardigans, T-shirts tucked into skirts. She was not one for unnecessary embellishment, neither in her appearance nor in her speech, but when she spoke, she was terse, forceful, and articulate. "Valentine's Day is an important date in the global feminist movement," she said of her decision to organize the performance. Since the feminist activist Eve Ensler, author of the 1994 play *The Vagina Monologues,* launched the first V-Day, to combat violence against women, on Valentine's Day in the late nineties, activists have held V-Day events worldwide from Afghanistan to Rome to the Congo. "So we thought, let's organize our own V-Day event. V for Valentine's, but also V for victory over violence."

Earlier in the month, Lü had stumbled upon news of three activists in Ankara, Turkey, dressed in bridal gowns and protesting domestic violence. Why not organize a Chinese rendition? She enlisted three volunteers to act as brides. For the venue, they picked Qianmen, where the LGBT NGO Common Language had organized a queer-wedding performance in 2009—a bold mix of protest and performance art.

She met the three women through *Feminist Voices,* the online magazine she started in 2009. After its founding, Lü wrote prodigiously (averaging three hundred thousand words per year), commenting on the news through a feminist lens, and urged her readers to suggest topics and send feedback. She tried all kinds of methods of disseminating the magazine—as an email thread, a website, a QQ group, and even by text message. On the eve of one Lunar New Year, she reached out to readers via a group text, asking them to weigh in on whether Central China Television's annual Spring Festival program was sexist.

But Weibo transformed *Feminist Voices* from a popular periodical into an online hub, a virtual gathering point for Chinese feminists to come together in the public domain. In 2010, Lü Pin created an @FeministVoices account on Weibo, and its following burgeoned. Aspiring Chinese feminists wrote to Lü, sharing how her ideas had reshaped their thinking and asking how they could contribute. One of *Feminist Voices'* avid readers, a high school student who didn't have her own computer, would go to her mother's office every weekend to read Lü's latest missives. Another, a twenty-three-year-old new graduate based in Hong Kong, asked Lü if she could intern for the magazine. Lü hired her at once, offering a salary of a couple thousand yuan ($278) per month.

Hoping to bring some of these women together in one physical space, Lü rented a two-bedroom apartment near the Second Ring Road in Beijing, in a building shared with the offices of several other grassroots organizations, such as the Anti–Domestic Violence Network and the Beijing LGBT Center. With a kitchen, a living room, and a small balcony, the space could fit up to thirty people. Lü named it the One Yuan Commune and asked each visitor to donate at least one yuan every time they visited to help with maintenance costs. The Commune hosted feminist book clubs, film screenings, and guest lectures, promoting events through the @FeministVoices Weibo account. At one lecture on domestic violence, a male police officer attended to learn how to address the issue from a law enforcement perspective. Every summer, the Commune hosted a "School of Feminism," a discussion-based seminar that met every Saturday for eight weeks. Students brainstormed topics that would form the curriculum, like domestic violence and sexual harassment, and invited guest lecturers to share their insights.

Feminist Voices' online presence connected a network of feminists through a common vocabulary; the One Yuan Commune provided them with a shared space to deepen those connections into friendships. Many of the women who became regulars at the Commune were young, idealistic college students born in the 1980s—part of the one-child generation—whose parents had poured all their hopes into them. They came of age at a moment when more women were enrolling in universities than ever before, exposed to new ideas about their womanhood, reading texts by Betty Friedan and Judith Butler. (In 1999, women made up only 20 percent of Chinese university students; a decade later, more than half.) Despite this newfound sense of empowerment, they stepped into the world only to realize that their gender remained an insurmountable obstacle to their success.

As a young girl growing up in Sichuan, Xiao Meili dreamed of her Prince Charming, fussed over her makeup to attract the right boyfriend, and carefully preserved her virginity for when she met him. But then she went to college. She read Simone de Beauvoir's *The Second Sex,* spent a semester in Taiwan hanging out with the local feminist community, and her attitudes began to shift. Then she discovered the Commune. She'd stumbled upon it by chance, through an ad for a film screening on Douban, which had evolved from its early days as a review site to a vibrant discussion forum. The Commune became a space where she belonged and felt understood. During one college calligraphy class, her professor explained that the Chinese character for "woman" was shaped like a squatting person; therefore, the essence of womanhood was obedience. Her classmates nodded in agreement. Xiao was infuriated. She went to the Commune to air her frustrations.

Growing up in rural Guangxi, Wei Tingting thought it was normal for women to get hit. Her father beat her mother; her neighbor hit his wife right on the street. Everyone in the neighborhood saw. Only later did she realize how wrong it all was—that intimacy did not justify violence. As a student at Wuhan University, she joined the theater club and organized the campus's production of *The Vagina Monologues,* in which taboos she'd learned never to speak about—sex, abortion, orgasms—were discussed openly onstage. After graduation, she threw herself into gender and sexuality advocacy, came to terms with her own bisexual identity, and found a job as a project manager at the Beijing Gender Health Education Institute, in the same building as the One Yuan Commune.

Li Maizi, from the rural outskirts of Beijing, had been born Li Tingting, a feminine name her father chose in hopes that she would grow into a virtuous lady. His hopes were dashed: In second grade, she was dressing like a tomboy, stopped wearing braids, and ditched her skirts. By middle school, she had also realized that she was a lesbian. She shed her old name and chose her own: Li Maizi, meaning "wheat grain"—free, resilient, and grounded. She enrolled in college in Xi'an, where she read queer theory and Foucault, organized lesbian groups on the messaging app QQ, and set up a sex-ed organization, which connected her to the Commune.

In bringing these women together, Lü had tapped into a nationwide feminist awakening. The Commune incubated a feminist community; *Feminist Voices* amplified their reach far beyond the city limits of Beijing. All across China, young women began to push back against the sexism and misogyny entrenched in their everyday lives: a society where sexual harassment was the norm, gender discrimination in the workplace was common, and a deepseated stigma existed against unmarried women over thirty, widely known as "leftover." These young women, armed with a strong sense of self-worth and ambition, were relatively independent and unburdened by familial obligations. They would form the future of the movement, because their hearts, bodies, and minds were freer.

"Our society does not allow for alternative views—be it about gender, sexuality, or politics—and those with different views find themselves isolated, rejected by the mainstream, with nowhere to go," Lü later wrote. "I wanted to create a space for these young people who refused to be absorbed into the system to come together."

Individuals need a flag to bring them together, she believed. Once you give them the flag, they rally around it.

. . .

In some ways, the February 2012 Bloody Brides protest was a success. The goal was to provoke attention—to get people talking, to attract the media, to start a conversation—and it did. Photos of the protest posted on Weibo instantly went viral on social media, sparking debate over China's overlooked domestic violence crisis. The activists were inundated with interviews, even from the state media outlet *Global Times*. Inspired by the activists, that December, young women staged their own Bloody Brides protests across the country, in Hangzhou, Shanghai, Guangzhou, Xi'an, and Dongguan.

The original Bloody Brides protest kickstarted what the young activists dubbed "Year One of the Chinese Feminist Movement"— the year that they stepped onto the streets and took their advocacy public, moving from the sidelines to center stage. Five days after, Li Maizi organized another protest: "Occupy the Men's Bathroom," a campaign calling for more women's toilet stalls. She mobilized a group of women to gather in front of a public bathroom in Guangzhou, holding signs that read THE EASIER IT IS FOR WOMEN TO USE PUBLIC BATHROOMS, THE MORE GENDER EQUALITY WE CAN ENJOY. They chose the issue of public bathrooms because they wanted to stir awareness but do so with an ostensibly light cause, so as not to provoke too much ire. The strategy worked: For more than a week, Occupy the Men's Bathroom was one of the top ten trending topics on Weibo.

This time, authorities intervened. The day after the Occupy protest in Beijing, two plainclothes cops escorted Li Maizi to their car. To her surprise, they took her to a fancy restaurant and treated her to a 600-yuan ($83) feast. At the meal, they told her to stop protesting, posting on Weibo, and giving media interviews. Later that night, uniformed officers arrived at her parents' home in Beijing, also taking her father out for a meal at a restaurant and telling him that if he could get Li to stop her activities, they could get her a respectable government job at the local Women's Federation. Li did not acquiesce but did learn when and how to lie low.

The young feminist activists continued to organize, undeterred, building on their momentum. Both idealistic and pragmatic, tech-savvy and entrepreneurial, they turned to social media as a tool to gain visibility and promote change through the court of public opinion. In June, they launched another campaign, to protest sexual harassment on public transportation, gathering at subway stations across the country, holding signs and handing out flyers that read "It's fine for me to be sexy. It's not OK for you to touch." In August, they spearheaded a nationwide Bald Sisters' Campaign, calling upon college students to shave their heads and sign a joint petition to the

Ministry of Education to address gender discrimination in higher education. In November, they compiled signatures online to petition for the passage of a domestic violence law. To drum up attention, they posted semi-nude photos of themselves, topless chests covered with the words SHAME ON DOMESTIC VIOLENCE in black marker.

The boldness of the activists paid off. The movement blossomed. New volunteers joined their ranks, the media flocked to cover their campaigns, and their efforts paved the way for concrete policy changes. In 2013, the Ministry of Education announced that universities could no longer set enrollment quotas based on gender (with the exception of those related to the military and to national and public security). Also that year, the Beijing court ruled in favor of Kim Lee, an American woman who sued her Chinese husband for domestic abuse in a high-profile lawsuit, issuing a three-month restraining order against her husband. Their high-profile actions helped pave the way for the 2015 passage of China's first Anti–Domestic Violence Law. Even the Occupy the Men's Bathroom campaign bore fruit: In 2016, the Ministry of Housing ordered the ratio of women's stalls to men's in all new public restrooms to expand to at least three to two.

In many ways, the activists had built upon years of efforts—from behind-the-scenes petitions to legal work—by the women's rights advocates who preceded them. The Anti–Domestic Violence Network, a coalition of NGOs formed in the wake of the 1995 World Conference on Women, in Beijing, had been spearheading anti–domestic violence initiatives for over two decades. Led by Feng Yuan, one of China's first women's rights advocates and Lü Pin's mentor, the organization conducted research on domestic violence, raised awareness among health professionals and prosecutors alike, and collaborated with the government to draft bills and push for legislation.

Like the women's rights advocates who preceded them, the young feminist activists also participated in a dance with the state, tackling issues that were not explicitly political but controversial enough to spark conversation. But unlike the previous generation, who believed that change could come from collaboration with the state, they saw themselves as "action-oriented feminists," wholly independent of the system. Their debates didn't take place in classrooms and academic journalism but unfolded on social media, thrust into the public spotlight. Weibo, free of traditional gatekeepers, enabled them to amplify their voices and spread a growing feminist consciousness later dubbed by the scholars Aviva Wei Xue and Kate Rose as "Weibo feminism."

In the 1990s, Lü was part of a nascent group of feminists who built a community of grassroots organizations from the ground up. Now, almost two decades later, she had brought together a younger generation, mobilized on the internet, gathered to propel the movement forward.

. . .

After moving to Beijing, Ma Baoli had come to a starkly different realization from Lü's: For an entrepreneur to succeed in China, he needed to gain the approval of the state.

Since Ma and the Danlan team had moved to the capital from Qinhuangdao, their optimism had been waning. They lived and worked out of a cramped apartment in Lishuiqiao, in the city's suburban outskirts, with a small yard, where they cleared the weeds and planted vegetables. They operated on a shoestring budget, supplemented by Ma's savings—barely enough to pay for rent and each employee's salary (a paltry 1,500–3,500 yuan [$208–486] a month). They picked an office space near the train tracks so that Ma could catch a four-hour train ride to Qinhuangdao whenever he was needed at the police bureau. They thought of themselves as *beipiao*, Beijing drifters, unmoored and unwelcome, part of the influx of migrant workers who arrived in the city only to realize that they did not belong. Ma barely slept; he was gaining weight and losing hair. The start-up's status was insecure. Any number of reasons—dwindling finances, demoralized spirits, Ma's responsibilities as a cop—could've forced them to abandon their plans.

He had little in common with the other tech entrepreneurs, like the founders of Sohu or Sina or Alibaba. He was a small-town cop from Qinhuangdao; they were college graduates from elite univer-sities like Peking and Tsinghua, with experience abroad, computer science PhDs, and venture capitalist funding. They worked out of the bustling new tech hub of Zhongguancun, bouncing from one start-up idea to the next, making and breaking companies without inhibition. Ma could not afford to fail, to shut down his website and start again. This was his one shot. His team was his family, the website his life's purpose.

But what Ma lacked in privilege, he made up for in street smarts. As a police officer, hypersensitive to the ways power moved in this country, he knew that he had to build the right alliances and align his goals with those of the state. The state and top tech entrepre-neurs forged a bond of cautious codependency: The state relied on its entrepreneurs to innovate and strengthen the economy, while the entrepreneurs benefited from the state's endorsement and patron-age. Key to Alibaba's success was not only Jack Ma's charisma but his willingness to participate in this tango. He cultivated strong relations at all levels of government—by offering the city of Hang-zhou its most important job creator, fueling the consumer economy, and backing state-owned conglomerates. "As always, be in love with them," Jack once explained of his strategy in dealing with the gov-ernment, "but don't marry them."

As a gay entrepreneur running a gay website, Ma Baoli had a much more challenging relationship to orchestrate. To succeed, Danlan needed to become *official,* to win the approval of the powers-at-large by offering something nobody else could. The question was how.

In 2010, Ma found an answer in public health—specifically, China's growing HIV-AIDS crisis. When he first arrived in Beijing, many of his friends had become infected with HIV and reached out to him for help. Awareness around sexually transmitted diseases was limited. Most gay men he knew did not wear condoms, which they believed were used simply to prevent pregnancies. Govern-ment interventions failed to adequately address a growing AIDS epidemic. Homosexual transmission accounted for almost a fifth of infections.

Ma called the county-level Center for Disease Control in Beijing's

Changping district. "I am the founder of China's largest gay website," he said, and he proposed that they collaborate on HIV-prevention nonprofit projects. More than any other organization, Danlan had built a tight-knit network of trust with the nation's gay community. The director of the Changping county-level CDC was delighted and invited Ma to the office to discuss their potential collaboration. "You have reached out at just the right moment," he explained. The CDC had just received subsidies from the Global Fund to Fight AIDS, Malaria, and Tuberculosis, and the director suggested that Ma submit a grant application for Danlan. He did, the grant was approved, and Danlan's first government partnership was secured. Danlan would offer Beijing's gay community HIV-prevention information, screenings, and anti-discrimination education; the CDC provided a 50,000-yuan ($6,940) stipend for them to do so.

"At first, everything was haphazard and improvised," said Chen Zihuang, a young physical education teacher from Jiangxi Province who was hired to run Danlan's new HIV-prevention nonprofit. When the company posted the job description on its Weibo account, he applied right away, taking the train one morning to the Beijing office for his interview. Ma had just rolled out of bed, groggy-eyed and hair uncombed. He asked a few simple questions, then said, "Well, why don't you grab a chair and get started?" Chen's first job was to administer HIV tests, so he set up an office on the first floor of a gay club, offering tests to anyone who dropped by during the day. Demand swelled. Soon, Chen was managing a team of a dozen volunteers.

The collaboration with the Changping Center for Disease Control paved the way for a city-level partnership with the Beijing CDC and eventually one with the Ministry of Health, at the national level, allowing Danlan to open testing centers across the country. It became the go-to organization for health professionals, experts, and scholars seeking to understand HIV transmission among men who have sex with men. Although the Center for Disease Control had nothing to do with internet regulation, it was still part of the official state apparatus. A government partnership gave Danlan funding, but also, most crucially, legitimacy. Ma changed the website's domain from .com to .org to emphasize Danlan's role as a public health organization. With a government partnership under his belt, he registered Danlan with the Beijing Municipal Public Security Bureau and established it as the first officially sanctioned gay website in China. In positioning Danlan as a crucial resource to the government's initiatives, Ma was making it indispensable.

. . .

In March 2012, Ma made a decision that changed his life. Three months earlier, a friend working at the social media platform Sohu had asked if he could shoot a documentary about Danlan to post on his site. Ma agreed, hoping that publicity might alleviate the organization's financial struggles: Perhaps a big brand would pay for an ad, or Sohu's CEO might watch the doc and invest in Danlan. Ma was still closeted and employed at the police bureau, shuttling back and forth between Beijing and Qinhuangdao to juggle his responsibilities. Qinhuangdao was far away and insulated from the world. Nobody back home would notice the documentary.

In it, Ma walked around the Danlan office—bare-walled, sparsely furnished. He showed viewers his bedroom, looking out the window at the city's smoggy skyline. "Look at Jiayuan.com, which was founded the same time as us," Ma said in front of the camera. "They just listed on NASDAQ, but we can barely keep our company afloat." Jiayuan was the largest dating website in China, founded by a journalism student out of her Fudan University dormitory. Ma knew that Danlan's lack of success was not for lack of effort but because of stigma and ignorance. "One day, people will look back and say this website changed people's lives," he continued. One day, the public would learn to love them, too.

The morning the documentary went live, it racked up so many clicks that it was featured at the top of Sohu's home page by the afternoon, under the headline GAY WEBSITE LEADER'S STORY. His phone was flooded with messages from friends and acquaintances. *Hey, Geng Le, I saw you on Sohu! Look, Baoli, you're famous now.* Ma was thrilled by the attention. Until a particular call came in.

"Baoli, are you in Beijing?" It was a colleague at the police bureau.

"Yes." Ma's face froze.

"Come home right away. The boss wants to see you."

The next day, he took the first train to Qinhuangdao. At the office, his colleagues either stared at him or didn't acknowledge his existence. His boss called him in to tell him that his decision to run the website was one of the most humiliating things he could've done—for his own reputation and that of the bureau. He gave Ma an ultimatum: Shut down the website right away or leave the bureau.

Ma had a night to think it over. His close friends and colleagues begged him not to quit, not to throw his life away. He desperately wanted to stay. The police bureau and academy had been his home and his life since he was a teenager. He'd lived and worked in the area for almost two decades. He knew every inch of the bureau by heart—the courtyard, the basketball court, the strip of barbecue restaurants across the road. To leave would be to let go of a home and abandon the place that had made him who he was.

Later in life, he would find that his role as a policeman was always a part of his identity. "I still have vivid dreams of that courtyard all the time," he told me more than a decade later in his glass-walled office overlooking Beijing's Central Business District. "In my dreams, I'll have returned to the bureau but can't find my office. I can't find my seat. I'll dream of my bosses calling me up, asking me to come back. 'Come back, Baoli,' they'll say. 'We want you to come back and work for us again.'"

The next day, he handed in his resignation, with the uniform that he had worn since he was nineteen. He left the bureau, gave up his health insurance, and filed for divorce from his wife. Spurned by his colleagues, ostracized by his friends, and estranged from his parents, he was a social pariah. But Ma had finally come out.

. . .

In August 2012, the Communist Party leadership gathered at its annual seaside getaway at Beidaihe Beach with its own pivotal decision to make: who it would select as part of its new lineup of leaders. After Mao's death, in 1976, Deng Xiaoping established new norms—like fixed term limits, a mandatory requirement age, and collective decision-making—that enabled smooth leadership transitions. In 1989, Deng passed the baton to Jiang Zemin; in 2002, Jiang stepped down to make way for Hu Jintao. This time would mark the second orderly leadership transition since the death of Deng, and the first time he did not handpick the Party's general secretary.

In 2012, China had reached a crossroads. Although some had called the ten years of Hu Jintao's leadership China's "golden age," others dubbed it its "lost decade"—a period of weak policies, limited reforms, and wasted opportunity. China had reaped all the low-hanging fruit of Reform and Opening's double-digit growth while failing to introduce deeper structural reforms to its political and economic institutions. Uninhibited growth gave the Chinese people gleaming skyscrapers and high-speed bullet trains but also a pollution crisis, deepening inequality, and endemic corruption. In March, the charismatic Chongqing party chief Bo Xilai, once widely regarded as a top contender for the leadership, was removed from his post amid a scandal involving his wife and the murder of a British businessman, laying bare the corruption rotting away the very core of his leadership. A year later, he was sentenced to life imprisonment.

The system was unstable and unsustainable. Simmering grievances exploded into protest; between 2006 and 2010, the number of "mass incidents" doubled. In 2011, the residents of Wukan, Guangdong, staged a months-long protest of illegal land grabs, demanding that local authorities grant democratic elections. The internet amplified the system's instability as Chinese netizens turned to new social media platforms, such as Weibo, to mobilize and protest. Days after Weibo users called for a Jasmine Revolution in China, President Hu Jintao summoned top leaders to step up internet controls, "guide public opinion," and address social problems before they became threats to stability. China could no longer afford to "cross the river by feeling the stones." The country needed to introduce immediate and drastic reforms or else risk another "historical tragedy" like the Cultural Revolution, the outgoing premier, Wen

Jiabao, declared. Whoever was selected as China's new leader would inherit an immensely difficult task: to guide the country to a more sustainable model of growth while maintaining the Party's tenuous control of its newly networked citizenry.

On November 15, 2012, the Party unveiled its selections. The new leaders, dressed in identical black suits, stepped onto the red-carpeted stage of the Great Hall of the People in Beijing. At the helm, as general secretary, was Xi Jinping. At his side was Li Keqiang, who would take the second-highest position of premier. Domestic and international observers alike immediately debated the lineup, speculating on what the new leadership would bring.

Some saw Xi as a cautious operator who would stick to the status quo. But many believed that he was a reformer who would push to further liberalize China's political and economic institutions. They pointed to his father, Xi Zhongxun, a Party elder who pushed for greater economic reforms. They cited the younger Xi's track record as the Party secretary of Fujian and Zhejiang, entrepreneurial hubs where he had introduced market-friendly policies. They gushed over his recent visit to Muscatine, Iowa—where in 1985 he'd spent two weeks as part of an agricultural delegation to study hog farms and feed plants—as evidence of his admiration of America. They also looked to his second-in-command, premier Li Keqiang, who was an economist by trade, known for his technocratic style of leadership. Xi seemed to confirm these beliefs when he traveled south to Shenzhen a month later, replicating parts of Deng Xiaoping's Southern Tour from two decades ago, visiting an internet company and laying a wreath in front of a bronze statue of Deng, expressing his continued commitment to reform.

Two weeks after the leadership transition, the Party unveiled its new slogan: The Chinese Dream. In a speech at the National Museum of China, in Beijing, Xi Jinping called the Chinese Dream "the great rejuvenation of the Chinese nation." The call for national rejuvenation was nothing new, echoing past leaders' calls for China to become rich and powerful. Xi's vision aimed for a "moderately prosperous society" by 2021, the Party's one hundredth anniversary, with doubled GDP and per capita disposable income, the people's social welfare needs met, and a military "capable of fighting and winning wars." Wang Huning, the stoic international relations professor who had since rapidly risen in the ranks of power to join the Politburo as the leadership's chief ideologue, was credited with shaping the idea of the Chinese Dream. Before long, the slogan had spread across headlines, roadside ads, school curricula, and even a chart-topping folk song. But what exactly did the dream entail? Was it a dream of constitutional reform, or one of sheer economic power and military might? Did it promise prosperity for all or only the elite? Did it include the dreams of China's entrepreneurs, dreaming of innovation; of its migrant workers, seeking fair opportunities and a just workplace; of its feminist activists, who dreamed of equality, or its queer communities, yearning for acceptance?

"Here is my prediction about China," Nicholas Kristof wrote in a *New York Times* op-ed. Xi "will spearhead a resurgence of economic reform . . . Mao's body will be hauled out of Tiananmen Square . . . , and Liu Xiaobo, the Nobel Peace Prize–winning writer, will be released from prison." In the coming ten years, he concluded, "China will come alive again."

Even Party insiders seemed to share this view. When Annie Jieping Zhang, a Chinese journalist who would go on to cofound the news site *Initium,* interviewed several Party princelings, they almost unanimously agreed that the new leader was a reformer. Only one person—Hu Dehua, the son of ousted party leader Hu Yaobang—vehemently disagreed with this assessment. The media had gotten it wrong, he claimed: As long as the Party's interests came before the people's, reform would not come.

. . .

On November 16, one day after the Party unveiled its new leadership, Ma launched his own creation: a gay dating app. Earlier in the year, one of Ma's colleagues, who had recently returned from a trip to Hong Kong, walked into his office bearing a gift. "You have to get a look at this," he exclaimed, gesturing at the object in his hand: Apple's latest iPhone. But it wasn't the hardware that he was excited about; it was the app displayed on the screen. The interface featured a black-and-white grid, each square depicting the profile of a young man, captioned with his name, age, height, weight, "scene" (i.e., Twinks, Bears, Strictly Friends), and, most crucially, his proximity. Named Jack'd, the app had been created by a Japanese engineering student at Cornell University and acquired by an American company. By the time Jack'd reached the Chinese internet, it was a popular download in China's app store that the queer community had dubbed the "Hookup King."

To Ma, Jack'd was a revelation. In contrast, Danlan's browser-based website was primitive. Connecting with other gay men involved chatting on a message board, then waiting for days, if not months, to connect with faceless users two provinces away. On Jack'd, you could meet the guy next door tomorrow. Ma still used a Nokia flip phone at the time. But he saw an opportunity. He tapped his best software engineer, recruited a handful of computer science undergraduates as interns, gave them 50,000 yuan ($6,940), and instructed them to "imitate Jack'd. Make an exact copy for China." When they were naming the app, Ma wanted something foreign-sounding that gave it a sophisticated ring. Since Jack'd was doing so well, why not riff on its name? They pegged the letter "d" onto Danlan's defining color and named their app Blued.

Ten days later, the Ministry of Health invited Ma to take part in a World AIDS Day conference. The organizers informed him that a high-level official would meet him, without mentioning who it would be. He walked onto the stage that day and found himself face-to-face with Li Keqiang. The newly tapped premier seemed thinner and shorter in person than when Ma had seen him on television.

"Greetings, Premier. I run a gay website," Ma said, starstruck, as Li walked over to greet him.

"Thank you for your hard work, comrade," Li replied as he shook his hand.

That night, elated, Ma called his mother and told her to turn on the television, where the handshake was aired on the evening news. The handshake was acceptance from the highest levels of power. It proved to his mother that there was nothing wrong with her son and that his work was worthy of the respect of someone like the premier. Far from having to be ashamed, she could be proud. She asked for a photograph of the handshake, printed and framed. She hung it next to their dining table at home.

The handshake, shared widely across the media, was a stamp of approval not only for Ma but for queer people across the country. Nearly a decade later, when I spoke to a young man from Hebei named Jeremy, he told me there were two public events crucial to his excruciating decision to come out: the queer wedding staged by activists in Qianmen in 2009 and Ma's handshake with the premier in 2012. In 2009, he was a depressed and closeted eighteen-year-old migrant worker, living alone out of a room on the outskirts of Beijing. He once visited a cruising spot in Dongdan Park, where he saw two elderly men having sex in the darkness, and felt such an intense sadness. "I realized that I never wanted to end up living my life like that, spending my entire life in the closet, living a lie," he told me. The staged wedding and the staged handshake—the first, an act of queer defiance, and the second, of queer acceptance—showed him that he did not have to.

But the handshake also embodied the intricate dance between the state and its private entrepreneurs. In contrast to activists like Lü Pin, who believed they could move forward only by unbinding themselves from the shackles of the state, entrepreneurs like Ma Baoli realized that they could achieve their goals only by collaborating with it. The state wanted to address a public health issue; Ma provided the tools to do so. Ma Baoli wanted official recognition; the Party gave him their endorsement. Once spurned by authority, Ma now found himself wrapped up in its embrace.

Having figured out the problem of political support, he still needed to address the other major obstacle: money. Growth was the goal, not mere survival. The success of Jack'd had been driven by the mobile internet boom, and China had just overtaken the United States as the world's largest smartphone market: 4G towers sprouted like weeds, and mobile traffic doubled annually. Every entrepreneur obsessed over the pressing question of how to go mobile. On Weibo, big-shot entrepreneurs and venture capitalists like Kai-Fu

Lee and Charles Xue, a Chinese American angel investor, declared that China was on the cusp of another revolution.

After Blued's launch in the Chinese Apple app store, it rocketed to ninth place in number of downloads. Users flooded the platform so quickly that the app often crashed, forcing programmers into frantic reboots. Ma pivoted away completely from the Danlan website to focus on the Blued app. They had to act fast. China had plunged headfirst into the mobile era, and imitation was no longer good enough. Just as Taobao had surpassed eBay, Blued needed to become more than just China's Jack'd. Chinese entrepreneurs were done playing catch-up with the world. This time, they wanted to get ahead of the curve.

Part II

CHAPTER 8

Going Public

I n the Chinese film *American Dreams in China*, a young man from the countryside lands a spot at the prestigious Peking University and launches a wildly successful tutoring company called New Dream. The film is loosely based on the real-life journey of Michael Yu, the founder of China's largest tutoring company, New Oriental. The character who resembles Yu studies Dale Carnegie mantras, tutors students over KFC, and woos a gorgeous classmate while preparing for a US-visa interview. By the story's end, he has swapped his schoolboy outfit for a business suit and transformed his tutoring service into a billion-dollar company. He ultimately doesn't end up with the girl or the visa, but he acquires glory, capital, and an IPO—the American dream, in other words, right at home in China.

The film, released in 2013, was an instant box office hit in China, capturing the wave of entrepreneurial optimism sweeping the country. Any underdog with enough savvy and hustle, the movie seemed to suggest, could rise to the top. By the time of the film's release, Yu was a household name and New Oriental a flourishing empire of learning centers, online courses, and bookstores, all built on the promise of leading students to self-made success.

Ma Baoli was fired up the first time he watched the film. "It captured the energy and dynamism of the entrepreneurial environment at the time, when everyone's eyes were filled with a kind of glow and confidence," he told me. Aspiring entrepreneurs gathered in

Zhongguancun's Garage Café—a start-up café the size of an Olympic swimming pool—cooking up new ideas. Ambitious Chinese coders studying abroad no longer aspired to go to Silicon Valley but began to seek opportunities back home. Wealthy investors hunted eagerly for the next founder to back and the next dream to fund.

Shortly after Blued's launch, in 2013, an investor at a Shanghai-based venture capital firm reached out to Ma with an offer. They'd noticed Blued's soaring rankings in the app store but were initially hesitant about investing in a gay enterprise, the investor explained. Ma's handshake with Li Keqiang changed their minds.

Ma was trained as a cop. He was suspicious. He had no clue about how investing worked. Of course it was a scam: cash in exchange for control of the company? So Ma turned the offer down. But the investor was persistent. To allay Ma's concerns, the investor invited him to visit Shanghai to attend a start-up conference for aspiring entrepreneurs. At the end of that trip, he presented Ma with a number he could not refuse. Once kept alive by 50-yuan donations, Blued received its first angel investment of 3 million yuan ($484,000). That was only the beginning.

In 2014, Blued raised a Series A round investment of $1.6 million led by the venture capital firm Crystal Stream. Months later, a few days after Apple CEO Tim Cook came out to the public, Blued received $30 million from the American venture capital firm DCM Ventures. "We knew that social networking sites were going to be verticalized and there were going to be niches," DCM founder David Chao told me, explaining his decision to invest. In other words, successful social media platforms would be targeting communities with niche needs, as opposed to a broad audience. In China—home to an estimated LGBT population of 80 million, larger than the population of France—"even niches would be massive."

With cash to spend, Ma leased a new office. After years of drifting from one cramped apartment to another, the company arrived at its final destination: a two-story glass building in Beijing's Central Business District. "We were finally rooted, finally official," Shen Wenjie, Ma's first Danlan colleague and now Blued's director of operations, told me. "This wasn't some part-time hobby but a real job, at a real company that you could tell your friends about." At the entrance of the office hung a framed photograph of Ma's handshake with the premier. It served as one of the most crucial artifacts of the company's legitimacy. Whenever investors doubted and questioned the political viability of his business model, Ma would reassure them by bringing up the meeting. "If Li Keqiang didn't meet us," Ma Baoli once said, "who would've dared invest in us?"

The premier didn't extend his handshake only to Ma. He extended it to wide-eyed entrepreneurs at start-ups across the country. In 2014, Li Keqiang announced a new policy of "mass entrepreneurship innovation." The government poured funding and resources into its burgeoning internet companies: In Shenzhen, authorities subsidized up to 70 percent of rent for "creative start-ups." In Chengdu, local officials set up a 200 million RMB ($27,800,000) entrepreneurship fund. In Hangzhou, the government launched a start-up called Dream Town, luring entrepreneurs in with cash handouts, courtesy of the city.

Suddenly, it became much easier for Blued to attract talented employees, most of whom were gay. With new funding, Ma poached Calvin Liu, a high-level employee from Baidu, to join as chief technology officer. As a fresh graduate student, Calvin had provided his coding expertise to Ma pro bono, as a contribution by a gay coder to his community. But now Blued had become a legitimate business—each investment a stamp of validation and public approval. When Calvin first met Lei Jun, the billionaire founder of the mobile phone company Xiaomi, at a gathering of prospective investors, he was starstruck. "If someone as popular as Lei Jun believed in us," he remembers thinking, "maybe Chinese society was more accepting of gay people than I thought." (Lei Jun's venture capital firm, Shunwei Capital, eventually invested in Blued.)

Most crucially, Blued's employees and investors believed in the company because they believed in Ma Baoli. "The CEO is a special guy—not a typical entrepreneur looking to make a quick buck, but an ex-cop," David Chao, of DCM Ventures, told me. "He knew how to work with the government and play the long game." In other words, Ma knew how to adapt to political constraints and seize every opportunity. In an environment as fast and capricious as China's, adaptability was key to a start-up's survival. When asked to share the secrets of his success, Xiaomi founder Lei Jun declared, "Every pig can fly, as long as it stands in the middle of the whirlwind." The word *fengkou*—"whirlwind," or literally "wind vent"—was immediately immortalized in the Chinese tech lexicon. It captured China's entrepreneurial ethos: Move quickly, try anything, and be ready. Any entrepreneur could succeed if they could seize the right tailwinds.

China's entrepreneurs had entered a new era, when the country's tech industry was stepping into the global limelight. If the 2008 Beijing Summer Olympics served as China's "coming-out party," 2014 marked the Chinese internet's coming-of-age. That year, Chinese internet companies listed IPOs in rapid succession: first Weibo, then the travel site Tuniu, the e-commerce platform JD.com, and finally Alibaba. In September, Alibaba raised an IPO of $25 billion, the largest ever in global financial history, making Jack Ma the richest man in Asia.

Ma Baoli was emboldened. An IPO was the ultimate marker of achievement for the Chinese entrepreneur. In the words of one of the characters in *American Dreams in China:* "Only when we stand in front of the New York Stock Exchange, striking the gavel, will they truly see us, recognize us, and respect us."

If Jack Ma could do it, why couldn't Ma Baoli one day take his company public and step onto the global stage, too?

· · ·

For decades, the world dismissed Chinese tech, like Chinese goods, as cheap knockoffs. Western scholars and tech entrepreneurs alike perceived Chinese internet companies as copycats of Silicon Valley offerings. They saw Chinese entrepreneurs as inferior, trained by an education system that failed to nurture creativity, instead rewarding conformity and rote memorization. In an influential article published in the *Harvard Business Review* in 2014, titled "Why China Can't Innovate," two professors at Harvard Business School and one at Wharton argued that real breakthroughs would be challenging in authoritarian environments, because innovation ran against "powerful currents that originate in China's Communist system and ancient culture." The problem is not "the innovative or intellectual capacity of the Chinese people, which is boundless," the authors concluded, "but the political world in which their schools, universities and businesses need to operate, which is very much bounded."

But inside China, this narrative was shifting. Chinese entrepreneurs realized that they didn't need to copy the West to succeed; instead, they could create unique innovations all on their own. By 2014, Alibaba had swelled beyond "China's eBay" into an empire of e-commerce and online banking. Tencent's WeChat grew out of a simple messaging platform into China's super app, rolling the functions of Facebook, WhatsApp, Venmo, Yelp, Uber, and many more apps into one. Xiaohongshu, which started out as a shopping guide for young Chinese women, morphed into their primary search engine and "lifestyle bible," where users could trade tips on everything from dieting to dating. Literally translated as "Little Red Book," the app's name was not a wink at Chairman Mao's compendium of Communist aphorisms, as many outsiders were led to believe; it was, instead, reportedly inspired by the signature color of cofounder Mao Wenchao's alma mater and his previous workplace, Stanford Business School and Bain Capital, respectively. The trio of Chinese internet leviathans—Baidu, Alibaba, and Tencent (collectively known as BAT)—had, in turn, paved the way for a new generation of giants: news aggregator Toutiao, food delivery platform Meituan, and ride-hailing app Didi (together, known as TMD).

Zhang Yiming, the young serial entrepreneur who founded Toutiao, was inspired by Silicon Valley but took its ideas further. In 2011, he noticed while riding the subway that nobody was reading newspapers anymore; they got their news on their phones. It gave him an idea: an app that would create personalized newsfeeds. "Just as Zuckerberg founded Facebook to connect people with people, and Travis [Kalanick] founded Uber to connect people with cars," Zhang would later say, "I want to connect people with information."

In 2012, he founded a company called ByteDance out of a four-bedroom apartment in Zhongguancun. His small team experimented with a number of apps: Gaoxiao Jiong Tu ("Hilarious Goofy Pics"), which served up amusing memes; Neihan Duanzi ("Subtle Jokes"), providing off-color jokes and short videos; and finally Jinri Toutiao ("Today's Headlines"), an aggregator that, according to Zhang, "let every user, at every moment, see their own front news page." There was nothing particularly remarkable about Toutiao's user interface or content. But its recommendation algorithm was innovative in its degree of granularity: It analyzed how users engaged with a piece of content—taps, swipes, time spent, pauses, comments—to determine what else to show them. The recommendation system improved with each use in a virtuous cycle: More users yielded more data, more data yielded a smarter algorithm, which yielded more users, and so on.

Toutiao became one of the fastest-growing Chinese apps in history: By 2016, it had 78 million daily users. The average user spent seventy-four minutes a day on it, twenty more than the average Facebook user. Beating Facebook was a big deal. Silicon Valley was a lodestar for Chinese entrepreneurs of Zhang's generation. One of his favorite books was *Winning,* the 2005 bestseller by the former General Electric CEO Jack Welch. ByteDance's guiding maxim, Always Day One, was borrowed from Amazon. "The golden age of Chinese technology is coming," Zhang wrote in a 2014 blog post after a trip to Silicon Valley. It was time to take his business global.

Toutiao's success was part of a broader social transformation in which the mobile internet penetrated every aspect of Chinese public life. Its rapid growth was propelled by an increasingly connected middle class, a vast population that provided an ample target audience to scale up new technologies. Among tech journalists, AI experts, and McKinsey consultants alike, "leapfrog" was the word du jour. Smartphones leapfrogged laptops, voice memos leapfrogged email, and mobile payments leapfrogged credit cards; in 2016, China's mobile-payments market surpassed that of the United States fifty times over. A cash-dependent country went cashless seemingly overnight. When I lived in Beijing in 2010, it was common to see people paying their rent with stacks of hundred-yuan bills. Five years later, farmers sold their produce on social media and panhandlers laid out printed QR codes on the street. More than anywhere else in the world, the line between online and offline life blurred: A smartphone served as a wallet, a transportation ticket, a means of communication, and a social world. With a few swipes, you could order dinner and pay rent, scout for dating prospects, and book a therapy appointment.

Chinese innovations soon proved to be popular outside its borders, too. In 2014, another Chinese entrepreneur, Alex Zhu, then employed as a project manager in the San Francisco Bay Area for a German software company, was on a train en route from the city to Mountain View, in Silicon Valley, when he noticed a group of teenagers. Half of them were listening to music; the other half took selfies. Why not combine both those features into a single app? Shortly after, Zhu moved back to Shanghai, where he founded Musical.ly, a lip-synching app for creating short videos paired with filters and soundtracks. It caught on quickly, particularly among American teenage girls, topping US app store charts within a year of its release. Avid users called themselves Musers. Many of them hoped to get famous, and some did, landing record deals, acting gigs, and sponsorships worth millions of dollars. Zhu compared them to "migrants chasing the American Dream."

Musical.ly came to Zhang Yiming's attention in 2016, just as he was looking for ways to expand worldwide, and around the time Mark Zuckerberg passed on acquiring it. ByteDance created its own app, using Toutiao's recommendation algorithm and imitating several of Musical.ly's central features, such as a full-screen display, an endless feed, and an emphasis on sound. It named the app Douyin ("Shaking Sound"). But ByteDance didn't just want Musical.ly's features; it wanted the app's clout and its 60 million users. So, a year later, it bought the company for $1 billion. The new, combined app would serve as Douyin's international counterpart and absorb Musical.ly's users. To name the new app, ByteDance came up with a list of English words that were short, catchy, and easy to pronounce across different languages. It settled on TikTok.

The rest of the world realized that the narrative had shifted. Driven by what some tech watchers called "WeChat envy," Mark Zuckerberg started pushing for Facebook to emulate WeChat's business model and offer a wider range of private services, such as mobile payments and e-commerce. International media no longer bemoaned China's inability to innovate but wrote about the Chinese internet in a tone of breathless awe. In March 2016, *WIRED* ran a story with the cover line IT'S TIME TO COPY CHINA. The cover showed a portrait of Lei Jun, founder of the smartphone company Xiaomi, against a large red, cartoonish sunrise, with the caption "Don't call me China's Steve Jobs."

The Firewall had remained permeable: Google, Facebook, and Twitter competed in China for years before they were blocked. Other platforms, such as Uber and Amazon, were never fully blocked but were beaten by local start-ups. This partially insulated environment—which prevented outside competition but also enabled access to new ideas—allowed the Chinese internet to evolve into an entirely separate ecosystem, a walled garden flowering with entirely new species of digital plants and fauna. To step within its walls was to inhabit a parallel world.

· · ·

From the inside, Blue City—Blued's two-story headquarters in Beijing—looked like "any other tech start-up, just slightly gayer," as Ma Baoli's personal assistant, Sifan Lu, put it. On the first floor, there was a lounge and recreation area with a gym and a foosball table; on the second, employees worked in an airy, open-plan office space with murals, gender-neutral bathrooms, and oil paintings of hunky, shirtless men. Employees enjoyed classic start-up benefits, like free lunch and company beach retreats, some with a queer twist, like a drag performance at the Lunar New Year; company swag included a plush toy unicorn with a rainbow horn. Conference rooms were named after queer films like *Brokeback Mountain*, *Prayers for Bobby*, and, of course, *Lan Yu*. At the entrance, next to a small shrine, on a wall next to a table with glass bottles of sand imported from Ma's hometown, were the words (in Chinese) "Qinhuangdao's sea and sand, that is the home of Danlan."

As the narrative of Chinese innovation flipped, Ma Baoli too transformed—from closeted leader of a scrappy start-up to openly gay CEO of the largest gay social networking app in the world. He swapped out casual T-shirts for a suit and tie, donned a pair of black rectangular glasses, posed for photos with his arms crossed, and adopted a more professional persona. By 2016, the team had swelled to about two hundred employees, its user base to 27 million (20 percent were international)—more than double the number for Grindr, Blued's largest competitor. Although other LGBT social networks emerged in China—such as Zank and Aloha, which catered to more urban gay communities—Blued was the most popular by far. If you opened Blued anywhere in the country, in the bustling Sanlitun area of Beijing or the Shanxi countryside, the app yielded an endless scroll of queer men, from proudly out college students to closeted middle-aged dads, from cosmopolitan yuppies in drag to rural blue-collar workers with faceless profiles.

The company's slogan, He's Right Next Door, embodied its ethos: to bring together gay men from all segments of Chinese society into its digital ecosystem. Like WeChat, Blued became a Swiss army knife for queer communities, absorbing features from other apps, like newsfeeds and live-streaming functions—as well as physical services like HIV testing centers—and integrating them into the app as quickly as possible. "Grindr crossed with Facebook" is how one former employee put it to me. "But more."

In 2015, having conquered the Chinese market, Ma Baoli had two major goals: to go global and to go public. By the end of the year, Blued launched the international version of its app, setting up local offices in Thailand, Vietnam, India, and the United Kingdom. Its European operation, based in London, was run out of a coworking space in the hip Shoreditch neighborhood and led by Charles Fournier, a French product manager who first learned about the app through his Chinese partner. By the time Fournier visited the Beijing headquarters to attend Blued's annual Spring

Festival party—a *baijiu*-fueled ceremony of dancing and drag—the international team had swelled to include employees from Mexico, Brazil, and India.

At one point, Ma seriously considered acquiring Grindr, but the Blued board of investors vetoed his proposal, wanting the company to focus on the domestic market. Years later, this move turned out to be prudent. (In 2019, the US government forced the Chinese company Kunlun, which ended up acquiring Grindr, to sell the company to American owners, citing the fear that the Chinese government could access sensitive data.) But at the time, Ma regretted what he saw as a missed opportunity. "If I had Grindr, I would have no more competition. I would go straight for the IPO," Ma said. "Who would have the power to beat me?"

For Ma and so many of his peers, an IPO was the ultimate marker of success. If a Chinese company—not to mention a gay Chinese company—went public, it would win the acceptance not only of the Chinese people but of the global marketplace. Ma was invested in the neoliberal logic that propelled China's rising class of entrepreneurs to stardom: The power of the internet, fueled by a growing economy, could serve as a force for liberal change. After all, entrepreneurs were expanding their influence well beyond the realm of tech, into education, entertainment, health care, and the media. Jack Ma founded a business school for entrepreneurs and a company that financed films from Wong Kar-wai's arthouse flicks to *Mission: Impossible—Rogue Nation;* he also acquired the *South China Morning Post,* the longest-running English-language newspaper in Hong Kong. When foreign dignitaries visited China, they stopped not just at Zhongnanhai—the nation's political center of authority—in Beijing but also in Hangzhou, the entrepreneurial center of power.

Likewise, Ma Baoli extended his queer business empire, producing queer television shows, collaborating with queer NGOs, and even partnering with Alibaba to bring ten gay Chinese couples to get married in California in a wedding officiated by the mayor of West Hollywood. Many of China's technology companies, from ride-hailing app Didi to restaurant review app Dianping, had begun to jump on the bandwagon of LGBTQ visibility, tapping into what they called the "pink economy."

There was a saying in China at that time that after decades of economic liberalization in China, "serving the *remnin*" ("the people") had taken a back seat to "serving the *renminbi*" ("the currency"). Blued was founded on the belief that to serve the renminbi *was* to serve the people. Proving gay China's worth in the global marketplace, the argument went, would allow for greater LGBT visibility, shift public perception, and pave the way for greater acceptance and freedoms. Becoming rich, in other words, would also help them become free.

· · ·

But Blued's relationship to the arena in which it operated remained precarious: It was a gay tech company operating under a one-party government whose stance toward LGBTQ issues remained opaque and ambivalent. Internationally, China publicly vocalized its support for LGBT rights at the United Nations, stating that China opposes all forms of "discrimination, violence, and intolerance based on sexual orientation." But domestically, gay marriage and adoption by same-sex couples were against the law; there were no openly gay public figures in the government and no expressed forms of legal protection against LGBTQ discrimination in the workplace. Censorship regulations expressly targeted same-sex relationships. But unlike their treatment of other minority groups, authorities had adopted an equivocal stance toward its LGBTQ communities, neither expressing explicit support nor seeking to crush them. "The rule is not that you're not allowed to be gay," Ben Mason, Blued's former international marketing manager, told me. "It just means that you have to play by the rules."

In this environment, Ma found himself in a peculiar position: He was the leader of the biggest app of its kind, but also the most precarious. His dance was doubly difficult. As a private entrepreneur, he needed to navigate government officialdom to survive. The Party endorsed its entrepreneurs because their goals—to innovate and make profit—were aligned. But this tango depended on forces outside his control: the success of the private sector, national security interests, changing vested interests. Imperative in order to survive on shifting terrain was Ma's ability to maintain a relationship with the Party that was both *qin* ("intimate") and *qing* ("clean"). Blued employed dedicated staff to liaise daily with various governmental departments—from the Cyberspace Administration to the Ministry of Culture—explaining the ins and outs of Blued's work in an attempt to destigmatize gay culture and prove Blued's social value. "I worked as a cop for ten years," Ma told prospective investors whenever they'd question Blued's feasibility as a company. "I know how they think inside the system."

As the leader of a gay organization, he needed to maneuver through the same confusing terrain that all civil society groups in China do, learning to read the shifting winds of relaxation and control. Ma exuded none of the brash swagger and hubris of some of his fellow entrepreneurs. His WeChat handle was Safety Superman; he was a cautious micromanager who left no stone unturned. Blued's content-moderation team worked around the clock, making sure that all content was impeccable and by the book. "On the Chinese app, the rules are very simple: If you show a bit of skin, you're gone," a Blued product manager told me. Most crucially, by framing the fight for gay recognition as a business opportunity, Blued pursued a strategy of pushing for greater LGBTQ visibility while avoiding political activism.

This strategy had limits. Social networks were still closed communities, not public forums where Chinese queer people could negotiate their rights. Queer identities were allowed to exist as long as they remained private, individual, and apolitical. Ma, now in a loving relationship with his partner—a man from the Northeast he met on Weibo in 2014—rarely discussed their relationship in public. According to a 2016 United Nations Development Programme report, "Being LGBTI in China," more gay people in China were choosing to come out to their family members, but the number who reported doing so was still no more than 15 percent of respondents. "The problem with being gay in China is that as long as you keep your sexual orientation private, you're fine," Wang Shuaishuai, a scholar of queer Chinese digital platforms, explained to me. "But you cannot receive public respect or recognition."

Like the gay bars before Stonewall that once served as "physical closets" for gay communities in the United States, social media platforms like Blued served as "digital closets" for those in China, explained Zhou Dan, a lawyer focusing on Chinese LGBTQ rights. Zhou wanted to see a more active and public-facing fight for LGBT recognition; if queer Americans were once encouraged to get out of the gay bar and take to the streets, he believed that queer Chinese should "get offline and go to the courts."

In 2014, a handful of brave young Chinese LGBTQ advocates took their grievances to court. In March, an openly gay man attempted to sue the Hunan government for refusing to register his gay rights organization. In July, the gay activist Yanzi Peng successfully sued a private clinic over forced conversion therapy. Whether they succeeded or not, these lawsuits put queer voices at the heart of public discourse. But once advocacy crossed the line into activism, risks skyrocketed. If there was an LGBTQ app or website whose main purpose was to mobilize queer activists, "it would be gone within a week," Zhou told me. "Every day, somebody could shut down your website without prior notice."

Even stepping into the realm of mainstream entertainment was risky. Blued produced a whole slate of LGBTQ web series, from a queer dating show to a gay high school romance called *Me and Mr. X* to a gay cooking show called *Little Fresh Meats' Kitchen*. This was until January 2016, when a web series called *Addicted*, featuring two gay high school boys who fall in love, garnered more than 10 million views on the first day of its release. *Addicted*'s sudden rise to fame embodied the paradox of visibility in China: What propelled the genre to the mainstream also invited the attention of the state. Three episodes before the season finale, the show disappeared abruptly from all streaming sites. A week later, China's top media regulator published an announcement banning all portrayals of "abnormal sexual relations" on television and online—including "sexual perversion," "sexual abuse," and "same-sex relationships." As always, Blued adapted: The company dropped all its film projects, retreating from the realm of film and television entertainment.

Ma played it safe, always staying in the government's good graces. To go public was safe only within the narrow arena of the market. To assert your presence in any other public setting—to chant a slogan on the streets, to wave a petition in front of a courthouse—placed you in risky territory. Ma put his faith in the power of the pink economy to nudge China's closet doors open—not just because money talks but because talking in terms of money was the safest option.

As Ma approached his late thirties, he was also entering a new phase of life—he longed to become a father. A friend had had a child via a surrogate, and that inspired him to pursue the same path. Since surrogacy was illegal in China, Ma went through California. As the baby's due date approached, he flew to Los Angeles, accompanied by a Blued colleague who acted as his translator. A few days later, a message arrived from the husband of his surrogate: The baby was on its way.

At the hospital, Ma was too nervous to cut the umbilical cord, so the doctor stepped in. The surrogate mother, already a mother of two, guided him through his first moments of fatherhood—teaching him to hold his son skin-to-skin so the newborn could recognize his scent. He named the child Xiao Shu, "Little Tree."

Ma returned to China with Xiao Shu in March 2017. In his son, he found more happiness than he ever could have imagined. But raising a family reconfigured his risk calculus. He was filled with joy but also had so much more to lose.

CHAPTER 9

Walled Garden

Eric Liu did not experience the optimism of China's tech entrepreneurs, enthralled by the blooming of the mobile internet. Nor did he share the hope of its online activists, still high on the promise of the Weibo Spring. In 2012, still working as a censor, he was deeply disillusioned. The Great Firewall had not yielded to the flood of new voices, as so many people had anticipated. In fact, the wall had only grown more imposing.

After the Wenzhou train crash, Weibo began to adapt. Eric estimated that the sensitive-keyword database swelled by 400 percent, from two thousand to ten thousand words. The company organized sensitive users on a spreadsheet, on tabs with different labels so their posts were more easily accessible to censors. The label "Sensitive VIP," for example, referred to verified users with large followings and reputations for criticizing the government, such as novelist Murong Xuecun; all posts by users had to be evaluated individually by Eric or one of his coworkers after they were published. After *The New York Times* published a scandalous scoop on Premier Wen Jiabao's massive family wealth, the company added a "*New York Times*" tab, treating the *Times*'s Weibo account and accounts of affiliated journalists as a special group.

Weibo also hired eighty more employees to join the team in Tianjin. An internet security officer took up a permanent cubicle in the office. He spoke to no one, and nobody ever explained why he was there and what he did all day. Eric guessed that the Ministry of State Security had dispatched him to learn how to use Weibo's backend so the ministry could delete posts and shut down users directly.

Eric kept to himself, staying out of office politics, but there was one censor who irked him. Like many of Eric's colleagues, the censor was just a classic shut-in who spent his weekends in front of a screen playing video games. But unlike the others, who were mostly apolitical, this censor was a proud nationalist who hung out online with the likes of Rao Jin and his fellow pro-Party agitators at the website he founded, anti-cnn.com. He saw his role at Weibo as more than a job—it was an honor, a chance to be a "gatekeeper of the web," as Eric put it. Eric recalled that the censor once gleefully shared in the office group chat a post he had deleted by a human rights lawyer. In the post, Eric remembered, the man discussed how his young child had been barred from attending school because of the lawyer's dissident status. Disgusted, Eric couldn't help but respond to the censor's message. "I hope a guy like you never finds love; it'll be better for the world," he shot back. The conversation ended. Back then, patriotic incels were still a rarity on the internet. Eric would soon encounter them everywhere.

One day at work, Eric realized that he still had dozens of censorship directives saved on his computer. The directives were handed to employees between shifts, compiled in a Word document, and shared in the office group chat. He often downloaded them, but he never bothered to delete them. He spent every day deleting things from the internet: news stories, sensitive posts, netizen voices. But these directives survived—months' worth of them, just sitting on his desktop. Were they not shards of history as well, worth being preserved for posterity?

He started collecting the directives deliberately—downloading the ones he received, asking colleagues to send him the ones he missed, and backing all of them up for future use. Eric never wanted to be a hero. But he no longer wanted to be a cog in the system,

either. And if he couldn't save the fruits of the Weibo Spring, perhaps he could salvage the fossils instead.

. . .

On January 3, 2013, the journalists at the Guangzhou-based newspaper *Southern Weekly* woke up to a devastating surprise: Without
their knowledge, the front page of their Lunar New Year editorial
had been changed completely.

Right before the paper went to press, the local propaganda chief
had allegedly intervened, forcing editors to make last-minute altera-
tions. In the original editorial, titled "China Dreams, Dreams of
Constitutionalism," *Southern Weekly* journalists, known for their
liberal views and hard-hitting investigations, called for political
reform and constitutional rights. Its replacement, titled "We Are
Now Closer to Our Dream Than Ever Before," was rewritten as a
puff piece exalting the Party.

For a year, officials had been stepping up censorship, routinely
tampering with their coverage. The previous summer, they had
forced the paper to cut out eight pages on a deadly flash flood that
hit Beijing. This latest intervention—a blatant distortion of their
words—was like a "fuse on a detonator," in the words of *Southern
Weekly*'s editorial staff. The journalists went on strike outside the
paper's headquarters and posted an open letter online, demanding
the immediate removal of the propaganda chief in charge of issuing the orders. On Weibo, the public chimed in to condemn the
infringement of free expression. The celebrity actress Yao Chen even
posted a photo of the *Southern Weekly* logo on her Weibo account,
with a quote by Soviet dissident Aleksandr Solzhenitsyn: "One
word of truth shall outweigh the whole world."

The paper eventually reached a concession with the local government: They would end their strike, and in exchange, *Southern
Weekly* staff who protested would not be punished and propaganda
officials would rein in intrusive censorship. Some viewed it as a
small victory for press freedom, while others feared it would lead
to tighter controls. Many of *Southern Weekly*'s journalists saw this

as the death knell for the paper and quit en masse, believing that its days as a muckraking watchdog were numbered. "I felt that the imagination [of the newspaper] had been depleted," one journalist who resigned told *Foreign Policy.*

On the other side of the Firewall, the orders rolled in. "As for the extreme posts that attack the party leaders and call for protests, make them invisible," the directives instructed. "Do not overkill."

The *Southern Weekly* incident was a turning point for Eric. Weibo ultimately would serve not to foster free speech but only to muzzle it—nothing more. "At the time, people clung to this belief that if we participated in civil society and public discourse online, the country would become more open," he told me years later. "The silencing of *Southern Weekly* was a painful slap in the face. I realized this wouldn't happen. Absolutely not."

It was time to quit his job. He planned to marry his girlfriend that summer. Soon, they would start a family. "If my future child asked me what I did for a living, I didn't want to tell them that Dad spent his days deleting posts, suppressing free speech," he told me.

By then, he had collected hundreds of censorship directives, backed them up on portable drives, and sent them as a compressed file to his own Gmail address via a full-tunnel (fully encrypted) VPN for extra security. He still had no idea what he would do with them beyond keeping them safe. During his last days at the office, his archival instincts kicked in. He even took photos of his surroundings: the fluorescent lights, the cubicle, the Weibo backend flashing on his computer screen. He felt like Indiana Jones gathering archaeological artifacts.

"I was no martyr, no whistleblower trying to overhaul the system. I never gave Weibo users the power to speak freely," he told me later. "I just saved the evidence of how that freedom was taken away."

. . .

Online, netizens compared the experience of being shut down on Weibo to being put to death. The act of registering for a new account was akin to being reincarnated. Those who revived their accounts said they were part of the "Reincarnation Party."

On the evening of May 11, 2013, Murong Xuecun, known for his viral posts and frank criticisms of the government, logged on to his Weibo to find that his account, too, had finally met its end. Without warning, all his public social media accounts—not only on Weibo but also on Tencent, NetEase, and Sohu—had disappeared. Minutes later, staff at each of the platforms relayed to him versions of the same message: His account had been shut down by order of a "superior department."

Murong grieved his loss. Years' worth of ideas, thoughts, conversations, his 8.5 million followers, the cultivation of an entire online identity, had been reduced to nothing in a split second. On Weibo, his loyal followers held virtual "memorial services" for his deceased account. Even his reincarnation attempts failed. When he tried registering for a new account, he found both his IP address and his phone number blocked. When he tried using different phone numbers, reincarnating as Murong Onecun, Murong Twocun, Murong Threecun, all the way up until Murong Fifteencun, each account was swiftly shut down. The worst part for Murong was not knowing exactly who had called for the shutdown, and why. "There is no procedure, no standard, and not a single explanation. It's as if you are walking into a minefield blindfolded," he wrote in *The Guardian*. "Not knowing where the mines are buried, you don't know when you will be blasted to pieces."

He suspected that the shutdown stemmed from his public criticism of an internal Party document that had been leaked online a month earlier. Known as Document No. 9, it warned that "Western anti-China forces" were "trying to infiltrate China's ideological sphere" and urged the Party's leadership to guard against seven forbidden perils: Western constitutional democracy, "universal values," neoliberalism, civil society, historical nihilism, the West's idea of journalism, and questioning socialism with Chinese characteristics. In response, he wrote on Weibo: "The seven no's can be summed into one: Don't be civil." Perhaps someone had been offended by the sentence.

Murong's account was one of several to perish. After *Southern Weekly* fell, China's most vocal liberals on Weibo, known as "Big Vs" for their large verified followings, fell, too, their accounts swiftly put to death and whisked away from the Weibo town square. In August, authorities took a step further when they not only silenced but arrested the Chinese American investor Charles Xue, a prolific Big V known for his scathing commentary on social issues, charging him with soliciting prostitutes. Given how common this practice was and how many others guilty of it went unpunished, the more likely explanation was that Xue was specifically targeted for his garrulity and influence on the internet.

Shortly after, he appeared on state television to "apologize" for his behavior, looking dazed. "My celebrity status got to my head. As an online thought leader, I felt like an emperor," he told the Beijing police in a videotaped interrogation. "With no online restrictions, people will become unruly. If the internet is not properly guided, it will go in the wrong direction."

Xue's arrest sent a chill through China's most vocal netizens, many of whom fell silent in its wake. The Great Firewall's true power lay not only in its technology and manpower but also in its ambiguity. "Clarity serves the purpose of the censoring state only when it wants to curb a very specific kind of behavior," the American professor and sinologist Perry Link once wrote. "When it wants to intimidate a large group, vagueness works much better."

After Murong's account was shut down, he received a message through a friend, passed on from an anonymous employee in Weibo's censorship department. It was a screenshot of the Weibo backend with the censorship directive that led to the shutdown. According to the directive, the order came directly from the top internet regulators: the State Council Information Office. He had offended someone at the highest levels of authority.

Murong asked his friend to thank the nameless censor. The screenshot gave him some clarity and allowed his online persona to rest in peace. But it would remain buried away forever. The Weibo Spring was over.

· · ·

In some ways, the rise and fall of the Weibo Spring seemed like déjà vu, a familiar, decades-old pattern in modern Chinese history—an undulating cycle between liberalization and retrenchment, freedom and control. In 1956, Mao launched the Hundred Flowers Campaign, encouraging intellectuals to speak out and freely express their criticisms, before changing his mind, silencing and punishing those critics only a year later. In the late 1970s, during a period known as the Beijing Spring, Deng Xiaoping allowed Beijing residents to erect a "Democracy Wall" in the center of the capital where they could share their grievances—only to shut down the wall and jail its most vocal participants shortly after. The Weibo Spring was a replay of this pendulum swing: a short-lived moment of free expression to allow authorities to gauge public opinion, followed by an abrupt crackdown to pull it back in.

But this time was different. The internet was fast, vast, and sprawling—a technology more powerful than anything the state had managed in the past. The Party feared that an uncontrolled cyberspace could threaten its authority by serving as a channel for "foreign hostile forces" to destabilize China. Outside the country, two events in particular alerted the Party to the dangers of the freewheeling internet. The first was the Twitter-driven "color revolutions" of the Arab Spring, which had spread across the Middle East and encouraged calls for a Jasmine Revolution on China's own soil. The second was Edward Snowden's June 2013 leak of thousands of classified US National Security Agency documents, which revealed that the NSA had been surveilling both Americans and foreign nationals and hacking into Chinese computer networks since 2009.

The Chinese government expressed "grave concern" over Snowden's allegations and held a meeting with leading companies to probe the impact of US surveillance. For the Chinese government, the implications were huge. First, the leaks exposed the US government's capacity to hack into China's critical infrastructure (according to the leaks, the NSA hacked into the servers of Chinese telecommunications company Huawei). Second, they revealed that the United States was monitoring its own citizens and relying on private tech companies, such as AT&T and Verizon, to help them do so. Together, these revelations strengthened the Party's belief that cyberspace must be controlled, surveilled, and shielded from foreign interference in the name of national security. In a speech delivered two months later at a national propaganda conference, Xi Jinping described the internet as the "main battlefield in the struggle for public opinion" and called on the Party to "unsheathe their swords" to defend it. They needed a more sophisticated system of control.

The Party's first move was to centralize control of the internet. Before 2013, the internet was still governed by an unwieldy and uncoordinated bureaucracy of different regulatory departments, which often clashed over decisions and competed over influence. Once, a public spat over online gaming licenses between the General Administration of Press and Publication and the Ministry of Culture led to a five-month shutdown of one of China's most beloved online games, *World of Warcraft*.

To address this problem, in 2014, the Party established the Cyberspace Administration of China (CAC), a central government agency responsible for regulating the internet and cybersecurity. Lu Wei, the man appointed to lead the CAC, would become known as China's "internet czar." Previously the Guangxi bureau chief of the Xinhua news agency before being promoted to Beijing's propaganda chief, Lu was a brash, chain-smoking workaholic who fervently believed in the importance of controlling information.

The CAC effectively centralized powers under one organization, streamlining the process of censorship. Kaiser Kuo, the Chinese American cofounder and host of the *Sinica Podcast*, compared the previous model of governance, under which you could play one regulatory agency against another, to asking your parents for permission to do something when they are on opposite ends of the house. The formation of the CAC meant that "your parents are speaking with one voice, in the same room."

The Party's second move was to strengthen the walls around Chinese cyberspace, defending it from foreign encroachment. Lu Wei championed a vision of "cyber-sovereignty," a model of governance under which individual nation-states regulated their own internet as they saw fit, much as they govern their own physical territory. Lu, who was prone to metaphor, compared Chinese cyberspace to a "spiritual garden" designed to "show the true, the good, and the beautiful" and "castigate the false, the bad, and the ugly." Like an Edenic garden, the Chinese internet would be carefully pruned of everything from fake news to nefarious hackers to foreign influence, walled off as a world of its own.

When Eric Liu first heard the leadership tout "cyber-sovereignty," he thought of it as a joke. "I believed that it was impossible to draw boundaries around something like the internet," he told me. "But then they went ahead and made it happen."

After leaving Weibo, he found a new job as an editor at Leshi, a video-streaming provider. He was still based in Tianjin, but on the other side of town, in the Binhai New Area, a newly built zone with favorable policies for trade and industry, filled with sleek modern buildings overlooking the waterfront. Eric remembered that many internet companies set up their censorship offices here: Leshi, the online video platforms Ku6 and Tencent Video, the social media platform Douban, and even the karaoke app Changba. Eric no longer worked as a censor but corrected technical and aesthetic mistakes like typos, grammatical errors, and broken links. But his department—"content optimization"—was housed in the same office as Leshi's "content moderation" department. So he received the same email thread sent out to the company's censorship managers, with all the censorship directives, and continued to compile them out of instinct.

In 2015, more than a year after Eric joined Leshi, the Cyberspace Administration started drafting a sweeping set of regulations, which would become known as China's first Cybersecurity Law, positioned as an effort to protect information security and the national interest. It required all companies—domestic and foreign alike—to store data on Chinese citizens on servers located inside the country. (To comply, Apple opened its first data center in China, in Guizhou Province.) The new law also required internet companies not just to censor public posts but also to monitor private chats and report unlawful groups; administrators were held personally liable for the content in the groups they ran. This was a powerful way to monitor WeChat—where many intellectuals had migrated after the end of the Weibo Spring, hoping to share their insights with a smaller, more intimate audience. If Weibo was the town square, WeChat was a private living room, where users were typically connected through shared acquaintances and had to request permission to enter somebody's circle. But from the censor's perspective, WeChat was in many ways easier to control than Weibo, Rongbin Han, a scholar of Chinese cyberspace, told me. "You are speaking not into a loudspeaker but at the dinner table—a level of discourse the government can manage."

The Cybersecurity Law paved the way for stricter control and enforcement against unauthorized use of VPNs; some Chinese internet users—albeit a small percentage—had long relied on unlicenced VPNs to bypass censorship. Because the government understood that many local companies and foreign businesses benefited from VPN access, it largely turned a blind eye, allowing unregistered VPNs to exist in a legal gray area—neither explicitly allowed nor banned outright. Still, they had the power to selectively control access, restricting VPN use more on some days than others. During China's Party Congress or the annual Two Sessions meeting of the nation's legislative bodies, for example, my VPN frequently glitched and browsing speeds plummeted. When the law came into effect, in June 2017, VPN use became more legally precarious: Several sellers of unlicensed VPNs were arrested and sentenced to up to five and a half years in prison. A year later, Apple announced that it had removed over six hundred VPNs from its Chinese app store.

The new law also enforced stricter real-name registration for social media users, which Eric believed drastically curtailed online expression. "As a result, heaven's net was cast much wider," he told me. "Even if your actions went unpunished before, real-name registration allowed them to eventually get to you."

Heaven's net eventually got to CAC head Lu Wei himself. In November 2017, a few months after the Cybersecurity Law was enacted, Lu was placed under investigation by the Party's anticorruption agency on suspicion of "serious violations of discipline," including pocketing bribes, violating party rules by visiting private clubs, trading power for sex, and deceiving investors. Netizens cheered his downfall. "He created his own mincing machine, then the machine crushed its own inventor," a scholar posted on Twitter.

But although the internet czar had himself been crushed, his vision of the walled garden remained firmly in place.

. . .

At 11:34 p.m. on August 12, 2015, four years after the Wenzhou train crash, another man-made disaster jolted Eric into action. This time, the calamity took place closer to home. In Tianjin's Binhai New Area, a chemical warehouse exploded. Two blasts ripped through the city, shooting fireballs into the air that reached hundreds of meters in height, so huge they could be seen from outer space. The explosions shattered windows, tore facades off buildings, and threw parked vehicles into the air. Toxic gas and debris shot through the sky into neighboring communities with the force of artillery shells. Survivors stumbled out of their homes, cut by shrapnel-like glass shards, covered in blood.

The city Eric woke up to the next morning looked like the aftermath of an apocalypse. Everyone within three kilometers of the blast site was evacuated, and all waterways were sealed off to curb contamination. Fires continued to burn through the weekend as rescue teams searched for bodies in the rubble. At a makeshift emergency center, people posted sheets of A4 paper with the names of missing loved ones on a cardboard wall. Eric lived a safe distance from the blast site, but at the Leshi office, eight kilometers away, an entire chunk of the ceiling had collapsed. If he'd worked his night shift that evening instead of a day shift and walked past his usual bus stop, perhaps his name would have been up on the cardboard wall, too.

The blast was China's worst industrial disaster in years, killing 173 people. Eight bodies were never found. Nuclear and biochemical experts arrived to assess the health risks from chemicals released into the atmosphere. Photos of fish carcasses washed up on the shore of a river near the blast site went viral. Eric stayed at home, stocking up on bottled water and compressed biscuits.

The Tianjin explosion, like the Wenzhou train crash, provoked an outpouring of online anger. Why was a warehouse carrying dangerous chemicals positioned so close to people's homes? Why was the company able to skirt safety rules?

The premier, this time Li Keqiang instead of Wen Jiabao, visited the site of the blast, vowing to get at the heart of the matter and punish those responsible. Investigations revealed that the warehouse that exploded, which belonged to Ruihai International Logistics, was located closer to residential neighborhoods than was permitted and had stored excessive hazardous chemicals, including seven hundred metric tons of sodium cyanide. Stocks of flammable nitrocellulose—a chemical used in nail polish—caught fire and spread to illegal stores of ammonium nitrate. Forty-nine employees and government officials were jailed for paying and receiving bribes and sidestepping safety regulations.

Again, the government tried to suppress public fury and move on as quickly as possible. The blast left behind a giant crater ninety-seven meters wide, a gaping abyss hollowed out from the earth. When Tianjin authorities proposed to repurpose the site of the blast into an "eco-park" and turn the crater into an artificial lake, the news drew derision—evidence of the authorities' attempt to "erase all trace of damage and memories," one user responded.

Again, internet regulators immediately issued orders to suppress the incident:

> Remove news and images from the explosions. Tidy up posts. Do not post articles that are not from Xinhua. If they have already been posted, please take them down from the backend.

Many of the censors tasked with "tidying up" worked only a few kilometers away, out of the content-moderation offices at tech companies in the Binhai New Area. Eric marveled at the irony of it all: thousands of censors forced to expunge their own experience of a disaster, right after it blew up in front of them. This time, it was their own fury that they toiled to erase. It was like that Soviet joke:

The Party secretary asked the worker: "Do you have any opinions about us?"

The worker replied: "I do have opinions, but I disagree with them."

He had to get the directives he'd collected out. By then, he had thousands—including Leshi's entire sensitive-keyword database, downloaded and stored in his computer. If he were ever arrested, it would all be destroyed along with him. All of it, for nothing.

On Weibo, he reached out to a reporter based in New York who was working for the Committee to Protect Journalists, which promotes freedom of the press worldwide.

I used to work as a Weibo censor and have saved all these censorship logs, he wrote. *Are they still valuable?*

Yes, the reporter replied. *Yes. They are very, very valuable.*

He gathered all the directives—no more than a few hundred megabytes—and uploaded them to Google Drive. Less than an hour later, the transfer to the waiting journalist was complete.

CHAPTER 10

Positive Energy

I n his self-help book *Rip It Up*, British psychologist Richard Wiseman championed a "radical new approach to changing your life." The core idea: Positive action begets positive thinking—not the other way around. People never smile because they are happy, he wrote, but, rather, feel happy when they are smiling. Repeating confident mantras sparks confidence. Psych yourself up, and sincere optimism follows. "Having people repeatedly sing a national anthem will make them more patriotic," he writes as an example. "Making children pray every morning increases the likelihood of [their] adopting religious beliefs." The book received a mediocre reception in the United Kingdom when it was published, in 2012, but its Chinese translation became an instant bestseller. The translated version was titled *Zhengnengliang* ("Positive Energy").

Little did Wiseman know that he had provided what would become one of the Communist Party's most important principles. The *Shenzhen Daily* newspaper reported "positive energy" as the top catchphrase of the year, and it caught the attention of the newly appointed head of the Cyberspace Administration of China, Lu Wei. In one of his first speeches, titled "Concentrate Positive Energy Online, Build the Chinese Dream Together," he called for the "spiritual garden" of Chinese cyberspace to be filled with "dew and sunlight." At the Party Forum on Literature and Art in 2014, Xi Jinping told a gathering of artists to create works "like sunshine in a blue sky or a fresh spring breeze, that should inspire the mind, nurture the heart, [and] cultivate our lives." Cultural creation, he said, should "generate the greatest positive energy."

Whereas the slogans of Hu Jintao's era, such as Harmonious Society, evoked Confucian ideals of stability and control, the "positive energy" of Xi's new era, borrowed from contemporary pop psychology, implied a more participatory form of control. It was not good enough to simply suppress critics into indignant silence; the Party must actively encourage them to sing praise. In this new framing, artists and censors were not opponents but collaborators, cheerfully cultivating China's gardens of art together.

As positive energy went viral, blasted on television and hashtagged on social media, it felt as if the country was engaged in something of a national self-help project. When online comedian Papi Jiang was censored for using vulgar language, she vowed publicly to "broadcast more positive energy"; when the United States sent warships to the South China Sea, Beijing urged Americans to show a little more positive energy. Successful salesmen were lauded for their #EcommercePositiveEnergy, and virtuous celebrities were praised as #PositiveEnergyIdols. The power of positive energy lay in its breadth; the same phrase used to extol the rise of China's economic growth was also used to judge everyday behavior. It also pushed the burden of well-being into the hands of the individual: If you are unhappy, it's on you.

．　．　．

Far from the political seat of power, the partygoers of Poly Center paid no attention to the nationwide call for positive energy. From the outside, it looked like one of the many nondescript office buildings lining the southwestern streets of Chengdu. But if you were to have walked past the sleepy security guard in the lobby and taken the grimy elevator up to the twenty-first floor, you would have discovered an entirely different world. Once the elevator doors opened, you would have found the air thick with laughter, strobing multicolored light, and the muscular *thud thud thud* of the bass booming from the speakers. Young people leaned against the walls of the cramped corridors, smoking weed, making out, taking shots of *baijiu* and hits of laughing gas from candy-colored balloons before diving back into one of the clubs in the vicinity: the Berlin-inspired techno club Tag, the rowdy dive bar Here We Go, and at the end of the hall, NASA, Chengdu's hottest hip-hop club, where the city's best-known MCs performed. By 2016, the building had transformed into the mecca for young Chengduers looking to party. When Kafe Hu performed at NASA, the club was so packed that people had to squat outside to watch.

Since he had moved to Chengdu a decade before, the city's hip-hop scene had continued to blossom. But Chengdu, still enamored by its youthful, rebellious ways, had also undergone a growth spurt. Thanks to hundreds of billions of dollars pumped into the region by the government's "Western development strategy" program—a long-term plan to boost economic development in twelve western provincial-level regions—the city had transformed into a commercial hub, shopping mecca, and source of two-thirds of the world's iPads. All around the city, one could find signs of its raging adolescence: stoic office buildings that hosted hip-hop bashes after dark, glitzy malls where underground fight clubs raged at night.

Kafe's own career was picking up. He'd released two albums in three years and established a distinct style: He mixed jazz inflections with old-school hip-hop, gravitated toward obscure and darkly humorous lyrics, and rapped with a low, husky tenor and a relaxed swing to his delivery as if he were a jazz musician riffing on an instrument. His second album, *27: The Code of Lucifer,* drew inspiration from the story of the archangel, which he first learned from a book on Western art history. He became fascinated by the idea of Lucifer as a countercultural spirit. ("He's not a bad guy, you know. He just challenged the status quo, lost his wings and fell into hell. Dude just didn't want to bow down to Jesus," he later explained his fascination to me.)

Drawn first to new opportunities and alternative lifestyles in Shanghai and Beijing, young people from all over the country followed in Kafe's footsteps and moved to Chengdu. Rent was cheap, food was good, and people were open to artists making a living from their music. They wanted money but also to take midday siestas. They wanted success but on their own terms. They didn't aspire to the state-sanctioned Chinese Dream of "national rejuvenation," whatever that meant, but to the Chengdu dream—of new opportunities, freewheeling creativity, and raucous play.

This combination of spending power, creativity, and free-spirited youth with something to say created fertile ground for hip-hop to grow. In the early 2010s, Chengdu gained a reputation as the proving ground for a new generation of Chinese hip-hop artists, who served as the face of a playful, provocative style—influenced by genres like trap—that was all their own. Instead of Mandarin, the language of school and national television, they rapped in Sichuanese, rich with rising and falling tones, which allowed for greater lyrical experimentation. The city's vibe was perhaps best captured by Fat Shady, in his viral track "Daddy, I'm Not Going to Work Tomorrow."

Daddy ain't going to work tomorrow, I'll rage all night
Daddy ain't going to work tomorrow, so I can live a little more
truthfully.

The track was so popular that in 2014, he was invited to perform a toned-down version of it onstage for the state-run China Central Television. Still, in front of a cheering crowd and a row of speechless, suited-up commentators, he railed against traffic jams and office sycophants. So that he could sleep in, he told his alarm clock "to go fuck itself."

In 2016, Chengdu hip-hop found its way to listeners outside China's borders, too. That year, VICE China, the Chinese branch for VICE Media, organized a "Motherland Tour," inviting Chinese-born musicians from around the world to return to their ancestral home and experience its music scenes. Bohan Phoenix, one of the artists invited on the tour, born in Hubei, raised in Boston, and living in New York City, was impressed by what he discovered. He met Kafe Hu and an up-and-coming four-man group called the

Higher Brothers. Their leader, Masiwei, with his sunken cheeks, dreadlocks, and raspy drawl, was the antithesis of a Chinese pop star. They named the group after Haier, one of China's most popular home-appliances manufacturers, because it was the brand of the refrigerator in the apartment they shared in Chengdu.

When Bohan returned to New York, he mentioned the Higher Brothers to his manager, Allyson Toy. Toy was one of the first employees of 88rising, an American media company focusing on discovering and producing the work of Asian and Asian American artists. Bohan's timing was perfect: It turned out that Toy was already looking for the group. Earlier that year, she'd heard one of its tracks on a Boiler Room mix in Brooklyn, commissioned by the Chinese music producer Howie Lee, and was hooked. When she showed 88Rising the group's music, the company knew that it had to sign them right away. "I grew up on Chinese hip-hop, and I never messed with it, because it never felt authentic," Jaeson Ma, cofounder of 88Rising, told me. But when Ma heard the Higher Brothers for the first time, he was impressed. "They're reppin' the city and the dialect. They had their own personalities and their own style."

More than anything, Bohan was amazed by the hunger he saw in China—the ravenous appetite for new music, new culture. The first time he performed there, the crowd was so wild he lost his voice. "I didn't know that kids in China were into hip-hop like this. Me and my bros went so hard last night," he told me. "When we got back to the Airbnb, I was like—China is lit, right? China is fuckin' lit, right?" He would move to China. His future as an artist wasn't in Brooklyn—it was in Chengdu.

. . .

The key driver of hip-hop's burgeoning popularity in China was the internet. Just as the rise of the mobile internet in the 2010s allowed new tech start-ups to flower, it provided fertile ground for new cultures to bloom. In contrast to the United States, where there were more established gatekeepers and institutions in the music industry—major music labels, bloggers, Kylie Jenner's Snapchat—

Chinese listeners discovered new music primarily through social media: WeChat, QQMusic, and Douban. Hyperconnected through these platforms, unknown artists spread quickly, without the help of powerful publicists and managers. "In the US, music media and editorial were still powerful, and getting a premiere on the FADER or Complex still carried huge weight," Allyson Toy, who followed Bohan to China, told me. "In China, I was primarily experiencing new music through my friend's WeChat moments."

Livestreaming and short video had become China's dominant forms of social media entertainment. In 2016, while streaming remained a niche gaming subculture elsewhere, it became a mainstream online activity in China, used by half the nation's internet users, for everything from education to news to grocery shopping. At least a hundred short-video apps vied for audiences' attention, the most popular being Kuaishou and ByteDance's Douyin. Short videos, easy to make and just a few seconds long, lowered the barrier to entering online participation. Ordinary users turned into instant stars, octogenarians launched second acts as fashion models, and farmers moonlighted as comedians.

Douyin, known at first for its viral lip-sync and dance videos, was driven by ByteDance's powerful recommendation algorithm. The app's main attraction, which would also fuel the power of its international sister app TikTok, was its "For You" page. Instead of showing users content based on social connects—accounts they followed and accounts that followed them—the app tailored it to their individual habits and instincts. If, for instance, a user engaged with content related to woodworking or a particular kind of dance, the algorithm served more content on these subjects, regardless of who created it.

Kuaishou, which targeted China's less economically developed and rural regions, propelled a whole genre of rural livestreamers to fame. One scroll through the app yielded a slice of Chinese society in its grassroots form: fishermen showcasing their daily catch, truck drivers livestreaming their commutes, teenage mothers showing off their babies, high school truants rapping into mics. The platform became a virtual carnival of crass and lowbrow humor. One woman, who called herself Gourmet Sister Feng, livestreamed herself gulping down light bulbs, feasting on live goldfish, and swallowing cigarettes. Another, named Liu Mama, a ruddy-cheeked farmer from northeastern China, posted videos of herself shucking corn, harvesting tomatoes, driving around fields, while composing crude rhymes about the glories of rural life: "You might have a Fe-la-li [Ferrari] / But I have got a *tuo-la-ji* [tractor]." Before long, she had garnered 14 million followers.

Online life in the parallel world of Chinese cyberspace felt faster, more chaotic, and more irreverent than its global counterparts, bombarding users with an onslaught of ever-evolving jokes and memes. Trying to keep up with even the most rudimentary forms of online jargon could feel like learning an alien language. It took me a while to figure out that 666 meant "well-played"; 3Q88, pronounced "san-Q-ba-ba-in" in Chinese, translated as "thank you, bye-bye"; and NB referred to *nuibi*—or, literally, "cow's cunt"— used to describe something awesome.

In this fast-paced online world, subcultures often blew up overnight, from the South Korean genre of *mukbang* (a genre of livestreams that involved people eating as much food on-screen as possible) to Peppa Pig (a sudden, inexplicable nationwide craze for the British children's cartoon pig, which transformed into a subversive symbol of Chinese "gangster life," inspiring delinquent youth to trade Peppa Pig memes and show off Peppa Pig temp tattoos). In 2016, *danmei*, or "Boys' Love"—a genre of fan fiction centered on romantic relationships between men—soared to popularity, swelling into a billion-dollar business of web novels, animation, and feature films, casting "little fresh meats" (the online buzzword for China's increasingly beloved fresh-faced, delicate-featured male celebrities) as their leads. One of the largest Boys' Love fan bases revolved around a queer reimagining of Benedict Cumberbatch's Sherlock Holmes and his intimate relationship with Dr. Watson.

Much like an out-of-touch parent trying to keep up with the younger generation, the Party tried to co-opt its people's tastes as its own. When China's top filmmakers were tapped by the state to create *The Founding of an Army,* a historical drama set during the revolutionary era, they cast the country's hottest "little fresh meat" celebrities to act as the founding fathers in an attempt to win over a younger audience. A military man was played by Lu Han, a Bieber-esque boy-band star whose crazed fans once crashed Weibo servers when he announced he had a girlfriend; young Mao was portrayed by Liu Ye, the long-lashed actor who had starred as the gay prostitute in *Lan Yu* more than a fifteen years earlier. The strategy backfired, inspiring mockery instead of patriotism. Gleeful viewers matchmade their revolutionary leaders as romantic partners, in both straight and queer iterations. The grandson of a celebrated Communist military commander was infuriated to see a finalist in China's *Super Boy* TV singing contest act as his grandfather. "Who are you trying to humiliate?" he posted on Weibo.

Hip-hop was no less exempt from the Party's positive energy drive. In 2016, the state news outlet Xinhua released a cartoon music video about the "Four Comprehensives," the Party's long-term development plan, featuring a middle-aged man and a little girl dancing to a hip-hop soundtrack that contained rap verses like "It's everyone's dream / to build a moderately prosperous society comprehensively." Unsurprisingly, netizens were unimpressed.

Direct methods of punishment also flopped. In 2015, the Ministry of Culture blacklisted 120 songs that "threatened public morality," scrubbing tracks with "negative energy" from streaming sites, concert halls, and karaoke parlors. Most came from Beijing's hip-hop underground, the first 17 from In3, one of the first and most notable of the city's hip-hop groups, as well as a slew of other forbidden tracks that ended up lending the banned songs a new round of publicity, such as "No Money No Friend," "Don't Want to Go to School," "I Love Taiwanese Girls," and "Fart."

Contrary to the ministry's intentions, the songs' popularity skyrocketed. "Thank you, Ministry, for the recommendations," a sarcastic Weibo user commented in response to the banned list. The censorship efforts fell victim to what was known as the "Streisand Effect," after Barbra Streisand. The term originated from an incident in which the singer tried to suppress photos of her Malibu cliff-top residence by suing the photographer, but the lawsuit backfired, spotlighting the very thing she'd wanted to hide.

. . .

"Rap music? China? What are they even saying?" the song began in a whiny American voice. "Sounds like they're just saying ching chang chong." Over a trap beat and a mandolin, the rappers proceeded to boast about how different types of Western products—chains, gold watches, toothpaste, umbrellas, and now hip-hop—were made in China.

The first time I listened to the Higher Brothers' breakout track, "Made in China," in the summer of 2017, I couldn't decide whether the song was brilliant or just outrageous. It was at once a bold and satirical assertion of Chinese pride, a comic riff on the Western stereotype of the quiet and inscrutable Oriental. But the sentiment bore no resemblance to the knee-jerk dismissal of the West that populated state media. The group boasted not about China's technological might or hefty set of military arms but the "mah-jongg set on the table" and the "jar of hot sauce so spicy foreigners start to burn" that defined daily life in Chengdu. They struck me as neither patriotic nor foreign loving, neither positive nor negative, but proud Chengduers, playful and provocative, holding fast to the city's irreverent spirit, not taking themselves too seriously.

Within a week of its release, "Made in China" had racked up 1 million views and was blasted in clubs from Beijing to Brooklyn. The Higher Brothers, newly signed to 88Rising, stormed the global stage, receiving enthusiastic praise from American rappers like Migos, setting up its first North American tour, and landing advertisement deals with the likes of Sprite and Adidas. For many listeners in the Chinese diaspora, it was a moment of pride and cultural validation that even rap music could be made in China.

That summer, Chinese hip-hop was propelled from the underground to the mainstream. One reason was the Higher Brothers. But the most crucial driver was *The Rap of China,* a reality TV hip-hop competition. The show went viral instantly after its debut in June on streaming site iQiyi, racking up 1.3 billion views in a month. Underground rappers like Vava and Tizzy T became major stars and house-hold names overnight, their performance fees increasing tenfold in a few weeks. "Do you freestyle?" became an online catchphrase, thanks to the show's celebrity judge, K-pop star Kris Wu, who would frequently ask the question of contestants. The show's slogan, R!CH, which stood for Rise! Chinese Hip-Hop, was registered by iQiYi as a trademark and street brand name and printed on hats, shirts, and cell phone cases. Douyin seized the opportunity to sponsor the show and gave Chinese creators the perfect tool to produce a churn of fast-paced rap, breakdance, and beatboxing videos on the web. "The internet and the reality TV show were like steroids for China's hip-hop scene," Wes Chen, the Shanghai-based Chinese American host of the hip-hop radio show *The Park,* told me.

Suddenly, Chengdu, a city known primarily among outsiders for its spicy food and large population of panda bears, became known as an incubator of trap music. NPR, *The New York Times, The Guardian,* and *Time* magazine all sent reporters to cover the burgeoning hip-hop industry. "Chinese artists were doing hip-hop way before *The Rap of China* arrived, but after the show aired, hip-hop suddenly became mainstream, became validated," Bohan Phoenix, the Chinese American rapper, told me. "Suddenly brands like Nongfu and Vitamin Water were all up in this bitch. People realized: Oh, there's a market for this."

Kafe Hu found himself swept up in all the attention, and his career as an artist accelerated. He was in high demand, called to perform across the country and invited to collaborate with fashion brands. Foreign reporters showed up at his doorstep asking for interviews—wanting to know his story, how many listeners he had, how much money he made. Riding hip-hop's explosive popularity, he signed with one of China's preeminent music companies and record labels, Modern Sky. For the first time in his life, he could make music full-time without worrying about how he would pay for food the next month.

As the hype around the Chinese hip-hop scene exploded, I couldn't help but feel the call to return to China, too. I'd just graduated from college in the United States with a degree in English literature, hoping to somehow make a career as a writer. I'd spent four years of my Yale undergraduate life reading Chaucer and Emerson and writing reported long-form articles on art museums and sustainable food initiatives for student magazines. Although the university offered many China-related courses—modern history surveys and Grand Strategy seminars—I mostly stayed away from them. It felt unnatural to try to make sense of a place I called home through textbooks, seminar debates, and the cold lens of geopolitics, and from hundreds of miles away.

I applied for a role as a reporting fellow at the Associated Press covering China but ended up being placed not in Beijing but back home in Hong Kong. Geographically and culturally, the city was closer to the subjects I wanted to write about than New Haven, but I still found myself covering the mainland from a distance. In many ways, Hong Kong had more in common with other global metropolises, like New York City or London, than it did with Beijing. Its internet, free of the Firewall, existed outside the walled garden of the Chinese cyberspace.

Not to mention, at the Associated Press, I was frustrated by the limits on what I could write. Of course, they were different from the constraints placed on my writing while I was an intern at *China Daily*—overt acts of political erasure by the hand of the censor. At the AP, I could write without inhibition on subjects that could never have been published in state media. But still, my writing was limited to the handful of topics about China deemed relevant to an international, which typically meant American, reader. To reduce huge concepts to a few hundred words, I had to describe Weibo as "China's Twitter," Sichuan as "the Chinese province the size of France," and Hong Kong as "the former British colony" and prescribe most problems to the "tightening grip of the ruling Communist Party." I wrote stories that felt meaningful to me—from a kindergarten abuse scandal to the devastating consequences of migrant evictions in Beijing—but mostly about how they "sparked public outcry," without delving into deeper systemic issues, such as the *hukou* ("household registration") system or the private education industry.

Meanwhile, I became fascinated by the unlikely creative explosion of Sichuanese trap, which completely defied my expectations of what popular music from China could now sound like. Who were the new voices of China's hip-hop scene, and how were they confronting, compromising with, and dancing around the red line of the censor? It had been almost a decade since my first encounter with the Firewall as a high school student in 2010. As a writer hoping to find my own voice in China's shifting cipher, I wanted answers. So, at the end of 2017, I decided to move to Beijing to write as a freelancer. The capital city would serve as my base to explore the rest of the country. As soon as I was settled, I booked a flight to Chengdu.

. . .

On July 1, 2017, a week after *The Rap of China* first aired, the China Netcasting Services Association—a state-backed industry body that regulates the online-media sector—published an expansive list of banned topics that needed to be scrubbed from the web. It laid out over sixty categories, including:

Depiction of male or female genitals

Depictions of underage drinking and drug use

Detailed plots involving prostitution, rape, and masturbation

Homosexuality, one-night stands, sexual liberation

Publicizing the luxury life

Reckless worship of celebrities

Depictions of killing or eating endangered animals

Defaming China's historical revolutionary leaders, or current members of the army, police, and judiciary

Blurring the lines between truth and falsity, good and evil, beauty and ugliness

Hurting the feelings of the Chinese people

The power of this form of censorship—dropped from above without warning—was that nobody could point to why exactly it had happened and who had called it in. Some attributed the tighter controls to official nervousness ahead of the 19th National Congress of the Party, a major leadership gathering in October. But they were also part of a growing list of regulations introduced to curtail online media. In May, regulators required online news providers to obtain government licenses, and in June, they introduced a ratings system for online bookstores and publishers based on such criteria as "focus on value guidance." Internet companies scrambled to interpret the new rules and preemptively sanitized their websites to avoid retaliation.

Blued was quick to react. Earlier in the year, internet authorities shut down the gay dating app Zank and the lesbian-dating app Rela, both for unclear reasons. Ma did not want his company to meet the same fate. Shortly after the new regulations were published, Blued scrubbed the words "gay" and *tongzhi* (a broadly used reinvention of the word meaning "comrade" to connote homosexuality) from its website. The official company description was changed to "The World's Leading Interest-Based Social & Health Education Network." In October, when the Party held its congress, the political event that determines national leadership over the next five years, Ma arranged a full staff screening of the event at Blued headquarters, a red Party flag erected next to its blue walls.

But the censorship directive did not stop at forbidden content; it also suggested categories of content that should be encouraged. These included:

Sing praise of the motherland

Applaud heroes

Celebrate the virtues of helping the needy, filial piety, and love for the elderly

Promote traditional Chinese culture

Contribute to the realization of the Chinese Dream

Promote truth, goodness, and beauty

Spread positive energy

China, regulators decided, would be lit. But it could be lit only in the way that they rigidly prescribed: positive, prudish, patriarchal, and, most crucially, patriotic. Although heavy-handed, the Party's positive energy efforts started to succeed. Although *The Founding of an Army* and its little fresh meat revolutionaries flopped, *Wolf Warrior II,* a jingoistic shoot-'em-up released in the same year, 2017, ascended to become the highest-grossing Chinese film at the time. The film, about a Chinese soldier who protects an unnamed African country from ruthless Western mercenaries, would go on to coin and popularize the term "Wolf Warrior diplomacy"—the combative stance and muscular patriotism that would characterize Chinese foreign policy in the years to come.

To reflect the Party's ideals, entire social media platforms revamped themselves. Kuaishou cleaned up its feeds, removing livestreamers who didn't fit the Party's vision of model Chinese citizens. Gone were the teenage mothers, cross-dressers, tattoo artists, and rappers who swore. Gone were Gourmet Sister Feng and her light bulbs. In their place, Kuaishou introduced a "Positive Energy" channel, which boosted the accounts of streamers who demonstrate the "everyday citizen's Chinese Dream." The feed featured videos of a master calligrapher inking a bird, a policeman helping a mother cross the road, a panda nuzzling its baby cub. Positive Energy produced its own online aesthetic: Pinterest meets Playhouse Disney meets the Communist Party.

This blend of patriotism and pop culture incubated one of the most powerful and organic collaborations between the Party and its netizens: Little Pinks. Little Pinks were the hybrid of the patriot and the contemporary stan. They adopted the Party as their idol, the nation as their team, and deployed the tactics of online fandoms, swarming the web to drown out their opponents' voices and defend all slights against China.

Unlike the 50 Cent Army, the moniker given to keyboard warriors paid by the government to pump out patriotic content, Little Pinks emerged from the grassroots and acted on their own, out of what seemed to be a sincere love for their country, like the "angry youth"—the online nationalists who, galvanized in the lead-up to the 2008 Beijing Olympics, preceded them. But in contrast to the angry youth, who engaged in often-earnest debate and called out media bias on older internet forums like Baidu Tieba, Little Pinks flocked to newer social media platforms like Douyin and Weibo, spamming opponents with crass slang and memes. They rose to notoriety in 2016, when they bombarded the Facebook page of Taiwanese president Tsai Ing-wen with insults after she won the presidential elections. Since then, they've targeted cosmetics company Lancôme for sponsoring Hong Kong pro-democracy pop star Denise Ho, attacked Lady Gaga on Instagram for meeting the Dalai Lama, and swarmed Australian swimmer Mack Horton's social media accounts after he criticized his Chinese competitor at the Rio Olympics.

"Little Pinks" originally referred to loyal fans of a starkly different team: a popular pink-colored literature website called Jinjiang Literature City, which featured Boys' Love fiction portraying romantic relationships between men. In popular lore, Little Pinks were foolish and fanatical young women who read fiction and chased celebrities, then transformed into online nationalists, projecting their affection for fictional protagonists onto the Communist Party. Later, media scholars would debunk this myth: Although the term originated on the website, the nationalists who became synonymous with it did not. A liberal blogger popularized the term after a dispute with online nationalists who had split from Jinjiang to create their own forum. It then became a gendered critique of online nationalists as frivolous, irrational, and unsophisticated. But in reality, most Little Pinks were men.

Older online patriots also upgraded their tactics, to adapt to not only the cultures of fandom but also that of the global web. Anti-cnn.com, for example, the scrappy independent website founded by Rao Jin in 2008, allegedly received $1.5 million from Eric Li, a Stanford-educated Chinese venture capitalist, to "upgrade the cultural industry of new nationalism." By 2016, it had transformed into April Media, a slick media company that produced TED-style talks on such topics as "resisting cultural colonization from the West," receiving praise from the Communist Youth League. The League also promoted patriotic hip-hop groups such as the Chengdu-based CDRev. Sporting ripped jeans and gold watches, the group rapped baldly nationalist songs with cringe-worthy lyrics criticizing the United States' antiballistic missile system in South Korea ("How many times do I have to warn you, my love little neighbor boy / you don't really want that toy") and glorifying a rising China ("Tell Uncle Sam / the red King's coming back").

Even the language of the Little Pinks borrowed not from Party platitudes but from the vocabulary of the global alt-right. They used terms like "feminist bitch" (*nuquan biao*) and "holy mother bitch" (*shengmu biao*) to attack feminists, and "white left" (*baizuo*) to refer to liberals who believed in immigration and LGBTQ rights. Fox News host Tucker Carlson would later bring *baizuo* up as an example of how the Chinese government was taking advantage of the weak, impressionable American left. The news ticker of his segment read CHINA'S WORD FOR WOKE AMERICAN LIBERALS: BAIZUO.

For all their clamor about China's unique standing in the world, Little Pinks represented an online presence that was anything but unique: angry young men, radicalized on the internet, fueled by the promises of strongmen to rejuvenate their dreams and make their country great again.

. . .

It was only a matter of time until the Party came for hip-hop. On January 19, 2018, just before I planned to fly to Chengdu in hopes of reporting on the growing hip-hop scene, the State Administration of Press, Publication, Radio, Film, and Television—the country's top media regulator at the time—announced new legislation forbidding TV programs from depicting hip-hop culture. Rappers' faces were crudely blurred in advertisements, concerts were hastily canceled, and the songs of PG One, winner of *The Rap of China*, were removed from music streaming platforms across the country.

PG One went silent before resurfacing with a Weibo post: "I will add more positive energy in my music works and serve as a better model for my fans." GAI, the other *Rap of China* victor, launched his own positive energy campaign to redeem himself, leading chants of "Long Live the Motherland!" on national television during a try-out performance for CCTV's Spring Festival Gala. An article in the *Global Times* declared that China hopes local hip-hop—"properly guided and purified"—can be "transform[ed] . . . into a positive influence."

Beyond the most visible victims of the ban, however, enforcement of the strictures remained ambiguous. I arrived in Chengdu a couple months later, in March, to find that most hip-hop artists continued to make music, albeit more cautiously. Most reacted in classic Chengdu fashion when I asked them about the ban: They shrugged it off. At most, it was a nuisance and an ineffective one, given that the ban was only for television. When I mentioned GAI, they wrinkled their noses, as if he reeked of the pungent odor of uncool. But they also understood: There was a sense that coolness had to make way for survival. "GAI's smart," said a Chengdu-based rapper called TSP. "He flipped a switch and decided to be a good boy."

I met Kafe Hu for the first time during that trip, at his friend's recording studio in a basement of a shopping mall called 339, next to a club. He was tall and tan, sporting a buzz cut and a sprawling patchwork of tattoos across the length of each arm: a half-finished dragon, a lion's head (modeled after the lion statues outside the Hemp House bar), a red Illuminati symbol (just for fun), and the word "Lucifer" (after his album *27: The Code of Lucifer*) spelled out in Morse code.

He seemed similarly unfazed by the ban. There were plenty of things to write about that fell into the category neither of contrarian dissent nor of commodity capitalism. His most popular track, "Hope and Reality," was recently censored because it explicitly criticized the government, but he continued to perform it live. The track begins with a list of hopes for the listener ("I hope you can breathe the air / I hope you can speak freely") before progressing into reality, where corruption is rampant and free speech can lead to imprisonment. His next track would be less confrontational, he said, addressing issues like Chinese society's discrimination against unmarried women, who were dubbed "leftover."

The previous year, Kafe had released his most experimental album to date, which featured a full jazz band and did not use any beats or samples. Titled *Kafreeman,* the album was named after his son, Freeman, born a few months prior. The lyrics were obtuse and introspective; his delivery was cool and unhurried, so they often sounded less like rap and more like spoken-word poetry. The album was released in three parts; the covers each bore a pop art–esque photo of his infant son but in three different colors: red, yellow, and blue. Some fans speculated online that the colors were chosen as a subtle critique of a recent abuse case that blew up in Beijing at a kindergarten that was part of the massive private company RYB (Red Yellow Blue) Education. The incident became a national scandal, one that I covered while I was at the Associated Press. Online, furious parents unleashed their rage at an education system that lacked official accountability and allowed the mistreatment of their children. Perhaps as a new father, Kafe wanted to express his outrage, too. "I didn't say anything explicitly," he told me with a sly grin, eyes twinkling with mischief. "But I'm not going to correct them."

He was ambivalent about Chinese hip-hop's suddenly being a focus of attention and had recently tried to shy away from it as much as possible. *Kafreeman* was lauded by critics, but the album wasn't a smash hit, and he seemed to like it that way. Onstage, he seemed almost disdainful of the idea of having a massive fandom and liked to engage in casual banter with his audience; a few years later, I would watch him perform in Beijing and call out overeager fans. "Who came early and lined up for the concert? And who came late?" he polled the crowd. "Late folks, I respect you. I'm fat and dark—it's not worth lining up for someone like me."

In some ways, he argued, the hip-hop ban allowed the subculture time to mature organically without the frenzied pressure of rapid commercialization. "The artists who were never really interested in hip-hop in the first place will move on," Kafe said. "And those who really love the art form will stick around."

Perhaps it was true. Perhaps the ban was no big deal—another one-off slap on the wrist to keep in check a subculture that had garnered too much attention. Or perhaps the nonchalance of all the artists I had met was a shrewd survival mechanism they had developed over the years in the face of the censor, founded on the belief that they could always continue to make music with a bit of grit and good humor. Instead of complaining about the constraints of the Great Firewall on the Chinese internet and on their music, they almost laughed them off. In the song "WeChat," the Higher Brothers sing praises—both ironically and earnestly—to the app: "There's no Skype, no Facebook, no Twitter, no Instagram / We use WeChat, yeah."

But I couldn't shake the feeling that the ban was but one tremor in a broader tectonic shift. I went to Poly Center in search of its storied hip-hop raves, only to find that the party was over. When the elevator opened to the twenty-first floor, I found the corridors silent and empty. The walls were peeling, and the doors to the defunct NASA hip-hop club were off their hinges. "Don't know," the guard at the lobby responded curtly when I asked him what had happened to the clubs.

On Poly Center's peak days, the line to the elevator had snaked for blocks past the building. The Tibetan rapper Young13DBaby told me that when he first moved from Lanzhou, in Gansu Province, to Chengdu, he rented out a cheap Airbnb in the basement of the building for an entire week. Every night, he made the twenty-one-flight pilgrimage to the top floor and danced till dawn. Now all that was left was one techno club, where the remaining stragglers bopped their heads to wordless beats. Electronic music was much more resilient than hip-hop to shifting regulatory tides, a local music producer told me, because it rarely used lyrics. "Think about East Germany when the Berlin Wall was still up," he said. "Why do you think there was only great techno at the time?"

I couldn't get a straight answer about why the clubs had disappeared. Perhaps it was something to do with drug use. Perhaps they were too rowdy and the city wanted to "purify" the gentrifying district of its negative energy. Perhaps the government was exerting its control, yet again, over a subculture it didn't understand. When I came back one night, stubbornly hoping to stumble into some sort of Poly Center revival, the guard looked incredulous. I asked him why they'd shut the parties down. "Who knows?" he asked in a way that sounded more like "Who cares?" Perhaps I'd arrived too late.

CHAPTER 11

Burning Out

In September 2016, China's first Science Fiction Conference launched inside the concert hall of Beihang University—a powerhouse of aerospace and astronautics engineering in the heart of Beijing's Haidian district, next to the Zhongguancun. For four days, the university buzzed with energy and anticipation. Banners emblazoned with the conference's theme, SCIENTIFIC IMAGINATION, ENCOUNTER THE FUTURE, adorned its walls. The campus gymnasium transformed into a full-blown sci-fi carnival, packed with booths showcasing the latest novels, video-game demos, and an exhibit on the history of science fiction. At the heart of the exhibit was Liu Cixin's 2015 Hugo Award trophy—chrome-plated, rocket-shaped, and the first of this prestigious science fiction honor ever bestowed on a Chinese writer—displayed in a glass case like a national relic.

When Stanley arrived at the conference, he was struck by the pomp and grandeur of it all. Science fiction had long been a fringe genre. Suddenly, sci-fi authors were being treated like rock stars. This wasn't a gathering of nerdy enthusiasts but a meeting of influential men and women shaping the nation's future. Attendees included sci-fi luminaries but also quantum physicists, film producers, and high-ranking government officials, such as Li Yuanchao, China's vice president and a self-proclaimed "science fiction fanatic." At the opening ceremony, Li delivered a speech urging the Chinese people to produce sci-fi works that "showcased the Chinese imagination, Chinese style, and Chinese spirit." The message was clear: Science fiction was no longer dismissed as escapist entertainment. It offered a vision of what China might become.

Just as Chinese hip-hop burst onto the global stage in the mid-2010s, so did Chinese science fiction. Overnight, it seemed as if a small circle of hardcore fans—nerdy college students debating the Fermi paradox on BBS feeds—blossomed into a full-fledged, multibillion-yuan industry of films, books, and video games. Sci-fi's soaring popularity captured the attention of all kinds of profit seekers, from film studios hungry for screenplay fodder to universities setting up sci-fi research institutions. The Sichuan government, hoping to tap into the nationwide sci-fi fever, poured 12 billion yuan ($1.7 billion) into building Chengdu Future Science and Technology City, a futuristic development outside Chengdu, with a science fiction museum, laboratories, offices, and an innovation center. In Beijing, a blast furnace at the abandoned Shougang steel plant, on the western outskirts of the city, was repurposed into a science fiction theme park; chimneys and chambers that once stockpiled iron ore now housed holographic art installations and fancy virtual reality theaters.

Crucial to science fiction's ascent in China was Liu Cixin, the lionized writer of the trilogy *The Three-Body Problem. Three-Body* was to Chinese sci-fi what the Higher Brothers' "Made in China" was to Chinese hip-hop: It propelled the genre to the mainstream. Fan clubs composed musical scores inspired by the novels; a string theorist wrote a book dedicated to explaining the physics of the *Three-Body* universe; Xiaomi CEO Lei Jun made the trilogy required reading for all his employees. After Ken Liu's English translation of the trilogy was published, Liu Cixin became the first Chinese writer to win the Hugo Award, in 2015, garnering praise from Mark Zuckerberg and President Obama alike.

Stanley also found himself in the spotlight. In 2016, he continued to work full time in the tech industry—he had left Google for Baidu in 2013, then joined a virtual reality start-up in 2015—while moonlighting as an author. He produced prodigiously, publishing his first novel, *The Waste Tide,* along with several short story collections. In doing so, he won virtually every science fiction literary award in China and established himself as a leading voice among the country's growing roster of acclaimed writers in the genre, such as Hao Jingfang and Han Song. Reviewers praised him as the William Gibson of China, in light of his cyberpunk style—futuristic stories that juxtaposed society's underclass (antihero protagonists and lawless underworlds) with cutting-edge technologies (artificial intelligence and cybernetic implants). Wang Yonggang, who led the AI research team at Kai-Fu Lee's venture capital firm Sinovation Ventures, was so impressed with Stanley's work that he gifted him with an intelligent algorithm, Chen Qiufan 2.0, capable of writing fiction imitating his voice.

In some ways, the ascendancy of Chinese sci-fi seemed not only unsurprising but inevitable. Thanks to the rise of the mobile internet, the country had undergone radical technological transformation—not only catching up with but surpassing the West. In 2016, when AlphaGo, Google's cutting-edge machine-learning program, beat the world's top player in the classical Chinese board game Go—China's "Sputnik Moment"—it served as a wake-up call that triggered a nationwide artificial intelligence fever. In hopes of seizing the next technological wave, the government published an ambitious plan laying out its agenda to become the world leader in artificial intelligence, pouring billions of dollars into AI research. Liu Cixin compared contemporary China to the United States after World War II, "during science fiction's Golden Age, when science and technology filled the future with wonder."

But unlike Liu Cixin, who grappled with the faraway grandeur of outer space, Stanley was drawn to the interior lives of characters struggling to anchor themselves at a moment of accelerated change. His fiction was often described as "science fiction realism." Although his job as a tech worker, which informed his writing, required an optimistic tech evangelism, his fictional futures were filled with cynicism, estrangement, and unease: burned-out office workers feeling spiritually impoverished, failed college graduates trapped in a rat race, sick citizens in smog-choked cities. He took as his subject not the dazzling wonder but the ugly underbelly of technological growth—rampant pollution, ecological destruction, soaring inequality. He channeled William Gibson's oft-quoted saying "The future is here, it is just not evenly distributed."

Stanley's novel *The Waste Tide*, for example, is set in the globalized, hypercapitalist near future. It follows the waste workers of Silicon Isle, based off Guiyu, a real-life island off the coast of southern China near Stanley's hometown, which served as the world's largest electronic-waste processing center. To research the book, he described his process as that of an "anthropologist conducting fieldwork," visiting the island to observe the workers lured there with the promise of job opportunities. Once he had a feel for the landscape of that world, he transported the scene into what he called the imagined "hyperreal"—a zone where the fantastical and factual are so blurred that it is unclear where one begins and the other ends. In the novel, corrupt government officials clash with greedy businessmen, eco-terrorists launch violent attacks, and a migrant worker—having toiled through so much toxic-laden trash—transforms into a cyborg.

Writing science fiction allowed Stanley to criticize society without being tied to any side of history. Veiled by the future, he had more room to obscure and complicate his views of the present. Although *The Waste Tide* could be read as a dark and scathing critique of the government's failure to deal with ecological destruction, the novel could just as easily be interpreted as an attack on American hypocrisy, a manifesto against global consumerism, or simply an apolitical exploration of posthuman consciousness. "With science fiction, I can probe real-life issues through an imaginary narrative," Stanley told me, "without explicitly arguing who is right or wrong, good or evil."

At their core, his stories were ultimately driven by a question that plagued everyone, not only in China but across the world: What were the consequences of human beings' relentless drive toward technological growth, and at the end of the process, who would we become?

.   .   .

Perhaps no work tackled the consequences of China's growth machine as directly as the novella *Folding Beijing*, by Stanley's peer and science fiction writer Hao Jingfang. Like Stanley, Hao wore many hats and worked with one foot outside the system and one foot within. After she graduated from elite Tsinghua University with an undergraduate degree in physics and a PhD in economics, she joined a government think tank as a macroeconomics researcher. In the daytime, she researched the effects of automation on the labor market; at dawn, she rose early to write science fiction.

In both roles, she was fascinated by inequality: how it worked, where it came from, and why it remained intractable. Living in Beijing, she was struck by stories of the city's migrant workers who, over the past three decades, were part of a migration of hundreds of millions of people moving from the countryside to the city in search of new job opportunities and a better life. They provided an endless supply of cheap labor—as construction workers, security guards, janitors, and factory workers—and formed the backbone of China's meteoric economic growth, building its skyscrapers and toiling in its factories. For decades, they lived within a deeply unequal system, deprived of an urban *hukou* (a household registration system that separated rural from city residents), making it much harder to access the city's benefits like health care and medical insurance and to send their kids to school. In hopes of bringing their experience to light, she sat down to write *Folding Beijing* and finished in three days.

The novella portrays an imaginary city, split by time and space into three distinct castes who inhabit three divided spaces, splitting allotted time on the earth's surface. At dawn, the city folds into itself, buildings twisting at their spines into compacted blocks and the grounds rotating inward like the tiles of a giant Rubik's Cube. The residents of the elite First Space stir from their slumber, waking up to a full twenty-four-hour cycle of blue skies, vast green parks, and gingko-lined streets. Meanwhile, the residents of Second and Third Space—the city's white-collar middle-class and its waste-worker underclass—go to sleep.

Lao Dao, the novella's protagonist, was inspired by a conversation Hao had with a Beijing taxi driver, who complained to her about the city's exorbitant school fees. A waste worker and single father, Lao Dao has lived in the Third Space since birth; his father arrived in the city as part of the first workers to build up its folding infrastructure. One day, Lao Dao discovers a message in a trash chute: A graduate student from the Second Space wants a letter delivered to his lover in the First Space. Traversing spaces is illegal, but if he succeeds, he could earn double his annual salary and pay for his daughter's kindergarten tuition.

He climbs over the edge of the rotating earth to the First Space, enchanted by a city of spacious, tree-lined streets and beautiful homes. But while eavesdropping on a group of officials, he learns a terrible secret: The city has developed a new green technology that could automate the processing plants but has chosen not to use it, because it would render the waste workers of Third Space useless and unemployed. The most efficient solution to an excess, idle workforce is to divide up the city across time and space. *Reduce the time a portion of the population spends living, and then find ways to keep them busy,* one of the officials explains bluntly. *Shove them into the night.*

Folding Beijing was an instant hit. University students, tech luminaries, and entertainment executives all loved it. Ken Liu translated the story, first published on a Tsinghua BBS feed, into English. Hollywood director Josh Kim announced that he would adapt the novella into a film. In 2016, the year after Liu Cixin's award, Hao won the Hugo for best novella, becoming the first Chinese woman to do so. In Hao's imaginary city, readers saw the Beijing—and the China—that they knew: the relentless pace of urbanization, the unfair treatment of the working class, and, beneath the glossy surface of "national rejuvenation," deep-rooted divisions that threatened to unravel the entire facade.

The ending of Hao's novella read like an eerie premonition. In 2016, the local Beijing government announced a cap on the city's population—a cut of 23 million by 2020. Population reduction would benefit all, it claimed; it would beautify the city, reduce traffic congestion, and make space for greenery. They demolished "illegal structures" the size of Manhattan, from fruit stalls to make-shift homes to entire apartment complexes—mostly occupied by the city's migrant workers. In official documents, the workers were referred to as *diduanrenkou*, or "low-end population." The local government appeared to have come to the same conclusion as the First Space officials Lao Dao had eavesdropped on. Like the waste workers of Third Space, Beijing's migrant workers had served their purpose. The skyscrapers were built; factories' need for cheap labor was dwindling. It was time to clear them out.

. . .

In November 2017, a fire broke out on the outskirts of Beijing, in the Daxing district, in a village that was home to many of the city's migrant workers. Firefighters spent three hours battling the deadly blaze, which ripped through a patchwork of makeshift homes, garment workshops, and factories. Nineteen people died, most of them migrants.

The government's response was swift. Shortly after the last flames were extinguished, Beijing's Party secretary launched a forty-day campaign to demolish the city's "illegal structures" in the name of clearing out "fire hazards." Authorities issued mass eviction orders, forcing thousands of migrant workers in the Daxing village, as well as other migrant enclaves across the city, to leave their homes. Given less than a day to get out, many were left stranded in the freezing winter night—so cold that roadside puddles had hardened into black ice. Entire buildings were sealed off, marked with the Chinese character *chai*, or "tear down," in red spray paint. "In 2008, you were welcome in Beijing," an evicted worker quoted the Summer Olympics slogan bitterly to a documentary filmmaker as he watched his home get bulldozed. "But in 2017, Beijing finds you disgusting and kicks you out."

As news of the evictions spread across social media, Beijing residents were horrified to see workers fleeing from their homes like a scene from a disaster film. In a rare moment of cross-class solidarity, poor and wealthy, blue-collar and white-collar, Third Class and First Class alike rallied together online to protest the injustice. On WeChat, volunteers created an online eviction map detailing the locations affected, so that people could supply shelter and aid. Journalists and documentarians flocked to the scene to amplify the voices of the evicted workers. Prominent lawyers and professors as well as ordinary Beijing residents penned open letters addressed to the Party leadership, condemning the "ruthless" campaign and demanding due process. "The bodies of the dead were not cold," they chastised in one of the petitions. "And yet some people in this fine capital cracked the whip to expel the 'low-end population.'"

Only days after the evictions, Beijing's Second Space became embroiled in its own crisis. Eight parents of toddlers at a kindergarten, part of the private education company RYB, filed a report to local police: They had discovered needle marks on their children, who also informed them that teachers had forced them to swallow tablets without explanation. Horrified, Beijing's parents lashed out at the country's fast-booming private preschool industry, which had been allowed to grow unchecked and unregulated in the service of profit. The scandal revealed that no amount of wealth or privilege could protect the people from a system that prioritized growth over justice and dignity. The twin tragedies, unfolding in separate spaces, brought Beijing's residents together in their anger. "Beijingers have a new greeting," went one widely shared WeChat post. "When you meet the low-end population, you ask, Have you found a place to live? When you meet the middle-class population, you ask, Is your child OK?"

But public protest, as always, was ephemeral. Migrants continued to be cleared out. Those who were able to stay considered themselves lucky, keeping their heads down. The lawyers and activists who spoke out for them were silenced. The labor NGOs that once could have defended them had long been incapacitated; new regulations had drained their resources and their ability to act. Online platforms such as WeChat and Weibo served as an emotional outlet, a cathartic valve to express grievance, but not a space for sustained mobilization. The hashtag #BeijingRYBCenterSuspectedofChild Abuse, which soared to one of the top-trending topics on Weibo, became inaccessible. "Low-end population"—which became a viral phrase laying bare the Party's hypocritical commitment to its working class—was quickly blocked on all forms of social media. The "delusions" of the capital, one WeChat user wrote in a post before it, too, was deleted, were being "folded away."

. . .

In the summer of 2017, Stanley quit his tech job to write science fiction full time. After more than a decade in tech, he was disillusioned with the industry's myth of ceaseless growth. His whole life, he had worked dutifully within institutions: acing his college entrance exams, enrolling in an elite university, working at highly respected companies. But what was it all for? He joined the tech industry to be a pioneer but ended up feeling like a cog.

The following summer, Stanley traveled to the Black Rock Desert in Nevada and spent a week at Burning Man. He was among tens of thousands of self-proclaimed "burners" who journeyed to the ephemeral "Black Rock City" seeking community, purpose, spiritual fulfillment—missing from their hypercapitalist world. He was a "virgin burner," attending for the first time with a group of other Chinese artists, filmmakers, and musicians. They built art installations and joined dance parties. They marveled at the values of this real-life utopia: radical self-reliance, communal effort, civic responsibility. Nothing was for sale except ice and coffee; in the festival's spirit of "gifting," all goods had to be shared voluntarily, bartered perhaps for a hug or a song. Stanley spent nine days wandering the desert, going with the flow. "It gave me a sense of what a utopian society could look like," he told me, "when no one gives you any external framework to shape your behavior."

But even utopias were imperfect. Despite Burning Man's reputation as an escape from the consumerist and stratified reality of the outside world, Silicon Valley elites from Elon Musk to Mark Zuckerberg to Elizabeth Holmes (who visited shortly after her grand jury indictment for defrauding investors in her blood-testing company, Theranos) loved the festival. Counter to its spirit of egalitarianism, tech bros and high-profile executives descended in their private jets, spending their days in tents with generator-powered air-conditioners.

Stanley discovered that the festival even attracted a large group of Chinese tech bro equivalents. Among them was an entrepreneur training camp of seventy start-up owners organized by a Chinese internet giant. The company they hired to organize their experience set up air-conditioned space-capsule tents, where they drank cold beverages, fiddled on their smartphones, and participated in entrepreneur training sessions. One tent even had karaoke. A slot at the camp apparently cost $20,000, compared to the regular Burning Man ticket of $425.

In stark contrast to Stanley's Chinese friends, the newly arrived Chinese tech bros had no intention of understanding or respecting the spirit of the festival. Many introduced themselves with their senior executive titles. Some took photos of other people's nude bodies without consent. Others refused to share food or take part in the collective work and called other burners *fuwuyuan,* or "waiter." "They either saw the festival as an exotic, lawless place, or as just another holiday getaway for business-related socializing," he wrote in an account of his experience. He compared them to "the first generation of pioneers journeying into the virtual New World. They imagine themselves as packs of wolves in the Mongolian plains who can only survive and emerge victorious through bloody combat, incessantly stalking new territory and prey."

Observing the behavior of the Chinese burner bros, Stanley felt as if he were "seeing something much larger played out in miniature." They exposed the worst traits of the tech elite—especially the cavalier and cutthroat competition that fueled their success in the Chinese tech industry's ascent. Chinese tech entrepreneurs admiringly used the phrase "savage growth"—a term borrowed from Liu Cixin's *The Three-Body Problem,* which described the aggressive expansion of an alien race in its efforts to eradicate humanity. ("That was *sav-*

age, man!") China's most successful tech companies thrived off this hypercompetitive mindset: The telecommunications giant Huawei proudly embraced a "wolf spirit," instilling an ethos of combativeness and opportunism among its employees; Meituan, China's largest food-delivery platform, cultivated a "victory or death" ethos and a strategy of "gladiatorial entrepreneurialism," ousting competitors by poaching employees, launching smear campaigns, and deploying "tactics that would make [Uber cofounder] Travis Kalanick blush," wrote Kai-Fu Lee in his book *AI Superpowers.*

But uninhibited growth was unsustainable. Stanley's concerns proved prescient. By the end of 2018, economic growth—the one vehicle that had kept China hurtling ahead—was slowing, falling to 6.6 percent, the lowest in three decades. Sectors that once served as sources of explosive growth declined sharply: Foreign investment plunged, and retail spending and the housing market slumped. Further exacerbating the slowdown, the Trump administration imposed punitive tariffs in June of that year, igniting what would become a long and messy trade war. As China grew at once more powerful and more assertive on the global stage, American attitudes toward Chinese tech shifted from one of awe to one of fear, from a policy of engagement to "decoupling." In response, the Chinese government doubled down on the need for self-sufficiency and "indigenous innovation" in core technologies.

Chinese tech entrepreneurs—who had long relied on an intermingling of Zhongguancun and Silicon Valley talent, funding, and resources—found themselves in a risky spot, both financially and politically. As venture capital dried up, they grew skittish, bracing themselves for what would be called China tech's "capital winter." Faced with funding shortages, hundreds of Chinese start-ups burned through cash, with many shutting down altogether. China's big tech companies started laying off employees and cutting bonuses while trying to speed up processes and boost productivity. Hard work and hustle no longer delivered corresponding returns. Whereas the tech industry's brutal "996" working hours (from nine in the morning to nine in the evening, six days a week) were once worn as a badge of honor, the phrase was now uttered by tech workers with frustration, disdain—and eventually, protest.

. . .

In March 2019, an anonymous group of fed-up tech workers took their grievances to an unlikely platform: GitHub, the world's largest open-source software site. Owned by Microsoft, GitHub was popular with programmers as a platform to crowdsource code. On the platform, Chinese tech workers created a "repository" or collaborative project called 996.ICU (based on the joke that a 996 schedule will send you to the intensive care unit) to share their grueling work schedules, crowdsource a "blacklist" of companies that illegally forced employees to work more than sixty hours a week, and drafted petitions to government ministries to demand better working conditions. Shortly after, Microsoft's US employees joined in by creating a Support 996.ICU GitHub project. In a matter of days, it was signed by hundreds of tech workers around the world, from Spain to Turkey to Singapore, becoming the largest online mobilization of tech workers in history.

The tech workers chose GitHub because it was one of the few global internet platforms that remained both uncensored and accessible within the country, known colloquially by Chinese internet users as the last land of free speech in China. Chinese authorities could not censor individual projects, because GitHub used the HTTPS protocol, which encrypted all traffic. But they were also unwilling to ban GitHub entirely, because it was invaluable to the Chinese tech industry. For the government, GitHub's continued presence on the country's internet embodied the delicate balancing act they had been performing since China joined the World Wide Web: Could it keep the internet just free enough to nurture economic growth but not so free that it opened the door to political instability? China's developers were both heavily dependent on and active contributors to the open-source community; blocking the site would have been too costly. GitHub therefore served as a sanctuary from censors and a platform for online resistance.

For all the rhetoric of "decoupling," "cyber-sovereignty," and the "splinternet," the 996.ICU protests on GitHub also revealed that American and Chinese tech ecosystems were more similar than they seemed. On opposite ends of the globe, tech workers rallied against the same problem: the unchecked power of tech monoliths and a toxic work culture that prioritized profit and efficiency over human dignity. As the 996.ICU protests exploded in China, tech workers in the United States protested Facebook's violation of data privacy, Uber's exploitation of gig workers, and Amazon's grueling work conditions in its fulfillment centers. Tech workers worldwide were resisting the idea that technological progress, fueled by single-minded market competition and the relentless hustle of its expendable workforce, would propel them into a future of wealth and ease.

On the final night of Burning Man, Stanley took part in the closing ritual, the Temple Burn. Each year, burners gathered at the Temple—a large wooden structure at Black Rock City's twelve o'clock, built as space for reflection, remembrance, and release. Some wrote letters to the dead. Others brought objects or offerings— totems of loss, past grievances, broken relationships—to burn in the flames.

Stanley sat in silence among them, the fire blazing under the vast, starry sky. For a moment, he felt as if they'd traveled thousands of years back in time, before smartphones and stock markets and steam engines, back when humans still met their most primal needs: to connect with one another, with their ancestors, and to the divine.

On a scrap of paper, he wrote: *Farewell to the old me, become the new me.* Then he stepped toward the Temple and cast the paper into the flames.

CHAPTER 12

Going Underground

Lü Pin planned to leave home for only two weeks. In March 2015, she was invited to New York City to attend the United Nations' Commission on the Status of Women. It was a big conference: first, a march to Times Square, followed by an opening ceremony in midtown Manhattan, then back-to-back panel discussions with feminist activists from around the world. For the trip, she packed the bare necessities, including three pairs of socks, two pairs of trousers, and a pair of slippers.

She didn't want to stay for too long, because her mind was still back home in China, where the young feminist activists were busy planning events for the upcoming International Women's Day. One of their campaigns, coordinated across ten cities, was to raise awareness against sexual harassment on public transportation. Its main organizer, Zheng Churan, known by the nickname Datu ("Big Rabbit"), who worked at a Guangzhou-based gender NGO, was in charge of printing and distributing colorful stickers; on WeChat, the group recruited and gathered participants—mostly university students—across the country to hand them out at subway stations.

Lü had left at an exciting but tense moment. Since they launched the Bloody Brides protest three years ago, the young movement had burgeoned; new volunteers eagerly joined their ranks, and the public was paying greater attention. But a higher profile came with the cost of increased government scrutiny. Online, *Feminist Voices*' following soared, but its posts were also more rigidly censored. Offline, police more frequently invited the women in to "have tea"—a euphemism for being summoned by authorities for a conversation as an informal method of intimidation and control—and demanded that they cancel events prior to sensitive anniversaries.

Somewhere, there was an ambiguous red line that they could not step over. What was the cost of crossing it? Nobody knew. They could only guess, tiptoeing along an invisible boundary.

On March 6, Lü's second day in New York, she received the news. Sitting in the lobby next to the elevator, preparing to attend a symposium surrounded by strangers speaking different languages, she felt as if her body were in endless free fall. *They've been taken in.*

· · ·

That night, security agents in Beijing, Hangzhou, and Guangzhou staged a high-profile arrest of five core members of the movement: Li Maizi and Wei Tingting, who once acted as brides in the Bloody Brides protests, as well as Zheng Churan, Wu Rongrong, and Wang Man.

They were taken completely by surprise. Li Maizi was getting ready for bed when half a dozen men—some uniformed police, others plainclothes agents—knocked on her door, barged in, and started searching the apartment to confiscate her phone and laptop. They brought her to the police station, drew her blood, tested her urine, took her fingerprints, and started interrogating her: Why was she organizing subversive activities about sexual harassment? Who was she working with? Who funded the organization?

All five were detained, interrogated, and charged with the crime of "picking quarrels and provoking trouble"—the all-encompassing term used by the government to condemn its critics—then moved to the Haidian District Detention Center in Beijing.

Wei Tingting became known as inmate #1203. Her cell was made up of a long plank on the floor, covered with a blue quilt. She was interrogated for several hours a day, sometimes past midnight. Her interrogators had done their homework: They asked about hotels she'd stayed in, workshops she'd participated in back in 2012, and

Weibo posts she'd made years ago. They'd even read through her diary, which was on the laptop they'd confiscated, looking for "reactionary" ideas.

Still, Wei found kinship and camaraderie among the detainees in her block, thirty or so women from diverse backgrounds: drug dealers, fake-ID sellers, and petty thieves. One of the oldest, whom they called Auntie, was a legal representative of a large company, in her sixties or seventies. The youngest, an eighteen-year-old they called Little Fatty, had been detained for stealing more than three thousand yuan. The women supported each other, sharing parts of their past lives, lending each other sanitary napkins, and giving each other legal advice. They fashioned a communal mirror out of the tinfoil wrapping of milk cartons. In the cold, isolated cells of the detention center, Wei even fell in love, meeting the woman who would eventually become her girlfriend.

Cut off from the world, without a phone or computer, the women had no idea whether they would be detained for a few days, for half a year, or even three. Little did they know that outside the detention center, their arrests had broken the global news. *The Guardian* and *Time* magazine jumped in to cover the event.

On the other side of the world, Lü Pin sent hundreds of emails a day, reaching out to the international community for support. On Twitter and Facebook, supporters posted images of themselves wearing masks that bore photos of the five women, now known as the Feminist Five. Lü got in touch with the American playwright V (formerly Eve Ensler), who issued a statement calling on the Chinese authorities to "recognize the Chinese Five, the extraordinary women who stood up not to antagonize their government but to liberate women." Hillary Clinton and then–US Ambassador to the United Nations Samantha Power publicly condemned the detentions. "If China is committed to advancing the rights of women," Power wrote, "then it should be working to address the issues raised by these women's rights activists—not silencing them."

Perhaps bowing to international pressure, authorities released the women thirty-seven days later. But they were scared, traumatized, and stripped of their support systems. One night in China, while

Lü was in New York, the police broke into her empty apartment in Beijing. Perhaps they were sending her a warning message, she feared. If she returned home, perhaps they would come after her. She'd be jeopardizing not only her own safety but also that of her friends.

Lü's days blurred into a sleepless frenzy. She had planned to be away for only two weeks. When the United Nations conference ended, she stayed on, drifting from one acquaintance's place to another, a single suitcase in tow. She felt guilty, unable to go home to help her fellow feminists work through their trauma. She also felt isolated, abandoned by former friends who'd cut her off out of fear of association.

More than a month into her stay, a telegram voice note arrived from Zheng Churan. She warned Lü, her voice hoarse and shaky: "You must not come back."

.   .   .

Back home, the crackdowns on civil society continued. On July 9, 2015, more than three hundred lawyers and rights defenders were arrested in a sweep, many on vague charges of "subverting state power" or "disturbing the public order." People called it the "709 crackdown," after the date it was launched. New lines had been drawn, and the feminists had crossed it; now they had to retreat.

The once-thriving feminist movement in China abruptly went underground—its activists scattering across the country, taking buses back to their hometowns, moving to smaller cities, lying low. They continued to pursue feminist work but on a smaller scale, moving from Beijing to cities like Guangzhou and Chengdu, relatively liberal havens away from the political center. In Guangzhou, Wei Tingting founded an NGO providing psychological support for victims of sexual violence. Others left China altogether, to study abroad in the United Kingdom and Hong Kong.

Lü stayed in New York, living in a transitory state. In China, she was a pariah. But in the United States, away from home, she was an alien, with no bank account, no support system, no long-term place to live. Without a working visa, she could not rent her own apartment. Without sufficient English-language skills, she could not find a job easily and make her own income. She was important in China—a respected leader within the feminist community—but in New York, she was nobody. "I felt like a grain of sand at the end of the world that could be blown away at any time," she said. "How do you replant yourself in a new place after you've lost everything you once had?"

Although she feared returning to China, she was just as afraid of losing touch with the place, fading away into irrelevance. She started writing in her diary a list of things that she'd left behind in China as a means of staying connected to her past life. When she got homesick, she would open Google Maps and zoom in on street views of her old apartment in Beijing. She thought of her cat, her companion for ten years, who had no idea where Lü had gone and whether she would ever return.

.   .   .

Two weeks turned into two years. Lü found a way to stay in New York after a professor at Columbia helped arrange for a visiting scholarship at the university. When those two years were about to run out, she enrolled as a graduate student at the University at Albany's Women's, Gender, and Sexuality Studies program to extend her stay.

If she'd felt lonely in bustling New York, she was lost in Albany. She struggled to communicate. Once a student of Chinese literature, proud of her command of the language, she now stumbled through broken English, mixing up her "he's" and "she's" because they were pronounced the same way in Chinese. She'd never learned how to drive, so getting around seemed impossible. "Even though I was free, in the United States, I still felt like a person being held captive," she wrote.

As the situation worsened in her own country, her adoptive country—whose leaders loudly touted their commitment to liberty and equality—was also regressing. In November 2016, the United States elected a sexual harasser, racist, and homophobe as its president. Just as in the States, in China, people projected wildly contradictory hopes and fears onto Donald Trump. Business elites hoped for a pragmatist willing to put aside ideological differences in favor of a good deal. Anti-CCP dissidents perceived him as a hawk who would take a hard line on China. The Communist Party itself saw an opportunity: Like the financial crisis in 2008, the election of Donald Trump to the US presidency, alongside the UK's vote to leave the European Union, signaled another step toward Western decline. Democracy did not yield wealth and power, it seemed, but instability and decay.

The feminists lamented Trump's ascent as the rise of another illiberal strongman. They called his behavior a form of "straight-man cancer," as Zheng Churan wrote in an open letter on WeChat: a chronic and infectious sexism that spread across borders, indiscriminate of nationality. "Straight-man cancer spreads everywhere, damaging feminist movements and undermining social equality," she wrote. "It is pervasive."

The day after Trump's inauguration, hundreds of thousands of women took to the streets of Washington in protest. At the time, I was a senior in college, celebrating my birthday. When I drove down that day from New Haven with my roommates, toting bright neon signs that read KEEP YOUR LAWS OFF MY BODY, Lü Pin was there protesting, too, amid a sea of pink hats, alongside a group of other Chinese-diaspora feminists.

In China, a parallel political strain was taking root. Although the Party continued to tout ideals of women's equality and liberation, it increasingly aligned itself with patriarchal, Confucian values. The Party encouraged the revival of traditional gender roles—namely, that women should embrace their "unique role in the family" as dedicated wives and child bearers to uphold the nation. The All-China Women's Federation—the country's official women's rights organization—not only warned of "Western hostile forces actively peddling Western feminism"; they partnered with a college to launch the New Era Women's School, offering courses that taught female students how to dress, pour tea, and sit properly.

The state was jarringly out of touch with the attitudes of Chinese women, who were increasingly asserting their desire (or refusal) to marry, have children, and raise families on their own terms. In 2018, China's marriage rate fell to the lowest point since 2012, and its birth rate to its lowest since the founding of the People's Republic of China, nearly seventy years before. Divorce rates were climbing, with women initiating most cases. Stories of female empowerment consistently found an enthusiastic audience: One of China's most popular online influencers was Papi Jiang, a wry and worldly comedian who garnered millions of Weibo followers for poking fun at sexist double standards. One of the most popular films of 2016 was the Bollywood hit *Dangal,* based on a real-life story about two young Indian women pushing back against gender stereotypes to become world wrestling champions.

But progressive feminism and archaic misogyny both had markets in today's China, and the growth of one did not negate the other. For a story I wrote for the Associated Press, I was struck to learn of the rise of "female morality schools," where women learned how to "shut their mouths and do more housework." *Don't fight back when beaten. Don't talk back when scolded. And, no matter what, don't get divorced.* I watched a female teacher at one of the schools lecture her students, captured on video footage taken by an undercover reporter. Under the right conditions, it was possible to turn back the clock.

. . .

On March 8, 2018, International Women's Day, the clock hands wound back again. All *Feminist Voices* social media accounts were permanently shut down, accused of posting "sensitive and illegal information." The living archive of the movement—a decade's worth of ideas, dialogue, and memories—was gone in an instant, like a magician's flash paper set alight. For Lü, the loss was devastating. "Losing *Feminist Voices* was like losing a loved one," she later wrote of her grief. "Like having a part of myself die before my eyes."

In the days that followed, the women tried in vain to resuscitate their accounts. They reached out to Weibo and WeChat, sent a letter to the Cyberspace Administration of China, and even filed a lawsuit with the Shenzhen Nanshan District People's Court and the

Beijing Haidian People's District Court, demanding that the two platforms restore their accounts, apologize, and pay compensation of one yuan. All attempts at outreach received no response. Before long, WeChat began shutting down accounts of those who spoke out in support, and Weibo started banning use of the *Feminist Voices* logo as an account avatar. Searches for the term "Feminist Voices" yielded the message *Sorry, no relevant results were found.*

Authorities continued to snuff out all forms of grassroots organizing. Even Guangzhou's status as a liberal haven for feminist activists did not last long. The Gender and Sexuality Center, established by Wei Tingting two years earlier, was shut down and listed as an illegal organization. Xiao Meili, who had been involved in the feminist movement since she marched down Qianmen in a wedding dress, also moved to Guangzhou and was forced by police to move apartments five times. To get her evicted, they told her landlords that she was a drug abuser or a lesbian. "They kick us like balls from one city to another, from one district to another," Xiao told the publication *ChinaFile*. "We are wanderers in our own country."

Lü herself remained in limbo, an outsider and an exile in two societies where different strains of misogyny continued to proliferate. *Take the firewood out from under the cauldron,* she quoted a Chinese proverb, *and its flames will extinguish.* Authorities did just that: They took out the feminist movement's organizers, drove them out of public spaces, and cut off their social network, trying to extinguish its flames for good. "Without its participants and places to gather," wrote Lü, "a movement will wither and perish."

On March 11, three days after *Feminist Voices* was shut down, the National People's Congress, China's legislature, voted almost unanimously to revise the state constitution and abolish the two-term limit on the presidency—reversing three decades of political precedent.

When the news was announced to the public, netizens turned to the one place where they could still voice their opinion: the internet. As usual, they engaged in a cat-and-mouse game with censors who moved in to erase them. Web searches for the term "emigrate" soared, until the word was banned, alongside the phrases "lifelong," "ascend the throne," and *daoche*, to "drive backward." Stripped of words, they started posting satirical videos of themselves backing up their cars—as if they were in the nation's driver's seat, jerking back the wheels of history.

. . .

Since Reform and Opening, Chinese society has moved in cycles of what scholars have observed of *fang* and *shou*, "opening" and "tightening." Deng's calls for the Chinese people to "emancipate the mind" followed the repressive era of Mao's Cultural Revolution. The freewheeling opening of the 1980s culminated in the Tiananmen crackdown of 1989. The chill of Tiananmen in turn paved the way for the market reforms of Deng's Southern Tour in 1992. The Communist Party theorist Deng Liqun was one of the first to observe this pattern of reform and retrenchment, in the 1980s. American scholars like Susan Shirk and Richard Baum expanded upon this idea, suggesting that ideological divisions within the Party, between reformist and conservative factions, drove these oscillations. When the system opens up too quickly, destabilizing power, the theory goes, conservatives step in to assert control. When their grip becomes too rigid, reformers call for change, provoking a loosening again.

Of course, academic theories serve as imperfect and simplified models of reality. On one hand, they explain undulations in the Party's governance, swinging from liberalization back to control. But they cannot point to the exact moment when tightening begins, when *fang* yields to *shou*. In a society as vast and diverse as China's, freedom and repression are not experienced uniformly. Ask the question of different people and they will respond with different answers. Ask the once-vocal journalists and liberal intellectuals on Weibo, and they would say the swerve hit over the course of 2013, after the downfall of *Southern Weekly*. Ask the musicians of Beijing's underground scene, and they might say they felt the shift in 2015 and 2016, in the wake of drug-related arrests in the city's clubs. For the feminist activists, the arrest of the Feminist Five in 2015 marked an abrupt turn, forcing the movement underground.

The theory is further complicated by external forces, part of a global authoritarian drift, that have amplified China's cycles of opening and closing. Many scholars, such as the American historian David Shambaugh, have pointed to the financial crisis of 2008 as a turning point between *fang* and *shou*. Disillusioned by the West's failure to handle the economic downturn, the argument goes, the Party decided to swerve off the path of liberalization into an entirely new direction. The failure of the Arab Spring of 2010 underscored the resilience of one-party regimes in the face of new social media platforms; Edward Snowden's 2013 revelations legitimized the use of technological surveillance by those in charge. The election of Donald Trump and the rise of illiberal populism in the West in 2016 only further emboldened authoritarians across the globe.

I felt the tightening most acutely in 2019, when I'd lived in Beijing for a year. At the time, I'd started covering China's queer communities—both because I believed the space was continuing to liberalize and open, against all odds, and because I wanted to figure out where I belonged. My college in the United States had been a queer cocoon: Pride month was something of a holiday, when I came out with little commotion and began to feel comfortable in my own skin. Now I'd returned to a city where I'd last lived when I was fifteen, at once familiar and alienating; I felt culturally confused and uncomfortably queer in a society where LGBTQ issues were neither forbidden nor openly recognized by the state. Which direction was society moving in?

As I always did when I wanted answers, I started asking questions, interviewing dozens of people involved in queer life in China: LGBTQ NGO volunteers, gay student groups, pink economy venture capitalists, impact-litigation lawyers. I wanted to understand their experience so that I could better make sense of mine and understand what possibilities lay in store. The details varied: the first crush was not the best friend but the popular class monitor; the social media platform of choice was not BF99 on a computer but Rela on a smartphone; sometimes the parents had come around, but more often they didn't. But each story pulsed with the same undercurrent of cautious optimism: that things were hard but much better than before and would only continue to get better—more tolerant, more free, more open.

"Right now, we're going through a period of winter," Duan, an NGO worker from the Beijing LGBT Center, explained to me. I first met him in the late spring of 2019, at a fundraising party hosted by the center at the local craft beer brewery Great Leap Brewing. Young people sporting rainbow armbands and pride stickers sunbathed carefree in the courtyard, drinking fruity IPAs. He stood by the keg station, dressed in a rainbow T-shirt.

Duan meant that China's political weather was shifting. Queer activists were more closely tailed and NGOs cut from sources of funding. Given that the weather was inhospitable during political anniversaries, the summer of 2019—the seventieth anniversary of the founding of the PRC and the thirtieth of the Tiananmen crackdown—was particularly precarious. In recent months, he erred on the side of caution, keeping event sizes small and promoting them through word of mouth.

But still, he remained optimistic. "Perhaps by the end of the year," he said, "the freeze will pass."

But when the summer arrived, the chill did not pass; it deepened. Weibo censored the word "lesbian" from its social media platforms; online stores removed rainbow-themed products from its shelves. Beyond China's borders, the geopolitical climate had chilled, too. In 2019, the United States raised alarms about national security risks posed by Chinese technologies, placing telecommunications giant Huawei on the Bureau of Industry and Security's "Entity List" over concerns of espionage. Gay dating apps became unwittingly implicated in the strife. The US government forced Chinese company Kunlun to sell Grindr to American owners, citing fear that the Chinese government could access sensitive data.

On June 4, 2019, Beijing summer in full bloom, I spent the night alone in my apartment. For the most part, the day had seemed to go by calmly and unruffled. As always, police guarded the periphery of Tiananmen Square, and the eighty-two-year-old founder of Tiananmen Mothers, a group of human rights defenders whose children were killed or injured during the Tiananmen crackdown, was whisked away from her apartment in Beijing for a quick, official excursion. Young men in large offices in the outskirts of Tianjin hunched over their computer screens, scrubbing the web clear of references to that day: "1989," "May 35th," "Tank," "Candle," "Never Forget."

Otherwise, the day went by as usual. On my WeChat feed, I scrolled through the usual stream of updates and advertisements, no sign of the trauma the city had suffered just thirty years ago. I lit a candle by my bedside table and tried to imagine its flame as one of hundreds of thousands flickering in living rooms and bedrooms and hallways in private vigils across the country. The world looked so different from when I attended my first vigil in high school, almost a decade ago, when I still naively believed in the romance: that both China and the world were on an inevitable path toward opening, spurred by the liberatory technology of the internet.

It is just as easy to fall into romance as to succumb to the apathy of inevitable decline. Depending on who you are and where you're from, each contraction hits differently—like whiplash, like heartbreak, or like the deep chill of an endless winter slowly sinking in. The most straightforward response would be simply to accept one's fate, to withdraw and retreat. But it is also possible to resist the trend: to refuse the rhetoric of inevitability, to reclaim one's agency and remain vigilant and awake. As the grounds shift, your dance steps quicken. You become alert to new hazards and new bounds that cannot be trespassed. And then you regain your balance and decide on your next move.

Part III

CHAPTER 13

Speech Tax

On the morning of October 1, 2019, the city of Beijing was ready to celebrate the seventieth anniversary of the People's Republic of China. Grocery stores touted National Day discounts, television shows aired National Day specials, and the mall down the road from where I lived erected a bubble-gum pink *I Love China* sculpture at its entrance. The flag hung on every streetlamp in every alleyway, a bright but monotone foliage. That afternoon, I set up for a party much earlier than usual; traffic would be tight. The big event was the official parade, an operatic spectacle of floats, tanks, and fighter jets rolling down Chang'an Avenue. Major roads were cordoned off, subway line 1 was shut down, and drones, kites, and homing pigeons were banned from the skies. Otherwise, planning my commute around the founding of the PRC was but a logistical inconvenience.

When I returned home that evening, it was easy for me to forget why the day had been so fraught. My WeChat newsfeed boasted a chorus of voices chanting the same patriotic song in seamless unison: videos of friends vacationing on Hainan beaches, photos of boozy brunches, China flag emojis, and #HappyBirthdayChina!s. But when I toggled onto my VPN and opened Twitter, a cacophony of angry tweets tumbled onto my screen: op-eds warning of a rising China, accusations of Chinese students operating as spies, photos of Chinese flag-raising ceremonies condemned by local residents in

Melbourne and denounced by diaspora demonstrators in Boston. From Hong Kong, footage streamed of masked protesters choking on tear gas, Mong Kok Station engulfed in flames, and on its walls, a scrawl of black graffiti, no genial hashtag preceding it: HAPPY BIRTHDAY CHINA.

Earlier in the summer, 1 million Hong Kongers had taken to the streets, marching in the summer heat, demanding that Carrie Lam, the city's chief executive, formally withdraw a bill that would allow the extradition of fugitives from Hong Kong to mainland China. In the months following, the protests would morph into a broader, more complicated, and more violent movement fighting for democratic freedoms, coalescing around five demands: the withdrawal of the extradition bill, amnesty for arrested protesters, investigations into police brutality, a retraction of the classification of protesters as "rioters," and universal suffrage.

In the wake of the protests, living within the bounds of China's Great Firewall, in particular on days like October 1, was a deeply jarring experience—a toggling between two conflicting narratives of the nation's future. In Hong Kong, outside the parameters of the Firewall, the more the Communist Party tried to force its residents to buy a narrative of a united, rising China, the more they rejected it. At soccer games, people booed the national anthem that so many had happily sung during the Beijing Olympics ten years earlier. Speaking Putonghua—the language of the mainland and not the local dialect, Cantonese—with young people today, a local activist warned me, was like "waving the red flag in front of a bull." One protester tossed the national flag into Victoria Harbor.

In stark contrast, on the mainland, it felt as if the country had been administered a shot of newfound nationalist fervor: Revolutionary films topped box-office charts and patriotic bloggers soared to online popularity. The more citizens witnessed Hong Kongers rejecting their Chinese identity, the more they rallied to defend it. Throwing the flag into the harbor was seen as not merely an act of defiance but one of desecration. In response, state broadcaster CCTV launched a "Five-Star Red Flag" campaign, calling upon its most influential celebrities to defend the nation's honor.

Beloved Hong Kong martial arts giant Jackie Chan and soap opera star Angelababy posted photos of the national flag on their social media accounts, paired with the hashtag #the-five-star-red-flag-has-1.4-billion-protectors. Victoria Song, a singer known more for her K-pop tunes than for her political views, declared on her Instagram account: "Hong Kong is part of China forever."

Even Chengdu's hip-hop artists, who once steered clear of politics, jumped on the bandwagon to voice their love for the nation. This time, it wasn't just the usual suspects, like the baldly nationalist band CDRev, which released a diss track titled "Hong Kong's Fall," criticizing the protesters as violent "splitists" manipulated by US Speaker of the House Nancy Pelosi. ("Yeah, I'm talking about American hypocrisy / they know nothing about love, just wars and casualties.") Vava, one of China's most prominent rappers, known for her hit "My New Swag" and bold songs about female empowerment, posted *People's Daily*–created memes with the words I SUPPORT THE HONG KONG POLICE. Jackson Wang, the baby-faced Hong Kong–born rapper once beloved on both sides of the border, declared his allegiance on Weibo as a "proud flag-bearer determined to side with China." Even Melo of the Higher Brothers, who rose to fame for his provocative, countercultural lyrics, parroted his peers' one-noted patriotism. He posted a national flag on his Instagram account with the caption "Once again, I'm proud to be Chinese."

. . .

In his seminal 1997 essay "The Silent Majority," the novelist Wang Xiaobo coined the term "speech tax." Having grown up during the Cultural Revolution in the 1960s, Wang learned to become deeply skeptical of all forms of public speech. During his teenage years, he watched people wield public speech as a tool of self-preservation and even self-advancement. Those who spoke out with the greatest zeal—hurling insults at political "struggle sessions," shouting slogans at student gatherings, quoting aphorisms from Mao's Little Red Book from memory—were appointed as cadres and rewarded with praise. To prove their devotion to the revolution, students spoke out to denounce their teachers; neighbors, to condemn each other; children, to turn on their parents. Chinese society became what Wang described as a "yammering madhouse," where language was hollow and bankrupt of meaning.

None of this was real speech. Instead, it was the payment of "speech tax," "coin-levied" by the state from its people by force, words often spoken contrary to the speakers' own hearts. According to Wang, "there is a tax official in the heart of all those who speak," calculating what he must say in order to get by, to survive, to evade scrutiny and denunciation. The model Chinese citizen was like the model greengrocer living under Soviet occupation described in "The Power of the Powerless" by the Czech dissident Václav Havel: The grocer must display a sign in his store window with the slogan WORKERS OF THE WORLD UNITE! Everyone else is doing it, and if he were to refuse, he would be reprimanded or lose his job. So he puts up the sign as a signal to the world: "I am obedient and therefore have the right to be left in peace."

When Deng Xiaoping came to power after Mao's death, he inherited a country impoverished by famine and chaos. Mao's aphorisms and slogans were materially useless, "all talk and no money," incapable of "building dams and power stations," as Wang wrote in "The Silent Majority." In contrast to his predecessor, Deng pursued a policy of pragmatism, prioritizing economic growth over ideological fervor. "It doesn't matter if it's a white cat or a black cat," he famously declared. "If it catches mice, it's a good cat." Adulation for Mao was redirected toward pop idols and basketball stars. Revolutionary slogans were recycled as ironic hip-hop lyrics and corporate mantras. Propaganda posters were resold as fine art and repurposed as wallpaper for kitschy cocktail bars.

In 2019, it seemed as if the Party was levying high rates of speech tax once again. Except this time, instead of having to speak out as good socialists, people simply had to assert their love for China and perform as good patriots. National pride, not revolutionary fervor, was the glue that bound people together. This time, the gains were also greater: People paid lip service not to win approval in a Communist system but to get ahead in a booming capitalist, platform economy. Paying your speech tax could propel your career, amplify traffic, bring in profit. Like the Soviet greengrocer, the model Chinese celebrity puts up the hashtag #five-star-red-flag on his Weibo feed to signal "I am obedient and therefore have a right to profit from this market."

Seen in this light, performing loyalty was a no-brainer. Those who paid their speech tax were more likely to land advertising deals, secure festival performances, and reach a broader audience. This process allowed GAI, the Chongqing rapper who fell from grace after the 2018 hip-hop ban, to claw his way back onto the mainstream stage. He covered up his tattoos, swapped his oversized basketball jerseys for crisp white blazers, and replaced hit songs like "Gangsta" with new tunes like "The Great Wall"—a rap song lauding China's "five-thousand-year history" and the "heroic blood spilled in defense of our great civilization." He landed sponsorships from sportswear giant Li-Ning and e-commerce company Tmall. In response to people who accused him of selling out, he posted on Weibo: "No matter what mean and sarcastic words they throw at me . . . I know where I stand when I look at my bank account."

On the other hand, those who refused to pay their speech tax were relegated to the margins. When Chinese American rapper Bohan Phoenix attended a meet-and-greet with the creators of *The Rap of China* in 2019 to discuss performing on the show, a producer asked him to take off the cross hanging on a chain around his neck, and he refused. "Just let me do my music first, and then we can talk about what I look like," he said. After the producers warned him that obedient artists were more likely to succeed on the show, he walked out of the room. "They took the coolest, dopest art form and ruined it by trying to control it," he told me. Cut off from one of the few paths to mainstream fame, he eventually left Chengdu and returned to Brooklyn to pursue his career.

Unlike in the Mao era, as the world's second-largest economy, China could levy speech tax from any stakeholder in the Chinese marketplace, not only inside but also outside the Firewall. Those who paid up were handsomely rewarded; those who didn't lost out. In October 2019, when Daryl Morey, then the general manager of the NBA's Houston Rockets, tweeted a slogan of support for the Hong Kong protests, he was vilified on Chinese social media and his actions were denounced by the NBA as "regrettable." LeBron James criticized Morey's words as "misinformed." Joseph Tsai, the Taiwanese Canadian billionaire and Alibaba CFO, who had recently acquired the Brooklyn Nets, posted an open letter castigating Morey for hurting the feelings of the Chinese people.

In response to Morey's tweet, Chinese state broadcasters suspended all NBA sponsorships and television broadcasts in the country. The decision ended up costing the NBA more than $150 million in lost revenue.

·   ·   ·

Three months later, in January 2020, when the coronavirus began to spread through Wuhan, I believed, perhaps naively, that this surge of performative patriotism would come to a halt. In the early days of the pandemic, the most dominant voices on Chinese social media seemed to signal a public turn against the government. Netizens criticized local officials for muzzling journalists, punishing whistle-blowers, and delaying their response in addressing the spread of the virus. The death of whistleblower doctor Li Wenliang from the virus on February 7 ignited widespread anger online, images of his masked face proliferating alongside the hashtag #WeDemand FreedomofSpeech on Weibo. When Fang Fang, a sixty-four-year-old writer from Wuhan, posted her diaries of the lockdown and criticized the government cover-up online, she was lionized as the nation's conscience. "Prohibiting people from speaking the truth leads to disaster," she wrote. "And now we are tasting the fruits of these disasters, one by one."

But by April, public opinion had shifted radically. As the virus began to ravage the rest of the world, China brought infection numbers to zero through swift implementation of mass testing, citywide lockdowns, and mandatory quarantines. Chinese students overseas were scrambling to find flights to return home. China's low fatality numbers, in stark contrast to the scenes of global chaos—of understaffed hospitals, bodies piling up in morgues, and violent anti-mask protests—confirmed to the Chinese people the West's complete failure and their own government's superiority in leading its people through crisis. A poll of Chinese citizens showed that half its respondents trusted their government even more after the outbreak.

Accordingly, nationalist sentiment skyrocketed. Critics vilified Fang Fang as a traitor after they discovered that she would publish her diaries in English for a US publisher. Online, netizens condemned her for working for the CIA, for "making the deepest stab in our back," and for creating "one of the biggest weapons used by anti-China forces to smear us." The attacks were so frenzied and vicious that Fang posted a plea online: "China cannot return to the Cultural Revolution." They reminded Fang of her experience in the 1960s, when Red Guards purged intellectuals with any tie to the West, driven by genuine ideological zeal whipped up into a toxic mix by groupthink and mob mentality.

But this time, many of China's vocal patriots came from a younger, worldlier generation who had come of age in a more stable, wealthier, and more powerful country and whose most salient personal memories were not of the poverty of the Great Leap Forward but of the glory of the 2008 Olympics. Many had studied abroad, worked at multinational companies, and jumped the Firewall with ease. And in 2020, it wasn't just the radical fringes of Chinese society—like the "angry youth" who emerged in 2008 or online warriors like the Little Pinks, who rose up in 2016—adopting this patriotic posture, but much of mainstream Chinese society. Emblematic of this perspective was Chairman Rabbit, the social media alias of Ren Yi—a Harvard-educated financier, grandson of a former Party official, self-described "cosmopolitan patriot," and intellectual pundit—who wrote a popular WeChat blog that appealed to educated elites. In Ren Yi's widely shared worldview, Fang Fang naively idealized the West and "served the anti-China industry"; the United States was a dysfunctional democracy in decay, plagued by systemic weaknesses, from the "supremacy of individualism" to "gun culture"; and the pandemic was a turning point that validated the superiority of China's top-down model of governance.

In 2020, I heard variations of this indignant pride in viral blog posts and state media broadcasts but also at dinner gatherings and during private conversations. Nationalism was not as simple as manufactured performance, dictated from above; it often drew from a deep reserve of sincere patriotic feeling, ignited from below. If the 2008 global financial crisis had sparked this pride, the Covid-19 pandemic of 2020 unexpectedly ended up pouring gasoline on the fire. It was an attitude of smug triumphalism laced with schaden-freude, fueled not only by confidence in China's rise but also by disdain for a West in decline. We were weak, but now we are strong. We were once poor, but now we can go to any country and buy whatever we want. Our young people wanted to move abroad, but now they're moving back home to make their fortunes. We once envied your freedom, but look where freedom has gotten you.

I heard this pride and indignation in Kafe Hu's voice, too, when I spoke to him on the phone in the fall of 2020 from my quarantine hotel in Shanghai. He was disgusted by the patriotic posturing tak-ing place in China. But he was equally disillusioned by the incom-petence and hypocrisy of the United States. When he first moved to Chengdu in 2000 and befriended his roommate, Charlie, America was the pinnacle of freedom and individuality, its culture singular. "I didn't just want to become another Chinese person. I thought that everything about America was amazing," he told me. To be Chinese was to be a conformist, a copycat, a creator of second-rate, saccharine pop. "But now I realized that's who I am—Chinese. I don't need to become more American. I don't need to speak better English. I don't need the American dream.

"Like, why did Americans elect Donald Trump? Everyone knows that he is a cartoon man," Kafe said with an almost gleeful incredu-lity. "When Americans criticize China, I don't trust what they say anymore. I'm, like, your government is pretty shit, too."

· · ·

It was hard to disagree with Kafe. Nationalism blazed on both sides of the Pacific. In the United States, the Trump administration fanned American fears of a nefarious China threat to deflect attention from its devastating mismanagement of the pandemic. The president's insistent use of the terms "Kung flu" and "China virus" fueled a spike of hate crimes against Asian Americans, and his administration's aggressive efforts to prosecute scholars through the China Initiative, launched by the Department of Justice in 2018, created a McCarthyesque environment for Chinese-born academics. The result of all this was, of course, a vicious cycle of hostility: rising Chinese nationalism and surging Sinophobia feeding each other's flames. According to a paper copublished by Stanford University and Sun Yat-sen University, Chinese students in the United States expressed more support for their own government after encountering anti-Chinese discrimination.

Just as public discourse within China had hardened into extremes, between dissident and patriot, loyal and traitorous, global attitudes toward China also ossified into binaries—pro-China and anti-China, apologist and opponent, hawks and doves. Conversations about China were framed in essentialist terms, as a zero-sum game between an enlightened, democratic West and a resurgent, authoritarian East. Descriptions of the Chinese people, Chinese culture, and intrinsic "Chinese values" were increasingly blurred together with the Party itself.

In a world in which conflict can be resolved only by victory and defeat, the enemy of your enemy becomes your friend. In 2020, in a surprising twist of allegiances, several famous Chinese dissidents and human rights activists abroad came out as staunch right-wing Trump supporters. Chen Guancheng, a blind human rights activist who rose to fame defending Chinese mothers from forced abortion before he was granted asylum in the United States in 2012, was now delivering speeches at the Republican National Convention, extolling President Trump as the man who would lead the effort to "stop CCP aggression." Chinese Christian activist Bob Fu, who once bravely championed democratic reforms back home and was exiled to the United States, went MAGA, lauding Trump's "decisiveness on China," condemning the left, and calling Biden's electoral win into question. "All their lives, they've been fighting for one thing—the fall of the Communist party," Murong Xuecun told me by way of explanation of this philosophy, which he sympathized with even if he didn't agree. "Trump is the branch they can hold on to at the edge of the cliff. To them, he is the last hope that might quash it out of existence."

In the eyes of many Chinese dissidents, Trump's hostility toward the Chinese Communist Party elevated him to the status not only of ally but also of role model—the ultimate beacon of freedom. Sun Liping, a prominent liberal intellectual, praised Trump for instigating a "profound transformation" in American society through his "attack on political correctness." He compared this to the dismantling of strict Maoist dogma during China's reform period. Guo Yuhua, a Chinese sociologist known for her tireless advocacy of workers' rights, compared Alexandria Ocasio-Cortez to the radicals of the Cultural Revolution. From this perspective, where the CCP is seen as the ultimate enemy and America as the world's salvation, rallying cries against "political correctness" and the "woke agenda" look like attempts to defend the free speech they have always dreamed of back home.

In some ways, the embittered, Trump-loving Chinese dissidents were not so different from the angry nationalists in China. The latter, so disillusioned with the United States' increasing dysfunction, morphed into ardent supporters of the Chinese state; the former, so disenchanted by China's authoritarian turn, transformed into vocal proponents of the American right, which they perceived as democracy's last salvation. Betrayed by shattered ideals and warped by the polarized lens of the internet, perspectives became hardened, myopic, and extreme.

. . .

When I met up with Kafe Hu in March 2021, the nationalist cacophony was deafening. That week, Chinese consumers were calling for a boycott of international brands, such as Nike, Adidas, and H&M, for accusing China of forced labor in Xinjiang's cotton industry. Ride-hailing companies wiped the boycotted brands off their app interfaces. Celebrities, eager to pay their speech tax, declared that they were ending partnerships with brands accused of "smearing"

China. H&M's revenue in the country fell by 40 percent. Shares of domestic sportswear brands, such as Li-Ning and ANTA, which proudly used Xinjiang cotton, doubled its growth in one year.

By then, Kafe had moved from Chengdu back to his childhood home in Jiangyou. The sleepy, county-level city he was so desperate to leave as a teenager now felt like a refuge, an escape from the swirl of commercialism and geopolitics that was now so noxious and distasteful. As I walked out of Jiangyou's train station, I was struck by how quiet the city was, its streets devoid of working-age adults. As in so many rural towns and third-tier cities across China, Jiangyou's young people had moved out in search of better opportunities, leaving behind the children and elderly. Its market was too small to be worth the attention of foreign brands: At the time, there was no McDonald's and no Starbucks, only a smattering of tea shops, hot pot restaurants, and a sneaker store called Old Beijing.

This was a welcome change for Kafe, who was no longer enamored of the idea of fame. Although in Jiangyou, he stuck out like a sore thumb—unusually tall, tan, and dressed in stylish urban garb—he rarely encountered hip-hop fans and was largely left alone. There were no parties to chase, no speech tax to pay, no *shabi* rules to follow, he told me as we sat in his grandmother's apartment by the river one morning having coffee. It was a classic Chinese elderly couple's living room, cluttered with trinkets, trays of watermelon seeds and biscuits. His grandmother sat on a cracked leather couch next to us, watching a soap opera. Kafe's father swung by the apartment, dressed in head-to-toe Nike—tracksuit, T-shirt, sneakers—seemingly unaware of the boycotts. A small-town hot pot restaurant owner, Kafe's father was freer to express himself than the nation's most famous celebrities. "Look at this guy," Kafe remarked. "He doesn't have to give a shit about what he wears at all."

But Kafe still had to. He'd stopped wearing his Nike high-tops onstage. A year ago, after joining *The Rap of China* as a contestant, he agreed to provide pretaped recordings of his performances, perform in long sleeves to cover his tattoos, and censor out lyrics deemed too sensitive. (One of his verses, "get some RMB into my hands," was swapped out for "get some *time* into my hands," because the producers said it was an example of "wealth flaunting.") He harbored no illusions that the show would allow him to grow as an artist. It was not a calling but a job—a low-stakes, low-reward way to pay his bills and survive as a working artist. "I am no longer only responsible for myself, like before," he told me. "Now I need to make money and raise my son."

In 2017, Kafe became a father, married his girlfriend, and then separated from her shortly after. Today, his son lives with his ex-wife and her family in Neijiang, a city a couple hours away by train, and Kafe visits him every other week. Although marriage was underwhelming, fatherhood was transformative, the "biggest turning point in my life," he said. It made him pragmatic, stripped him of his ego, his desire for fame and recognition, but also his idealism, his belief that he could make music that would challenge the status quo.

Kafe once aspired to be like Kendrick Lamar, because Kendrick was commercially popular but also spoke truth to power. Now it was clear to him that this would no longer be possible. "China probably has ten thousand artists who could be as influential as Kendrick Lamar, but none of them will ever reach their full potential," he said. "Real hip-hop is sung by those who are truly suffering, by those who are marginalized, by ethnic and racial minorities. Do you think those people would dare to speak out now?"

In the afternoon, I accompanied Kafe to the local hospital for a doctor's appointment. For over a year, he'd been suffering from tinnitus, a ceaseless ringing in his left ear. It buzzed throughout the day and kept him awake at night. I sat in the waiting area as the doctor poked around Kafe's ears with an otoscope. Five minutes later, he emerged with a prescription of sleeping aids and a vague diagnosis.

"Probably anxiety or depression or something." Kafe shrugged.

The tinnitus was only one of the ways in which his body had been acting up. Lately, there had been a strange out-of-body sensation, as if he were dreaming in the middle of the day, untethered to reality. The feeling hit him once while he was onstage for *The Rap of China*.

"I was onstage, freaking out, thinking, *What the fuck was I doing here?* Then I took some deep breaths and it passed."

It sounded to me like the symptoms of a depersonalization disorder—the feeling of being detached from one's own body, like an observer watching oneself from a distance. As Kafe described his symptoms, I couldn't help but recall something Stanley once said: that many artists in China lived with a split mind, constantly juggling personas, playing roles, concealing their private selves behind a public mask. How did the body respond to an environment that curtailed the expression of one's authentic self?

We left the hospital for his apartment, a new two-bedroom twenty minutes away from his grandparents, which also served as his recording studio. One shelf by the entrance boasted rows of Nike high-tops, collecting dust until the boycotts were over. Another shelf displayed a handful of books—an Adele biography, a translation of Nietzsche.

He'd just ordered new speakers, so I asked him to play his favorite track. He chose his "Far," a fast-paced mumble set against a synth beat, a jazzy saxophone, and a woman's eerie falsetto. The lyrics painted a scene of him wandering through Chengdu's streets at night, walking past the white Mao statue in the city center. He compares the city to a spider web that traps its prey and consumes them.

Tonight, the lights in my studio shine
More brightly than the five-pointed red star.

"Far" was one of his most critical songs, he said. It was unlike his now-banned track "Hope and Reality," which explicitly dug into problems like corruption and air pollution ("Hope you can speak freely / hope the air is clean"). Nor was it like his more recent crowd favorite, "Economy Class," a motivational uplifter for all who find themselves falling behind on the ladder of social mobility ("Phones that won't connect, signals lost in the clouds / aspire to be a better person / even when you're in economy class"). "Far" was one of his least popular songs, because nobody—neither censors nor listeners—had really picked up on what it meant ("You know which five-pointed red star I'm referring to?").

During the Cultural Revolution, when Chinese society devolved into a "yammering madhouse," Wang Xiaobo had lost faith in the spoken word. The more vehement the voice and the more fervently it was pitched, the more he doubted. He admired Dmitri Shostakovich, the Soviet composer who refused to speak out publicly, quietly dictating his own memoir to be published after his death. Remaining silent was the only way to protect his humanity.

Today, the Chinese public sphere, once again a "yammering madhouse," has shifted online. The internet has made the collection of speech tax even more pervasive and insidious. Authorities outsource taxation to social media platforms; platforms in turn supercharge the process with algorithms. Artists endlessly compromise their speech both to evade censorship and to compete for visibility in the politicized attention economy, funneled to fame through entertainment gatekeepers like *The Rap of China*. In this artistic landscape, "dumber people speak more, their voices louder, and they make more money from it," Kafe Hu told me. "And smarter people are quiet and do not speak often."

It is perhaps no surprise that the most creative music has eschewed the mainstream for the underground: basement concerts, small-scale jams, and independent labels. "If it's small and marginal, it can keep its edges," Krish Raghav, a writer and music festival organizer based in Beijing at the time, told me. "Because the pandemic has pathologized togetherness, the music scene has further fractured into thousands of tiny denominations. Going to a gig has become akin to being in an underground church, a space where people can come together. People recognize that mass visibility is dangerous. But they also need to remain accessible, to allow more people in."

In these smaller spaces, quiet songs of resistance persist. J-Fever, Kafe's friend and part of Beijing hip-hop's old guard, recently kick-started small, freestyle rap concerts. He first posted a recording of himself freestyling a verse on WeChat, then invited people to respond to it live, onstage. "If they start monitoring hundred-person concerts, I'll just keep going smaller and do dozen-person ones. If they control dozen-person ones, I'll perform one-on-one," he told me. "Like that artist Marina Abramović. Or like a priest, providing a space for people to open up and be themselves."

As space to dance has shrunk, artists like Kafe were faced again with a choice: to accept their shackles, pay their speech tax, and perform their loyalty or to keep quiet—to lie low, write obscured lyrics, sing quiet songs for a small audience. Although music couldn't serve as the vehicle of social change Kafe once imagined, at the very least, it could serve as a hidden transcript and a cathartic valve, a place where he could project feelings of suffocation onto the cityscape, gesture at the oppressor through subtle metonymy. For now, music was an expression of private pain, not of public protest. "I've realized that I absolutely cannot change the world," he said. "All I can do is work on myself."

CHAPTER 14

Swimming Against the Current

In the spring of 2020, as the pandemic unfolded in China, reality began to imitate science fiction. Bustling metropolises transformed into ghost cities overnight; airport and train stations were deserted. Cannon trucks sprayed down empty streets with plumes of disinfectant; AI thermal scanners were dispatched across public checkpoints to sound an alarm if anyone was detected to have a fever. Locked down at home, people spent their days sinking into their desk chairs, eyes glued to their screens.

Stanley's science fiction, which I was reading for the first time, seemed to me more like nonfiction. His short story "The Year of the Rat," published in 2009, eerily echoed the present day: Amid a trade war between China and a NATO-like "Western Alliance," a mutant rat escapes a Chinese lab, unleashing an epidemic that thrusts the global economy into crisis. The story's protagonist, an unemployed college graduate, joins the Rodent Control Force, a national army deployed to kill rats—blindly following his commander's orders to tally kill counts and compete with rival squads. Even "The Bait," the first story Stanley ever published, as a sixteen-year-old, was uncannily prophetic: Humans are bestowed with an invaluable new technology, only to find themselves enslaved by it.

But no story felt as prescient as "The Fish of Lijiang." In 2005, Stanley took a trip to the southwestern Chinese province of Yunnan and noticed that time seemed to slow down as he reached the city of Lijiang. He was then a recent college graduate, working at a soul-sucking job in real estate, and Lijiang was a backpacker's refuge. Wandering through the city, he was enchanted by the serrated rows of snowcapped mountains on the horizon and the schools of fish swimming through meandering canals. But he was also unnerved by the other tourists, visiting city dwellers like himself—burned out, spiritually lost, adrift. When he returned home, he wove his observations into a short story about an overworked office worker who travels to a vacation town, only to discover that everything is artificially engineered, from the blue sky to the fish in the streams to the experience of time itself.

Fifteen years later, this imaginary world of Stanley's had transformed into reality. In the fall of 2020, after Covid numbers had been brought to zero and lockdowns had been lifted, Stanley returned to Lijiang to find that the city was a digitized, commercialized tourist trap where self-driving cars shuttled smartphone-toting visitors around and local delicacies were prepared by automated bots. It wasn't just Lijiang. Technology had radically reshaped the fabric of Chinese society across the country. Walking through the streets of Beijing or Chengdu often felt like inhabiting one of Stanley's works of cyberpunk fiction: Bright yellow shared bikes lined the streets, facial-recognition cameras hung on streetlamps, and robot servers delivered hot pot dinners to your table.

"Today, we live in a world dominated by technology, where everything is driven by data, productivity, metrics," he told me. With a swipe of a touchscreen, we could order a Luckin coffee that appeared wordlessly on our doorstep and hail a nameless Didi driver whenever we wanted to go somewhere. The tech industry had learned to monetize not only consumer goods but also experiences, attention, relationships, so that we turned to algorithms for all the answers: where to eat, what to watch, whom to love. In many ways, we'd become just like our devices: efficient, optimizable, operating faster than ever, caught in the endless churn of increasing productivity.

In China, this transformation had been so fast, complete, and bewildering that netizens started using a viral word to capture this sense of sped-up purposelessness—an arcane, academic term that exploded on social media: involution. The American anthropologist Clifford Geertz first popularized the term in the 1960s to describe the dynamics that prevented agrarian societies in Java from progressing. His theory of involution holds that an increase in labor does not yield an increase in innovation. Instead, a society involutes. The Chinese term for involution, *neijuan,* which is made up of the characters for "inside" and "rolling," suggested a process that curls inward, ensnaring its participants within what the anthropologist Xiang Biao has described as an "endless cycle of self-flagellation." Involution is "the experience of being locked in competition that one ultimately knows is meaningless," Biao told me.

The concept of China as a society beset by involution first gained traction in the spring of 2020 on Douban, a social media site popular among college students, in a discussion thread called "985 trash." The name referred to Project 985—a consortium of elite Chinese universities similar to the Ivy League, including Stanley's alma mater, Peking University—and the shared reality that many students at these institutions felt like "trash": anxious, stressed, overworked, trapped in a status race. The thread grew as participants bemoaned the involuted job market (finance or data analytics— which path is more involuted?), criticized involuted entrance examinations (taking and failing the CPA exam five times), and lamented the involution of the pandemic economy. A student at Beijing's Tsinghua University, caught on video riding his bike at night while working on a laptop propped on his handlebars, became a viral meme dubbed "Tsinghua's Involuted King." "Young people can see only one way that they can make claims for their dignity and be recognized as a person," Biao said. And, most often, that way was to earn top grades, land a well-paying job, buy an apartment, and find a similarly high-achieving spouse.

Unsurprisingly, the idea resonated most deeply among those who worked in the next destination for many of China's top college graduates: the hypercompetitive tech industry. They described themselves ironically as *manong* ("coding peasant") and *dagongren* (which translates as "worker," but typically refers to blue-collar laborers); their employers are *hulianwang dachang* ("big internet factories"), to poke fun at the poor working conditions once associated with the country's assembly lines. At the short-video platform Kuaishou, employees were infuriated to discover one day that the company had installed digital timers in their office cubicles to monitor the length of bathroom breaks in order to boost productivity.

In December, a twenty-two-year-old employee surnamed Zhang at the e-commerce company Pinduoduo collapsed on the ground in the middle of the night on her way home from work and died six hours later, apparently from exhaustion and overwork. Two weeks later, another Pinduoduo employee leaped to his death, reportedly after he was fired for criticizing the company's work culture. In response to an outpouring of anger and grievance, the company appeared to dismiss Zhang's death, posting a comment on its official social media account: "Who hasn't exchanged their life for money?"

Involution came to the fore once again as online commentators tried to make sense of the deaths of these two young people. I compulsively read posts on WeChat with titles like "A Pinduoduo employee has died; why did we descend into an era of involution?" and "Workplace involution under the Pinduoduo model." In contrast to words like "exploitation" or "suppression" or even "alienation," involution was presented as a part of the natural order of things—like bad weather. You couldn't protest an abstraction or rally against a fusty term from an anthropology text.

In many ways, China's affliction of involution was a universal problem, no different from America's burnout crisis. In a 2021 survey, over half of 1,500 American respondents reported feeling burnout from their jobs. In December of that year, 4.3 million Americans quit their jobs as part of "The Great Resignation." The American sociologist Corey Keyes coined the term "languishing" to name this anxiety and stagnation. The engineer Zaid Khan popularized the phrase "quiet quitting" on TikTok to describe the process of working just enough to get by; *The Guardian* soon explained the trend in an article titled "Quiet Quitting: Why Doing the Bare Minimum at Work Has Gone Global."

But China's crisis was unique in the severity of its myopia and its methods of entrapment. The young high schooler, disillusioned with the monotony of school, could no longer as easily access subversive subcultures or explore alternative ways of living, because, increasingly, that information was deemed "vulgar" or "immoral" and scrubbed from the digital sphere in the name of "promoting positive energy." The delivery driver, seeking better working conditions, could not organize his fellow workers into an independent union, because he rightly feared detention. The disillusioned office worker, instead of taking action, would more likely sink deeper into his desk chair.

When Stanley met up with his friends for dinner, they all seemed to be racing against time—scrambling to keep pace with grueling jobs, soaring real estate prices, and expensive tutoring for their kids. Like the burned-out wanderers of "The Fish of Lijiang," they all seemed lost, desperately looking for something to hold on to.

. . .

When I first met Stanley, in 2020, he was turning thirty-nine, but at first glance—lithe and graceful, sporting candy-colored Adidas high-tops—he could easily have passed as a man in his twenties. He lived in Shanghai but came to Beijing for two weeks in October, where I met him at a café. Writing science fiction kept his mind roving and energetic. He switched seamlessly between languages (English and Mandarin) and dialects (Teochew and Cantonese). He moved with ease among conversational topics, from autonomous terrorism to Freud, and midway through our discussion of Taoist philosophy, he excused himself to take a quick call from his investment adviser. He also read voraciously—citing Aldous Huxley, the Chinese novelist Lao She, and a ten-thousand-word academic paper on asteroid mining. A self-described INTJ on the Myers-Briggs test, he spoke carefully and deliberately, with the intense, focused gaze of someone who seemed to exist in a constant state of measured thought.

When I saw him next, he was standing on a neon-lit stage in the banquet hall of the Grand Millennium Beijing, a slab of glass and steel in the Central Business District, giving a speech titled "Mind Reset and Embracing the Unknown: The Way of Science Fiction" to an audience of suited-up professionals. The *Financial Times* had organized the conference, inviting a lineup of modern-day oracles—the CEO of a health care start-up, a professor of economics, a machine-learning expert, and Stanley—to prognosticate about the near future. Dressing for the occasion, Stanley donned a blazer but still sported the high-tops.

It seemed as if everybody now wanted to hear Stanley prophesy. His visit to Beijing in October was packed with similar engagements. Tencent, the tech monolith behind China's super app WeChat, had invited Stanley, a literature major, to join a panel alongside world-class biophysicists to predict developments in genetic engineering, because he once wrote a story about genetically modified "Neorats." Kai-Fu Lee summoned him to the glassy offices of his company, Sinovation Ventures, to join another panel, this one on AI–human cooperation in the creative arts, and to demonstrate the algorithm that wrote fiction like Stanley.

Lee and Stanley were collaborating on a book, *AI 2041: Ten Visions for Our Future,* that would be published in September 2021. The book paired Stanley's speculative fiction with Lee's real-life technical perspective, exploring how artificial intelligence would transform humankind and the global order in the next twenty years, in areas ranging from contactless dating to natural language processing to job displacement.

"Computer scientists and science fiction writers don't speak the same language. If I describe how speech recognition works, it'll go right over people's heads," Lee told me in a glass-walled conference room called Back to the Future (all the rooms at Sinovation were named after science fiction films: Total Recall, Cloud Atlas, Star Trek). "I needed a writing partner who understands the technology but can also tell a good story."

"I tend toward darker endings, and Kai-Fu toward the positive," Stanley said. "He thinks of the narrative as a step-by-step process, like a manual, and I prefer to preserve a story's ambiguity."

Given all the time he spent at tech companies, Stanley was both an insider and an outsider in an environment like Lee's; he was fluent in the language of data and metrics and KPIs. But he wasn't at home only in tech. I noticed that in any new environment, he was observant and open-minded, careful to absorb its rules and rituals before he synthesized them as his own. As he zipped from one engagement to the next, I watched him make a straitlaced professor feel at ease, charm a hippie Mongolian shaman over lunch, then pen an op-ed for a state-run newspaper at night.

His ability to dance between disparate worlds proved useful for navigating the perilous waters of China's political landscape. Chinese writers had to be sensitive not only to commercial pressures but also to shifting political winds, evading the ever-watchful eyes of the censors. They had to gauge what the government was thinking, pay attention to developments on the international stage, and discern what to play up and play down and when. In recent years, science fiction's popularity had piqued the interest of authorities, who were eager to use its skyrocketing profile to boost their agendas. "If I'm speaking to the government," Stanley told me, "I emphasize the importance of sci-fi as a tool to strengthen innovation and promote creativity. I fill my message with *zheng neng liang*," he said wryly, quoting a hackneyed catchphrase of officialdom. "How do you say that in English?"

"Positive energy," I responded.

Lately, though, the leeway afforded to science fiction had narrowed. In the summer of 2020, the China Film Administration issued a set of guidelines on how to make sci-fi films, urging filmmakers to "highlight Chinese values," "cultivate contemporary Chinese innovation," and "thoroughly study and implement Xi Jinping thought." These measures have made writers and publishers more paranoid about making a misstep. (Stanley wanted to write a story about California's secession as an independent nation, but he was advised against it by his publishers for fear that it would not get past the censors. "It wasn't even about China," he exclaimed, rolling his eyes.)

Abroad, China's science fiction writers now found themselves caught in a tug-of-war between competing geopolitical agendas. The Western world had always perceived China as a monolith, reading Chinese literature through the lens of Western dreams and fears and viewing Chinese authors as either romantic dissidents clashing with the regime or soft-power tools parroting the Party's agenda. Recent developments—the US–China trade war, the closed borders from the pandemic, China's aggressive posture as a technological superpower—had only exacerbated the situation. Hawkish academics penned reductive op-eds with subtitles like "To Know What the Chinese Are Really Up To, Read the Futuristic Novels of Liu Cixin," as if one novelist could demystify and represent the voices of an entire nation. Whereas in 2017, President Obama touted *The Three-Body Problem* as one of his favorite books on his reading list, in September 2020, Republican senators condemned its Netflix adaptation, criticizing Liu for his politics.

"We do the works a disservice when we . . . focus on geopolitics alone," Ken Liu once wrote. But as much as China's science fiction writers aspired to transcend the boundaries of nationalism, they found themselves swept up in a whirlpool of forces outside their control. According to Stanley, the timing of *The Three-Body Problem*'s publication was crucial. If it had come out today instead of in 2008—the days of bilateral relations, economic cooperation, and the Beijing Olympics—perhaps it would be censored by the Chinese government or condemned by the US one, targeted by both. "I stay away from politics because—what do I know?" he said. "Sometimes I feel like I'm just being pulled along by the strings of history."

I was reminded of a passage toward the end of "The Fish of Lijiang." The protagonist discovers schools of fish swimming in the waterways. At first sight, they seem to be hovering calmly in the water, but as he looks closer, he sees that they are struggling to maintain their position. Once in a while, a fish gets pushed out of formation. "But soon," the passage continues, "tails fluttering, they fight their way back into place."

.   .   .

In the three decades since Stanley first watched *2001: A Space Odyssey,* his understanding of the film—and the world—shifted. When he was younger, he was drawn to its depictions of technology: the sleek, cylindrical *Discovery One;* HAL 9000's operating system; the underground lunar base. Now he paid much less attention to the shiny technology and more to the film's spiritual arc. What once seemed like a story about technological progress now felt more like a religious quest, an odyssey in search of answers to the most fundamental, most elusive questions: Who are we? Where are we from? Where are we going? "The times have changed," Stanley told me. "And the story needs to be renewed."

In the past year, Stanley had become interested in shamans. He went on several field trips, interviewing and shadowing shamans in hopes of understanding the rites, rituals, and traditions of China's Buddhist and Taoist past. In the summer of 2020, he met a shaman named Aodeng Toya through a WeChat group, and the two became fast friends. He stayed with her in Mongolia and spent a night at the foot of the sacred Bogd Khan Mountain, where thousands of villagers gathered to pray to the mountain gods, drinking, eating, and dancing under the stars. For most of the year, Toya practiced in Beijing, helping urbanites through all kinds of spiritual ailments. "Depression, overwork, bad luck with love, to ward off evil spirits, to commune with the dead," she told Stanley and me over lunch. "I'm booked up every day for the next month."

In our accelerated transition to a technological culture, Stanley believed that we had lost so much—our relationship to our bodies, to nature, to our roots, to our faiths—and he set out in search of them. "Shamans used to predict the weather, prevent disease, counsel leaders, show us how to coexist with the natural world," he said. "Today, technological tools have replaced those functions but not all. Why do we still go to them? What are we looking for?" We thought we could divine, precisely and quantifiably, where we're headed but instead find ourselves hurtling toward an increasingly volatile future: skyrocketing housing prices, soaring unemployment, deepening inequality, accelerating climate change, and a shattering global pandemic.

It wasn't surprising that people were turning to shamans—and to science fiction writers like Stanley. "They are treating sci-fi as an anchor to reality and science fiction writers as prophets to help them make meaning of an unfolding future and navigate a treacherous world," Emily Jin, Stanley's translator, told me. How do we reclaim meaning and purpose in the age of computers? What does spirituality look like when everything is mechanized and mass-produced? When our lives are so deeply embedded in our devices, how do we preserve what makes us human?

Like Stanley, young Chinese from all walks of life started seeking answers to these questions—searching for ways to slow down, hold on to meaning, and reclaim their humanity in a system that demanded ruthless productivity. In search of alternatives, some embraced Marxism, organizing *Das Kapital* reading groups and revising leftist revolutionary songs from the Soviet Union. Some developed a "Buddha-like" (that is, a laid-back and laissez-faire) approach to life. Others adopted the more pessimistic *sang*—an attitude of sardonic apathy and nihilism. "I wanted to fight for socialism today," Zhao Zengliang, a twenty-seven-year-old *sang* internet personality, wrote in a representative post. "But the weather is so freaking cold that I'm only able to lie on the bed and play on my mobile phone."

Many adopted coping mechanisms similar to those of Silicon Valley dropouts: quitting their jobs, prioritizing self-care routines, joining remote communes. Stanley's tech friends left the industry in droves. They resigned from Big Tech companies like Tencent and Alibaba to write astrology blogs and start life-coaching businesses. They moved from pressure-cooker metropolises like Beijing and Shanghai back to their childhood homes, as Kafe did, or to smaller cities like Jiangxi's Jingdezhen or Yunnan's Dali.

Just south of Lijiang, Dali became the go-to getaway for urban migrants, dubbed "Dalifornia" for its mild climate, proximity to nature, and laid-back West Coast vibes. By the time I visited, in the summer of 2021, although Dali had not been fully gentrified like Lijiang, it was filled with all the trappings of yuppie bohemia: yoga studios and craft beer shops, cloth-dying workshops and Montessori schools, glamping tents and eco-tourism sites. I attended the China Vegan Society's inaugural gathering, hosted at a vegan community complex with an organic farm, a homestay facility, and a dyeing workshop. Attendees included robed Buddhist monks, representatives of the oat milk brand Oatly, and a steel drummer who identified as a fruitarian.

Like the members of the Back-to-the-Land movement in the United States in the 1970s, or the Arts and Crafts movement in the UK in the nineteenth century, Dali's urban migrants sought to return to a simpler, pastoral life, far away from their high-pressure, time-constrained lives in the city. This nostalgia was evident in the soaring popularity of rural vloggers like Li Ziqi, the Sichuanese vlogger who rose to viral fame during the pandemic sharing videos of her life in the countryside. In one classic Li Ziqi video, she spends her morning riding through a misty forest on horseback, collecting magnolia flowers in a wooden basket to prepare magnolia pastries on a traditional stove from scratch. Dressed in a sweeping red cape, she looks like a cross between a Disney heroine and a mythological Chinese princess, tapping into a recent craze for *hanfu*—traditional Han clothing—popular among young people nostalgic for a preindustrial past of rites and etiquette. At the home where she lives off the grid and entirely self-sufficient, there are no signs of modern life: no smartphone, laptop, money, or microwave.

By 2021, scenes of Li's life—harvesting jujube dates, hatching ducklings, and simmering peach blossom wine—were mesmerizing audiences around the world, drawing 55 million followers on Douyin and a YouTube subscriber base of 16 million. She was beloved by fans from China to Portugal to Bangladesh, was named an "ambassador" of Chinese culture by the Communist Youth League, and was dubbed "Quarantine Queen" by *The New York Times*. She was an oasis of calm in her followers' high-pressure, screen-centric, time-constrained existences. Through her, they lived vicariously in an online Eden, where pollution, corporations, and coronaviruses ceased to exist.

. . .

Trapped in an involuted system, many young Chinese realized that the most realistic and accessible way out was simply to do nothing at all: to *tangping,* or "lie flat." The term was coined in 2021 by a factory worker named Luo Huazhong in a social media post titled "Lying Flat Is Justice." Luo quit his job and moved to a small village, where he read philosophy, tended his vegetable garden, and took on odd jobs, living on $28 a month. "I've been chilling and don't see anything wrong with this," he wrote. He compared himself to Diogenes, the Greek philosopher who embraced self-sufficiency, "sleeping in a wooden barrel, enjoying sunshine."

"Lying flat" soon became a viral philosophy, and Luo's post an anti-work manifesto for young Chinese looking to exit the rat race. Poets drafted lying-flat couplets; musicians composed lying-flat songs. A video game producer created *Exhausted Man,* featuring a limp avatar skulking around his room trying to accomplish tasks with as little effort as possible. Lying-flatists, as its adherents called themselves, celebrated quitting their jobs, cutting costs to a minimum, and withdrawing entirely from competition. One popular slogan defined "lying flat" as follows:

Don't buy an apartment.

Don't buy a car.

Don't get married.

Don't have children.

Don't consume.

Maintain the lowest possible standard of living.

Don't become a machine for others to make money or a slave to be exploited.

Lying flat was a form of economic action—to exit an economy demanding that people endlessly compete and consume—but also inherently political, a refusal to comply with the state's demand to be productive and fertile members of the workforce. Lying flat was a passive form of resistance—a way to reclaim one's humanity by opting out of the system altogether.

Not long after the term went viral, embraced by young Chinese across all walks of life, I attended a feminist workshop, where everyone was asked to introduce themselves by their nickname and with an adjective. For example, I was "curious." Another participant was "caring." One woman's response struck me in particular. She described herself proudly as "useless."

At first, I was confused. Then I realized what she meant by being "useless": She could not be used. She could not be exploited—neither by the market nor by the state. By lying flat, in other words, she felt free of her shackles.

CHAPTER 15

Retreating Ashore

In the summer of 2020, Blued went public on NASDAQ. Ma Baoli, ex-cop and keeper of secrets, finally stepped onto the global stage. The company had originally planned a trip to New York but decided to stay at home after the pandemic hit. On the eve of the IPO, the entire team gathered to celebrate in the ballroom of the China World Hotel, a glamorous five-star hotel in the heart of Beijing's Central Business District. It was like the final scene of a queer Hollywood romance, complete with a red carpet, spotlights, clinking champagne glasses, and the Beijing Queer Chorus performing Gloria Gaynor's "I Am What I Am" in the background. Dressed in a tuxedo and a rainbow corsage, Ma, the protagonist, arrived with his partner and young son by his side, surrounded by teammates cheering him on. As he stood on the stage in the center of the ballroom, a stock exchange executive in New York announced the IPO via a large-screen livestream. "Welcome to the NASDAQ family!" he declared when Blued's logo appeared as a rainbow on a shimmering Times Square marquee.

Ma felt like he was dreaming. He'd worked toward and sacrificed for this moment for decades—from his teenage years as a cadet to his present day as a gay tech mogul—yearning for the acceptance of his peers. Going public won him the recognition of the global marketplace. Once closeted, he was proudly out. Once sustained by $6 donations, he'd raised an $85 million IPO. Once shunned by the mainstream, he was now welcomed into communities he never would have imagined being part of, from government pandemic-prevention efforts to national cyberspace conferences to United Nations gatherings.

Two years earlier, in 2018, Ma had been admitted as a student to Hupan University, in Hangzhou, Jack Ma's prestigious school for top entrepreneurs. This was as sure a sign as any that he'd joined China's business elite. Named after Hupan Gardens, the sweaty, haphazard apartment complex where Jack Ma founded Alibaba almost two decades earlier, Hupan was created as "China's answer to Harvard Business School." The university admitted fewer than forty students each year, at a 4 percent acceptance rate. Applicants had to be founders of companies with revenues of more than $4.5 million and be recommended by one of the university's sponsors. Hupan's alumni were the victors of China's meteoric growth: the CEOs of top tech companies and the founders of unicorn start-ups, from the president of China's largest ride-hailing app, Didi, to the CEO of one of its largest food-delivery platforms, Ele.me. During the three-year program, students were required only to fly in to take classes for four days every two months, so that they could return to their day jobs as tech moguls.

Jack Ma sat in on the first lecture of Ma Baoli's Hupan cohort.

"If we didn't accept you because of your sexuality, how would you feel?" one of Hupan's professors asked Ma Baoli during the lecture.

"I've always admired Hupan as one of the best business schools in the world, inclusive and open. So if you didn't accept me, I would realize that I was wrong," Ma responded. "And as for how I would feel? I would feel the same way that Jack Ma felt when he got rejected for his first job at KFC—because he was too ugly."

Everyone laughed. Jack laughed, too. The joke landed. *Good answer.*

I first visited Hupan University in 2020, tagging along with a gathering of Ma's classmates, slated to graduate in the spring of 2021. Located a twenty-minute drive from Alibaba's headquarters, in the Future High-tech City, Hangzhou's techno-suburbia, Hupan's campus was a cross between an Apple Store and an imperial Chinese garden, complete with floor-to-ceiling glass walls, meditation rooms, and an antique pavilion. Next to the campus coffee shop, a wall was covered in the quotes and mantras of Hupan students, which captured their unique ethos:

Since I was small, I wanted to be a boss, I never wanted to be a laborer.

For love, I decided to become an entrepreneur.

If I want wonderful things, I need to keep improving myself.

Can I hang my computer screen on my bed? That way I can write code in bed.

NEVER GIVE UP

Plunging into the sea is the path to serving our country.

Hupan's students, who like Ma Baoli had grown up in the 1980s, were part of a generation that reaped the benefits of economic reform; they responded to Deng Xiaoping's call to "plunge into the sea" of the private sector, seized the rise of the mobile internet, and emerged wealthy and victorious. It was no surprise that their mantras blended the bootstrapping neoliberalism of their era with Silicon Valley's culture of experimentation and the Chinese tech sector's self-flagellating work ethic. They believed in the narrative that with enough hard work, ambition, and capital, any underdog could rise to the top and change the world for the better. They bought into the myth that if Jack Ma could work hard enough to transform himself from KFC reject to one of the most influential men in China, so could you.

Every year, freshly admitted students were asked to stand before all their classmates and answer the question "How has the world changed because of me?"

. . .

In some ways, Ma Baoli could not have imagined a more fraught moment to take his company public: While China halted the spread of the Covid virus, it did so at the expense of its economic growth. Consumers were tightening their spending, investors were wary, and workers were bracing for layoffs. For all the nationalist triumphalism that the pandemic had ignited, young Chinese appeared not to be hopeful but to be increasingly disillusioned with their future prospects. Outside Hupan's walls, the myth of entrepreneurial ambition had become outdated. A new narrative—of burnout and stagnation—had sunk in.

The entrepreneurial elite continued to tout their ambitions, oblivious to the fact that their employees no longer admired but resented them. Tech workers pointed fingers at Hupan for being a "lakeside clubhouse" or "CEO club," feeding into a growing sense that the tech industry was an exclusive network for a concentrated elite, not a path of social mobility available to the ordinary worker. Anger once targeted toward the *guanerdai* ("second-generation political elite") and *fuerdai* ("second-generation wealth") now included a new group: the *chuangerdai* ("second-generation entrepreneurial elite") and their various connections and privileges. The tech elite seemed dismissive of their employees' grievances. In 2019, when tech workers protested the industry's brutal 996 hours, Jack Ma called 996 a blessing, claiming that long hours were vital to Alibaba's success. ("Well, for him it's a blessing," one contributor shot back on Reddit. "Just not for his employees.")

Meanwhile, Jack Ma seemed as confident and ambitious as ever. After all, for Jack, hard work continued to pay off: He was planning to take his fintech company Ant Group public on the Shanghai and Hong Kong stock exchanges, in a $34 billion IPO slated to become the largest in global history. On October 24, 2020, days before the IPO, Jack delivered a bold and blistering speech at a financial conference in Shanghai, in front of the key figures of China's financial establishment, criticizing the financial system as antiquated, blasting government regulators for stifling innovation, and accusing state-owned banks of behaving like "pawnshops." The audience was shocked. He'd bitten the hand that fed him, so sure was he of his own authority.

He was wrong. One week later, authorities summoned him for questioning. Ant Group's IPO was suspended just two days before its debut. Two months later, they launched an antitrust investigation into Alibaba. Four months after launching the investigation, they fined the company $2.8 billion for monopolistic practices. Hupan University was forced to suspend enrollment. Videos on Chinese social media showed a worker using a blowtorch to remove the university's name from a large stone sign in front of its campus. Jack himself, a national celebrity who dominated the spotlight, disappeared from the public eye.

.   .   .

After Jack Ma's disappearance, it quickly became clear that the Party wanted to tame not just Ma but the entirety of China's Big Tech sector. In 2021, regulators initiated antitrust investigations into not just Alibaba but also more than thirty other tech companies, from Tencent to Baidu to JD.com. Four days after Didi's IPO in the United States, the Cyberspace Administration of China suspended the app for violating data security protocols, eventually forcing the company to delist. The government introduced a slate of new guidelines to regulate the tech industry, requiring companies to ensure that algorithms didn't promote addictive behavior, ordering platforms to guarantee transparency in recommendation algorithms, mandating improved working conditions for delivery drivers, and ruling the 996 work hours, much despised by China's tech workers, illegal.

China's tech sector appeared to be only one example of what the Party had repeatedly called a "disorderly expansion of capital" in memos explaining the slate of new policies. That summer and into the fall, authorities unleashed an onslaught of regulations so broad and drastic in scope that they were described by international news outlets as a "crackdown on everything": cryptocurrencies, real estate speculation, high-frequency stock trading, wealth-flaunting celebrities, online idol fandoms (organized fan communities), and use of video games by minors on weekdays.

In July, the government kneecapped the tutoring industry by introducing a policy known as "double reduction," ordering schools to limit the amount of homework assigned to students and banning all private tutoring companies that taught K–12 from making a profit. Overnight, it thrust China's multibillion-dollar education industry into an existential crisis. New Oriental, China's largest tutoring company, let go of sixty thousand staff members. "The era of private tutoring has ended," wrote its founder, Michael Yu, the rock star entrepreneur who inspired the 2013 film *American Dreams in China,* in a somber post to his WeChat account.

In August 2021, the Party gave the regulatory blizzard a name: "common prosperity." For three decades, the country had lived the first half of a famous saying by Deng Xiaoping: "Let some people get rich first." The summer of 2021 marked a swerve into the second half: "for the purpose of achieving common prosperity faster." The old bottom-up, laissez-faire "to get rich is glorious" ethos of the Dengist era was out; Xi's top-down, tightly controlled vision of equitable development was back in. Some commentators called common prosperity the coming of a second Cultural Revolution, like the ideological cleansing of decadent Western values that took place under Mao in the 1960s. In a WeChat post that went viral, the retired editor Li Guangman wrote that the country was going through a "profound revolution." "The red will return," he proposed, and the Chinese capital market will no longer be "a paradise for capitalists to get rich overnight."

But in reality, the common prosperity campaigns looked nothing like the Cultural Revolution, and Xi was a drastically different leader than Mao. Common prosperity was not an end to China's market economy but, rather, a curtailing of its excesses—not a reversion to a Maoist utopia but a pivot to a more tightly controlled form of state-led capitalism. As Dan Wang, a technology analyst, explained to me, the leadership was discarding what it viewed as capitalism with American characteristics, driven by Wall Street and Silicon Valley; it now favored a capitalism with German characteristics, featuring a strong ecosystem of industrial firms and a more equal society. The Party wanted to build a development model that prioritized what it defined as "high quality" growth, such as electric vehicles, solar panels, and the industrial internet, over "inflated growth," such as cryptocurrencies, online tutoring, and the consumer internet. In the new era, the Party's ideal young entrepreneurs weren't joining hedge funds, flipping properties, or listing gay dating apps; they worked in what Wang called "the physical world," called upon to "make babies, make steel, and make semiconductors."

In Xi's speech, he stated that "common prosperity" was not "welfarism" or "falling into the trap of lazy people." His language reflected less the ideas of Maoism than the ideas of the Party's top ideological adviser, the conservative Fudan University professor who now sat in the highest ranks of the Politburo Standing Committee, Wang Huning. When Wang first visited the United States, in 1988, he was impressed by the nation's immense wealth and technological prowess but disillusioned by what he believed to be liberalism's great unwinding: crippling inequality, racial strife, homelessness, crime, powerful corporate monopolies running amok, decadent attitudes toward love and sex, a loss of core values in the face of "spiritual openness." His takeaway was clear: China had to surpass the United States in technology, but these new technologies could not allow Chinese society to unravel in the same way.

Thirty years later, although China remained a one-party state, it resembled in many ways the America that Wang once so vehemently condemned. Tech monopolies wielded unbridled power, businesses exploited workers for low pay and brutal work hours, and the country had become one of the most unequal societies on earth. Devoid of "core values," young Chinese were driven solely by profit instead of virtue, worshiping online celebrities and fandoms instead of historical heroes and national leaders, rejecting marriage and childbirth in favor of divorce, singledom, casual sex, and "abnormal," "Western" ideas like feminism.

If liberalism had enabled China's great unwinding, the Party's solution was "common prosperity": to reel in the free market and the moral excesses it unleashed, and wind the coil back tighter.

Its goals were therefore not only "economic" but "political," as Xi declared in his speech—to "prevent the tearing of the social fabric" with a unified set of cultural values. New regulations were therefore both technocratic and ideological, a restricting of the market but also a cleaning of its "spiritual pollution." The Party clamped down not only on tech entrepreneurs and Big Tech monopolies but also on idol fandoms and video games. It punished not only Jack Ma but also the billionaire celebrity actress Zhao Wei—scrubbing all mentions of her from the internet.

Most notably, the Party also espoused a conservative gender ideology to address what it saw as a national masculinity crisis. According to a proposal by the Chinese People's Political Consultative Conference, China's top political advisory, which consults with the government in policymaking and governance, Chinese schoolboys had become "weak, self-effacing, and timid." The "feminization of boys," like unfettered capitalism, was a "threat to the development and survival of the nation." The ideal Chinese man, in the eyes of the state, could not be like the "little fresh meats"—the androgynous, delicate-featured, K-pop-inspired stars popularized on social media—but should be macho, dominant, and virile. In response, the Ministry of Education called for more physical education in schools to improve boys' masculinity. Media regulators banned from television what they dubbed "sissy men"—*niangpao,* a slang term referring to effeminate and queer men.

To watch the film *American Dreams in China* now—with its scenes of wide-eyed college students sporting John Lennon haircuts and memorizing Dale Carnegie quotations, filled with dreams of going to America—is to revisit a faraway past. Today's version of the film would look more like *The Silicon Waves,* a television series announced in 2021 that featured two Chinese scientists who are lured back home from the West to help realize China's dream of becoming self-sufficient in semiconductor technology. In stark contrast to the *American Dreams* poster, featuring three young Chinese founders squatting in the middle of Times Square, the *Silicon Waves* poster featured a giant semiconductor chip sandwiched between two steel-blue skyscrapers in Shanghai's Pudong district and is absent of human presence.

.   .   .

When I stopped by Blued's offices to see Ma at the end of 2021, he looked anxious and exhausted. It felt like an entire era had passed since I'd seen him at Hupan University a year earlier. He was coming down with a cough, dealing with midnight cold sweats and a muscle on his face that wouldn't stop twitching. It reminded me of Kafe's tinnitus: the cumulative stress of dancing in shackles one's whole life manifesting in the body as illness. Ma's dance had higher stakes now. Although he no longer lived the double life of his youth—cop by day, underground website leader by night—he still had to don different masks and juggle conflicting roles: the CEO of a private enterprise, a spokesperson for China's queer communities, a model collaborator with the state.

As a former police officer, Ma told me, he had an occupational disease: He was always cautious. He constantly repeated three mantras to himself: *Be fearful. Stay vigilant. Tread carefully on thin ice.* "I know what is OK, what is not OK, and I stay at least one meter away from any red line drawn by the government," he said.

But during the previous year of regulatory upheaval, new red lines abounded, and every step felt treacherous. As the ground shifted, all entrepreneurs could do was adapt: lie low, downplay their wealth, and realign themselves with government initiatives of "poverty alleviation" and "rural revitalization." Tech giants from Tencent to Alibaba announced they were setting up "common prosperity funds"—multibillion-dollar pledges toward "high-quality growth" initiatives, such as revitalizing rural villages and improving gig-worker welfare. New Oriental founder Michael Yu pivoted to a new venture: an online farmer's market. Instead of tutoring English, his employees were reassigned to new jobs assisting him in peddling rice, apples, and beef. Jack Ma finally resurfaced, embarking on a trip to Spain to study farming technology.

"Is Jack Ma still the person you admire the most?" I asked Ma Baoli.

He chuckled uncomfortably. "I guess I shouldn't dare to say that anymore, right?" he replied. "But I still abide by his saying that today will be hard, tomorrow will be worse, but the day after tomorrow will be sunshine. To have hope that things will be OK."

I asked Ma what gives him hope now.

He paused for a long time, struggling to find the right answer. "Honestly, I can't think of anything," he finally replied. "This year has been so hard, I haven't thought about Jack's words in a long time."

Like his peers, all Ma could do was adapt. But it was now risky not only to run an internet company but also to run an LGBTQ organization; his position was doubly precarious. His old strategy—of raising LGBTQ awareness through the private sector while steering clear of political advocacy—no longer felt like a viable way forward. China had gone through a paradigm shift: The old vision of tech entrepreneurship and innovation—that an unfettered market and the power of the internet could serve as a vehicle of disruptive social change—no longer aligned with the Party's vision of state-led capitalism.

Being a successful entrepreneur felt less like a privilege and more like a liability. Young people no longer dreamed of plunging into the sea of the private sector to become the next Jack Ma. Instead, they ditched their entrepreneurial get-rich schemes for low-paying but stable government jobs. In 2021, a record 2 million applicants registered for the national service exam, seeking the security of state employment. They called this pivot *shang'an,* or "retreating ashore."

. . .

In the summer of 2022, less than two years after Blued went public, Ma Baoli took it private again, delisting the company from NASDAQ. The reasons were ostensibly technical, financial: In the lead-up to the IPO, Ma had signed a contract agreeing to cover losses personally if stock prices fell below expectations. They did—within months, the company's share price plummeted to $1.65, less than 10 percent of its IPO price. Unable to fulfill the contract requirements on his own, Ma brokered a deal with another social media company, which bought out a majority of the shares and took over ownership of Blued. Then, at the request of its new owners, he resigned as CEO, leaving the company for good.

Ma's departure was bitter, anticlimactic, with no farewell party. The Omicron variant of the virus causing Covid had begun to spread, and new, rigid pandemic controls were in place. During his last trip to the office, he tore down the company's history wall—a timeline of photos documenting his journey. Two decades of a life's work dismantled in one day. Only a handful of people responded to his farewell message in the company's group chat. Some wanted to distance themselves from him so the new management wouldn't fire them; others were simply angry, holding him personally responsible for the company's unraveling. Calvin Liu, his CTO, quit and moved to Canada with his partner and child. Shen Wenjie, Ma's first business partner, stopped talking to him altogether.

He deleted the Blued app from his phone. It made him too depressed. After his departure, many of the app's old functions had been eliminated; rainbow flags had been removed. Users could no longer identify as a 1 or a 0 (a top or a bottom), state that they were HIV-positive, or use the phrase "coming out."

"Blued was my life. Every part of its DNA, its services, its employees, its users, the names of every office in the building, had a part of me," he said. "To let it all go is devastating."

Ma blamed his own inexperience and naiveté—for signing the wrong contracts, trusting the wrong advisers, making the wrong moves. But how much of Blued's fate was truly for Ma to decide? He came out, connected China's queer communities online, and took a gay company public during an era when China came out to the world, embraced the rise of the internet, and stepped onto the global stage as a technological powerhouse. But as the country entered a new era, closing off and turning inward, he had no choice but to withdraw and retreat.

When I called Ma in the fall, he was back in Qinhuangdao, his hometown. He had bought a new house next to the police academy, returning to where it had all begun—the place where he nursed his first crush, read his first gay novel, and walked away from his job to plunge into a new life as an entrepreneur. But the hope and possibility he once felt had long faded. From his window, he could see the police academy's old courtyard, a relic of the past. The rest of the buildings were gone, torn down years ago. Only tarp-covered remnants of the structures remained, hollowed out, their indigo walls peeling.

Since stepping down from Blued, he'd sunk into a depressive funk, mourning the loss of his company, his community, and his sense of purpose. Just a year ago, his days had been booked up from morning to night, an endless stream of tasks and responsibilities. Now he slept past noon and spent his days looking through old photos and flipping through *Chicken Soup for the Soul* for inspiration. Even if he had the energy, his options were limited. The takeover locked him into a noncompete agreement with Blued's new owners, barring him from working on any LGBTQ ventures. Outside the business world, his hands were tied, too. The advocacy work he'd once thrown himself into—speaking at universities, running corporate diversity workshops—was no longer possible. There was no space for him in queer public life to dance anymore.

"Society will become more conservative," Ma told me. "Homophobes who were once afraid to speak out now feel free to bully queer people." He raised an example of a nineteen-year-old student at Shandong University who took his own life by overdosing on insecticide after being bullied for his sexuality. When an LGBTQ WeChat account posted about the suicide, it was swiftly suspended.

"How does that make you feel?" I asked.

"Like it's impossible to reverse the tide," he responded. "Like the only thing left to do is to watch and accept this new reality."

Other LGBTQ advocates I spoke to also seemed at a loss. They were no longer thinking about how they could push for greater progress, as they were a couple years earlier, but simply about how to survive—how to help support the next generation of queer Chinese through a long and uncertain winter. "I feel like I've always lived in a dark room, but I used to have a big window with lots of sunlight," Ah Qiang, the cofounder of PFLAG China, told me. When we spoke on the phone, he was living in New Haven, doing a semester-long research fellowship at Yale Law School's Paul Tsai China Center. "Recently, that sunlight has faded away. Any light that must be generated must come from myself."

But though Ah Qiang was pessimistic about short-term prospects for LGBT advocacy in China, for the long term, he remained hopeful. After all, compared to three decades earlier, queer life had radically transformed. Surveys showed that young Chinese were more open and tolerant about LGBTQ issues than ever before. Queer Chinese were more accepting and affirming of their sexuality; they would scoff at norms of his generation, like cooperative marriages to appease their parents and hide their sexual orientation. For all the tightening the Party had exerted on the public sphere, Ah Qiang did not believe they would intrude on queer people's private lives. "We will not regress to what it was before 1997, when homosexuality was persecuted and gay people went to public bathrooms to meet," he said. "The nation's hands have stretched out far and wide, but they won't reach into my bedroom."

Yanzi Peng, the founder of the now-shuttered legal rights NGO LGBT Rights Advocacy China, who recently moved to the Netherlands, pivoted to supporting and researching the legal needs of queer families and same-sex parents in China, such as child care and custody. Queer family life was still possible and growing; given the number of participants Yanzi had encountered in lesbian- and gay-parenting WeChat groups, he estimated that there were at least tens of thousands of such families living in China today.

Ma Baoli was, of course, part of such a family. Although his public life had shrunk, his personal life had blossomed. For the first time in years, after shuttling back and forth between Beijing, where he worked, and Qinhuangdao, he now lived with his family under one roof. He could support his father, who was suffering from Alzheimer's, hang out with his partner, and take care of his young son, Xiao Shu.

Eventually, Ma would want to start a new internet enterprise— perhaps something for the younger generation of queer Chinese. But for now, fatherhood had shifted his priorities—from running a company to walking his son to school. At school, Xiao Shu is still unaware that his family is different from others; he calls Ma "Daddy" and Ma's partner "Uncle"—a label that Ma explains is "more convenient" than calling him a second father. He doesn't want his son to be discriminated against by people who have never met a queer person, let alone a queer family. "I'll explain it to him when he's a teenager," Ma said.

But what would China look like then? How would he be treated as the son of gay men? Would his peers accept him? His government? It was hard to imagine his generation facing the same challenges as his father did in his teenage years, when simply being gay could be persecuted as both a crime and an illness.

Despite the government's tightened grip on LGBTQ advocacy, surveys continue to show that the public has become more supportive and affirming of queer identities. Online, young Chinese now turn to an array of different platforms, like Douyin and Xiaohongshu, to post journals of gender-transition experiences, share guides on coming out, and swap advice on surrogacy services for queer parents. They continue to dance in shackles, carving out spaces of freedom within constraints.

Like all of us, Ma had no idea what the future would hold. But he did know that Xiao Shu filled his life with a light and joy he had never known. "He gave me something new to live for," Ma said. "A new beginning."

CHAPTER 16

Groundfire

After the shutdown of *Feminist Voices,* Lü Pin soon discovered that the feminist movement had not been extinguished. Instead, it had gone underground, regained its balance, and resurged in a different form. This time, it existed to a greater extent online: It was more decentralized and, with its network now scattered across the globe, more resilient. It had laid the kindling for a large, unexpected awakening to come.

The first sparks ignited in China on January 1, 2018. Luo Xixi, an alumna of Beihang University, accused a former professor of sexually harassing her when she was a PhD student, sharing her experience on Weibo. She was inspired by the thousands of women around the world who spoke out before her: the women who came forward to accuse American entertainment mogul Harvey Weinstein of sexual misconduct, who were emboldened to share their own experiences using #MeToo as a status. By the beginning of that year, they had brought down hundreds of powerful men from their positions of authority—producers, actors, senators, journalists, politicians—stopping short of President Trump himself. The flame of #MeToo had raced through American borders to the rest of the world, from France to Egypt to Japan—#MoiAussi, #QueVoltaChe, #AnaKaman, #YoTambien—before finally lighting up in China as #WoYeshi.

Luo's post went viral, and shortly after, the professor was dismissed from his position. Dozens of Chinese women came forward to share their experiences of sexual harassment, with thousands more chiming in to support them. Previously, a core group of activists spearheaded the feminist movement; this time, young women who perhaps never previously considered themselves activists drove the movement forward—speaking out on Weibo, circulating petitions, demanding that institutions do a better job of combating sexual harassment.

Authorities had to perform a delicate dance in response to the sudden and fiery outbreak. On the one hand, they had to present themselves as paragons of morality; the Ministry of Education published an official statement expressing zero tolerance for sexual misconduct. On the other, they had to prevent the fire from growing out of control, causing "social unrest" and threatening their legitimacy. Censors acted quickly to delete social media posts; petitions disappeared from the web; searches for "MeToo" were blocked.

But netizens deployed an array of digital and linguistic tricks, refusing to be snuffed out. When "MeToo," or *Wo Yeshi* in Chinese, was blocked, they replaced it with slang from other dialects, such as the Sichuanese *Laozi Yeshi* or the Northeastern Chinese *An Yeshi*. When censors rushed to delete an open letter, one innovative user rotated the document and sent it to herself on a tamper-proof Ethereum blockchain, impossible to erase from the web. Many others turned to a simple act of wordplay: the Rice Bunny. The characters for "rice bunny" are pronounced "mi tu" in Chinese, a homonym of "MeToo." Soon, rice bunnies multiplied across social media platforms, sometimes simply represented as an emoji of a rice bowl and a bunny head. *Rice Bunny says the only thing I want for the coming Lunar New Year is anti-sexual harassment rulings,* began one discussion thread on Weibo. *You can take my plate away, but you cannot shut my mouth.*

By summer, the movement had erupted into a full blaze, fueled by the highest-profile #MeToo accusation in China to have emerged. A woman known as Xianzi, whose real name was Zhou Xiaoxuan, accused the nationally beloved talk show host Zhu Jun of sexually harassing her four years earlier, when she was a college intern at CCTV. That day, she found herself alone in his dressing room with him; he grabbed her hand, reached under her dress with his other hand, and forcibly kissed her on the lips. When she reported the incident to the police the next day, they dissuaded her from pursuing the case, because Zhu was a national example of "positive energy" whose reputation should not be sullied. So she kept quiet, until #MeToo.

Empowered by the women who spoke out before her, she stayed up all night writing down her thoughts. She posted her story on WeChat before dawn broke at 5:00 a.m. "I was numb to things like this," she wrote. "But in the past year, the feminist movement started little fires all over the place, giving me guidance. By tonight, I've seen so many women coming out about what they went through, I think it's time for me to record mine. To tell you something about the world we live in."

After a friend of a friend shared Xianzi's post on Weibo, it was reposted more than ten thousand times before the censors took it down. *Immediately delete all information related to Zhu Jun. Leave no area neglected.*

But Xianzi's post was only a first spark. In April 2019, Chinese feminists mobilized to support Jingyao Liu, a twenty-one-year-old Chinese student in Minnesota, who accused Richard Liu, the CEO of Chinese e-commerce giant JD.com, of sexual assault. After news of the allegations splashed across the Chinese internet, many netizens called her a slut, a whore, a liar, and a gold digger. But among an increasingly vocal community of Chinese sexual assault survivors and feminists, her story prompted an outpouring of support. Inspired by protests taking place at the time against Supreme Court nominee Brett Kavanaugh, they defended Jingyao from social media harassment by building a global movement around the hashtag #IAmNotAPerfectVictimEither. "To Liu Jingyao," they wrote in an online petition. "You are not alone. We believe in survivors, we believe in your bravery and honesty, we will always stand with you."

Although they could not explicitly agitate for political rights, women turned to social media to push back against the misogyny embedded in their everyday lives. Many turned to lifestyle apps like Xiaohongshu and film-review sites like Douban to criticize mansplainers and rail against social conventions that required women to dress up for men, and they created discussion forums for single women pushing back against marriage. "I'm not a domesticated animal," one woman posted in a Xiaohongshu single women's forum. "I don't want to be a wife. I want to live freely, to explore this world, to make full use of my life and live like a free bird." Even as the space for feminist activism shrank, feminist ideals continued to proliferate on the web, building solidarity among women through a common language.

The Rice Bunny, or the *mitu*, remained the symbol of the Chinese feminist movement: adaptable, agile, capable of propagating quickly across national boundaries. Anybody could participate, from online influencers writing about feminist issues in Shanghai to college students participating in feminist workshops in Hong Kong to young Chinese professionals attending a feminist winter camp in New York City, where they gathered for a weekend to discuss plans for activism and to build up the Chinese feminist community in the area. The movement continued its work as a decentralized "guerrilla network," as Lü Pin described it, organizing independently without a core leadership, with nodes all over the world.

· · ·

In February 2020, Guo Jing, a twenty-nine-year-old feminist activist and social worker living in Wuhan, woke up to new regulations: Residents were banned from leaving their homes without permission. Under lockdown, with their movements surveilled and restricted, everyone in the city could viscerally feel the limits on their freedom. "The new rules remind me of Margaret Atwood's novel *The Handmaid's Tale,* where women are gradually stripped of their freedoms by a patriarchal government during a state of emergency," she wrote in her diary. Cut off from the outside world, she felt isolated and powerless.

I first stumbled upon Guo's diaries shortly after Covid-19 broke out in China. I, too, was in lockdown, but at home in Hong Kong.

She started posting them on her public WeChat account, documenting details of daily life in the epicenter of the pandemic: her trips to the grocery store, conversations with frontline workers, observations of how the city of Wuhan was changing. Her readership snowballed as the posts were shared across the country and the rest of the world, reposted on international news sites like the BBC. But unlike Fang Fang, the renowned Wuhan diarist, lionized by admirers and decimated by her critics, Guo experienced a much more muted, less polarized response: mostly messages of gratitude and support. Her diary entries focused on the intimate and the personal, from her perspective as a feminist.

Guo grew up in rural Henan, where her parents worked as farmers. As a child, she never understood why she wasn't allowed to run around outside like her brother or why only the women in her family did any housework. "It's just the way it is," her mother explained when she asked. Only four girls from her village graduated from junior high school; she was the first to attend university. On campus, she started using the internet in the computer lab and, later on, her first OPPO mobile phone. When she stumbled upon *Feminist Voices'* Weibo account, she discovered a gender training workshop, where she met a broad community of feminists. She was delighted by the workshop: Unlike her college lectures, where the professors lectured a passive audience, in the workshop, everyone spoke up and shared their thoughts freely.

In 2014, after graduating from college, Guo applied for a job at a cooking school in Hangzhou, which had advertised for a male administrative assistant—because the male director needed a man to carry his suitcases on business trips. In response, she filed a gender discrimination lawsuit at a local court—and won. The court ruled that the cooking school had violated the applicant's equal employment rights, a landmark victory. "This feeling that I could act, and that those actions would lead to change," Guo told me, "that feeling was addictive." She filed an appeal for more compensation (the court awarded her a small sum of $300 in damages), but in 2016, the year after the Feminist Five were arrested, she left Hangzhou and moved to Guangzhou. In 2019, when feminist organizations were getting squeezed out of Guangzhou, she left the city for Wuhan, arriving just a month before the pandemic hit.

If the pandemic emboldened the Party to stoke nationalism among its artists and demand obedience from its entrepreneurs, it enabled them to further clamp down on all forms of civil society. In Shanghai, the city's annual pride event, which ran unhindered for eleven years, was abruptly canceled. In an open letter posted online titled "The End of the Rainbow," the organizers said they were "taking a break from scheduling any future events," without giving a reason. In Hong Kong, the annual Tiananmen vigil was banned for the first time in three decades, under the pretense of controlling the virus. To prevent people from congregating, police lined the perimeter of Victoria Park with metal barriers.

But even as the walls closed in on Chinese civil society, Chinese feminist activists—long cut off from public spaces and well-versed in the skill of building trust and solidarity across boundaries—had learned how to adapt. Offline, Guo lived an isolated existence, but online, she led a vibrant social life. During the pandemic, she ran a WeChat hotline for victims of domestic violence and launched a social media campaign to raise awareness of the issue, posting an open letter online and mobilizing thousands of volunteers to share it with their communities. One feminist activist, named Liang Yu, organized the Stand By Her mutual-aid initiative to donate feminine-hygiene products to female medical staff working in Wuhan hospitals; another launched the #SeeFemaleWorkers project on Weibo, to bring attention to female frontline medical workers, who were largely overlooked in the media but formed two-thirds of Hubei Province's medical workforce.

I visited Guo in Wuhan in late November 2020. We met at a hot pot restaurant in a mall. For several months, Covid cases had been brought to zero. Life seemed normal. Although she lived and worked at home alone, Guo was deeply connected with friends and colleagues scattered around the country and the globe. She checked in nightly with a circle of like-minded feminist friends, exchanging exercise routines, sharing cooking tips, and swapping answers to the *New York Times*'s "36 Questions That Lead to Love." The feminist movement's resilience lay in the strength of relationships, she explained, built on trust, shared experience, and mutual vulnerability. It served as a tight-knit network of solidarity, invisible to the outside eye, but strong, supple, and sprawling across geographies— from Wuhan to Chengdu to New York.

Although Guo was deliberately vague about whom she worked with, she did say that crucial to holding these relationships together was the woman she admired most in the world, a name I had heard repeatedly from feminists in China and across the diaspora: Lü Pin. "No one has sacrificed as much as she has sacrificed, and given what she has given, in terms of time and emotional labor," Guo told me.

Lü was, of course, thousands of miles away from Wuhan, in Albany, New York. By 2020, she was used to being alone. Even before the pandemic broke out, her life was marked by social distancing. Other than attending class on the University at Albany campus, where she was completing her master's degree in gender studies, or getting groceries at the closest Walmart, she spent most of her time alone. Albany's gray winters and wide, empty streets reminded her more of colder, sparser cities in China's northeast like Shenyang than the bustling Beijing she had left behind.

"I have no friends here," she told me bluntly over the phone when I called her earlier in the year, when the pandemic had just hit New York. "The professors and students in my department don't talk to me. Language is a barrier. We have nothing in common." She spoke with a distinctive cadence: in clipped phrases, curt and matter-of-fact, not a word wasted, as if her speech had become slimmed and hardened after years of self-exile.

She was spending every ounce of warmth and energy, I realized, on supporting her fellow feminists back home, who still subsisted on her convictions and depended on her guidance. She stayed up late every night, always online, liaising with people in China, facilitating group chats, hosting workshops, and responding to interview requests. She lived her life in a perpetual state of jetlag. Although her body was in the United States, her spirit remained firmly rooted in China; even her circadian rhythms ran on China time.

If extinguishing a social movement meant removing its participants from their site of contention, reviving a movement meant creating a new site—entirely in the virtual realm. "If your body cannot participate," said Lü, "then you have to re-create the front line elsewhere."

.   .   .

Sustaining a movement online was both empowering and challenging. On the one hand, it allowed for broader participation, unconstrained by time and place. On the other, without a clear center or leadership, it became chaotic, uncoordinated, and with no clear processes to manage disagreement. In the United States, Lü Pin created a WeChat group for Chinese-diaspora feminists based in North America, which quickly swelled to nearly five hundred members and proved challenging for larger-scale mobilization. She spent hours each day managing the group—sharing articles and responding to individual questions. Once, one member demanded that another be removed from the group, claiming that she was sexually harassed by her when they were in high school. When Lü, unable to verify the claims, did not immediately remove the accused woman, the accuser launched a smear campaign against Lü for condoning sexual abuse. Lü herself left the group, which eventually disintegrated.

For Lü, living abroad as an activist created a whole set of logistical and emotional hurdles. First, there was the constant anxiety over her visa status. (Once, when the university failed to process her visa in time, they suggested that she "go back to China and return in a few months," which was clearly not possible for her. She ended up taking a last-minute trip to Mexico.) She did not feel welcome in either her home country, where she could be perceived only as a loyal patriot or a traitor, or in her adopted country, where she could be seen only as an apologist or a dissident. When one of her Chinese friends posted a picture of herself on Twitter participating in a protest against anti-Asian hate, she received many offensive comments, claiming that "Chinese were not eligible to participate in US social movements unless they label themselves as Anti-CCP."

"To be a Chinese person with a conscience is a path destined to be unfree and painful even if you have physically left the country," Lü wrote in a Twitter post. "The way you love your 'homeland' is not allowed by the government. But the 'free world' has never understood what you are going through."

She thought of herself as distinct from Chinese dissidents in the United States—mostly men, many of whom embraced Trumpism as their beacon, and almost all of whom had cut ties with Chinese society and were therefore free to say whatever they wanted. She was not. She needed to think about how her words and actions affected the safety of her community back in China. Her relationships, much like the web itself, were both transnational and intimate—impossible to neatly divide or sever along national boundaries. And as long as she maintained connections on the Chinese internet, she could not extricate herself from its system of control, no matter how many miles away she lived. "I came to the feminist movement in search of freedom," she wrote in a Twitter post. "Yet many times in it, I felt like I had lost the option of speaking freely."

Online movements were also vulnerable to transnational surveillance, online harassment, and intimidation. After the crackdown on liberal influencers in 2013, Weibo lost its status as a town square of meaningful public debate and discourse. To survive both politically and commercially, Weibo has not only censored critical dissenters but also amplified patriotic voices. While the platform remains one of the noisiest hubs for pop culture and celebrity gossip, it has also become a "huge camp for Little Pinks and Wolf Warriors, where they smear, slander, and attack those who tell the truth," Guo Yuhua, a disillusioned Chinese intellectual, wrote in a farewell letter announcing her decision to leave the platform for good.

In this sense, Weibo's decline reflected developments that were not unique to China but taking place all over the world, in autocracies and democracies alike: the drowning out of meaningful discourse with illiberal furor and the erosion of consensus reality. One of the Chinese government's key censorship techniques is what the scholar Margaret Roberts calls "flooding": a coordinated effort to drown out another perspective by overwhelming the public with distracting information, be it "positive energy" news reels or posts by patriotic influencers. This technique is increasingly being deployed in open information environments (Donald Trump's erratic tweets being a prominent example). In China, of course, flooding out unwanted voices altogether is completely within the Party's power.

In March 2021, China's feminist movement encountered a crisis when it was hit by this flood with full force. Xiao Meili, one of the young feminist activists who took to the streets of Qianmen in Beijing in 2012, was having a meal at a hot pot restaurant in Chengdu with a group of friends when she asked a man smoking at the next table if he would mind putting out his cigarette. They were sharing a public space; smoking indoors was illegal. She was completely caught off guard by what followed. In a burst of rage, the man unleashed a barrage of insults at her, calling her an "infertile woman." When Xiao pulled out her phone to record him, he stood up and hurled a cup of hot, oily liquid on Xiao and her friends.

Xiao uploaded a video of the incident on Weibo. A few hours later, she discovered that her post had gone viral and her account had been bombarded with hateful messages attacking her, her appearance, her friends and family, calling her a "feminist bitch" and telling her that she "should die." A prominent nationalist influencer named @ziwuxiashi posted a photo of Xiao from 2014, of her holding a poster with the slogan PRAY FOR HONG KONG during the city's Occupy Central protests, accusing her of supporting Hong Kong independence, being funded by "foreign enemies," and "inciting conflicts between men and women in China so Western countries can benefit." Other users piled on, calling Xiao and her friends "CIA agents" and reporting on their accounts to get them shut down.

Two days later, Xiao Meili and fifteen other feminist activists discovered that their Weibo accounts had been shut down. Other platforms quickly followed suit. Discussion forum Douban shut down a dozen feminist group forums for containing "extremism and radical political views." E-commerce marketplace Taobao delisted all products from Xiao's online store, where she sold feminist-themed tote bags and keychains to support herself financially. Over secondhand cigarette smoke, China's most influential feminists were silenced in one blow, their voices—and in some cases, their livelihoods—erased from the public sphere.

Authorities had effectively adopted a more sophisticated censorship playbook: Instead of simply deleting the voices they didn't like, they cultivated an online ecosystem that incentivized online nationalists and incels to do the dirty work for them and drown those voices out. Although nationalist influencers like @ziwuxiashi were not direct employees of the state, they received other benefits: promotions by Communist Youth League platforms or invitations to special workshops hosted by internet regulators on how to boost their followings. On social media platforms like Weibo, where nationalist content—uninhibited and amplified—generates the most traffic and therefore advertising revenue, patriotism became a weapon wielded by misogynists to turn harassment into a lucrative business under the guise of loving the nation.

"This attack tells abusers the world over that as long as you're waving a red flag, violence is not a crime and misogyny is justified," wrote Zheng Churan, one of the Feminist Five, in response to the attacks after her Weibo account was shut down. "I'm afraid that if we silence ourselves, our gains in women's rights, hard won from the 1995 UN Women's Conference to the student activism of today, will gradually be erased. Companies will start to overtly hire men only. Men who beat their wives and children will face no serious consequences. Repeat sexual harassers will have no need to keep themselves in check. Anyone with power and authority will consider it their right to pick on the weak."

. . .

Late on the night of November 2, 2021, Chinese tennis star Peng Shuai took to Weibo. In a public post, she accused Zhang Gaoli, former vice premier and member of the Party's most powerful seven-man Standing Committee, of sexually assaulting her. In Peng's post, she wrote that Zhang first had sex with her more than a decade ago in Tianjin, when he was the city's Party chief. Then, three years ago, he invited her to have dinner with him and his wife and then forced her to have sex with him in his bedroom while his wife kept watch at the door.

"You were always afraid that I would make recordings and keep them as evidence. In fact, I have no evidence or proof other than my own word. All I have are the true experiences of my own twisted self," she wrote. "I know that you, the high and mighty Vice Premier Zhang Gaoli, have said that you're not afraid. But even if I'm like an egg cracking against a rock or a moth to the flame, bent on self-destruction, I will speak the truth about you and me."

The post lasted thirty minutes before it was deleted. By the end of the night, Peng Shuai was scrubbed clean from the Chinese internet, her name unsearchable. In the hours that followed, censors kicked into overdrive, erasing every reference to Peng in a game of cat and mouse with creative netizens. Peng Shuai and Vice Premier Zhang Gaoli's names were censored, so netizens used their initials, PS and ZGL, until those, too, were deleted. Netizens then tried using the names of those who shared their initials—Pusa (the Chinese name for the Bodhisattva, an enlightened being in Buddhist tradition) and Zhuge Liang (a famous Chinese military strategist and statesman from the second century)—as well as subtle euphemisms of the tennis player and the vice president—such as "Mike Pence and Serena Williams"—until those, too, disappeared. After netizens turned the Korean soap opera *The Prime Minister and I* into a code word for news about Peng Shuai, Tencent removed the drama from its streaming service altogether. Before long, searches for the word "tennis" itself were restricted to showing posts only from verified accounts.

Inside the firewall, Peng no longer existed and seemingly never had. A month after her post, I brought up the case with a group of acquaintances at a bar in Beijing, and one woman—a recent graduate of a college in the United States who worked at a foreign multinational company—was shocked. What was I talking about? She had no idea. She was busy with work and didn't use a VPN to access most things she needed online, and her Chinese social media feeds and news channels were so cleanly scrubbed that the most significant #MeToo accusation to have embroiled China barely registered a blip on her radar.

Outside the firewall, Peng's disappearance stirred up international outrage. Chinese-diaspora feminists and tennis luminaries alike demanded her whereabouts, tweeting out the hashtag #WhereisPengShuai; the Women's Tennis Association (WTA) chairman responded by suspending all tournaments in China. Peng was included in *Time* magazine's "100 Most Influential People" list; Lü Pin wrote her introduction. In response, authorities switched tack: Instead of burying the accusations, they changed the narrative to pretend that nothing nefarious had happened at all. Suddenly, Peng "reappeared" in the public eye, paraded on state-media channels, denying all her allegations. On Twitter, state-media journalists circulated videos of Peng at a dinner with friends, and photos allegedly from her WeChat account of her smiling in her bedroom, posing next to a coterie of stuffed animals, with the caption "Happy Weekend." She video-called the chair of the International Olympic Committee with an unwavering smile on her face, declaring that she was "safe" and "happy." "Can any girl fake such a sunny smile under pressure?" Hu Xijin, the garrulous editor of the state-run *Global Times,* posted on Twitter. "Those who suspect Peng Shuai is under duress, how dark they must be inside." Less than two years later, when the world had long moved on from the news, the WTA announced its return to China. A Weibo search of Peng's name still yielded no results.

This combination of censorship and gaslighting was a crude strategy, but it worked again and again. In 2022, two incidents of sexual violence also sparked uproar on Chinese social media. In January, a woman was discovered in a dirty shed in Jiangsu Province, chained by her neck to the wall by her husband, who had also forced her to birth eight of his children. In June, a woman having dinner in the city of Tangshan, Hebei, refused a man's advances; he and a group of other men dragged her onto the street and beat her, blood streaming across her face, as shocked bystanders looked on. In both cases, horrified netizens voiced their outrage online and muckrakers flocked to the scene to expose the truth; but in each case, censors stepped in to delete posts, authorities muffled the muckrakers, and the outrage was suppressed to a quiet simmer, as if nothing had happened at all.

. . .

I finally met Lü Pin in person in the summer of 2022, during a visit to New York City. She had recently moved to New Brunswick, New Jersey, where she was completing her PhD in the Political Science Department of Rutgers University. Of all the disciplines she had explored through her coursework in Albany—anthropology, sociology, public policy—she felt most aligned with political science as a frame of thinking. It focused on the issues that mattered most to her: the state, political power, and social movements.

When I asked Lü if I could interview her in person, she was reluctant—and understandably so. After years of corresponding online, I had asked to enter her physical space, a refuge she'd carved out for herself from the chaos of the virtual realm and state encroachment. I came filled with questions about the future of the feminist movement when there was no clear path forward. I was curious about the specifics of her organizing work—what she was working on and who she was working with—at a time when her biggest priority was to protect her community from the hostile public sphere. To a journalist, specific details breathed life into and gave color to a story; to an activist, it meant greater risk. "It is not helpful for you to know the internal affairs of an activist movement," she responded curtly when I asked about current projects she was thinking about. "All you need to know is that we're still here."

Lü agreed to meet me as long as I did not ask about her work. So I didn't. I left my notebook and recorder behind and took the train from Penn Station to New Brunswick, where she picked me up at the train station. She'd learned to drive the year before; being able to get around in her own car had made her life much easier. We ate at a Sichuanese restaurant near the university campus, then walked along the Delaware Canal, the path quiet and secluded, lined with a canopy of sycamore and maple trees. For one afternoon, I was no longer a disembodied voice on a Signal call, another journalist extracting information about the future of feminism, but just another feminist seeking her counsel and camaraderie.

Before I left, I gave her a book of poetry I'd bought in a bookstore in New York City's East Village: Ada Limón's *The Carrying*. I knew that Lü was swamped with things to read—long PhD dissertations and other dense academic writings. I wanted to ease, not add to, her burden. Limón's poems—taut, piercing, each no more than a page long—would provide solace. *The Carrying* was about all the things that women had to carry in their bodies through this cruel and unstable world—joy, grief, anger, loss, fear of violence, children, families, the emotional and physical labor required to take care of the communities that depend on us—and how it was impossible to carry it all. "What if instead of carrying / a child, I am supposed to carry grief?"

I thought of everything Lü carried with her: the faded memories of Tiananmen Square as a young college student, the waning idealism of the 1995 UN World Conference on Women, the deleted words of *Feminist Voices,* the well-being of each feminist activist who still depended on her support, the grief of exile. She still carried the key of her home in Beijing—a token of hope perhaps, of a future return.

Lü once told me that she had not spoken with her family for years. "They have their own life, and they don't understand my work," she said. "We don't talk anymore."

"Not even during the Spring Festival?" I asked. It was, after all, for so many, the one time in the year that people traveled home to reunite with their families.

"No, not even during the Spring Festival."

"What about friends back home?"

"Friends? I don't have any friends outside the movement," she said. Then she paused. A faint, knowing smile appeared at the corner of her lips, but as always, it didn't linger long. "Only secret friendships, I guess. Friendships from shared experience, from going through things together, from supporting each other through repression."

Like Ma Baoli, who became a custodian of China's gay community, creating an online space for gay men to seek kinship, Lü had dedicated her life to nurturing China's feminist activists, providing them with a platform to speak out. He was empowered by his decision to have children; she was by her freedom not to. But they also adopted different dances: Ma believed he could lift up China's queer community only by collaborating with the state; Lü believed that the only way to empower China's feminists was to hold the state accountable. Decades later, both approaches seemed increasingly difficult. The feminist movement had retreated into a mode of self-preservation. Forced underground and abroad, Lü understood that the only way to sustain the movement was to protect its participants and maintain "secret friendships"—invisible but tight-knit relationships of trust and solidarity.

Even if a movement cannot be surging forward with great momentum, Lü once wrote, it is enough that, for most of the time, it remains a "groundfire." Groundfire: kindling, forest duff, deep organic soil, and coarse, woody debris, hard to see with the naked eye, but burning at a low temperature underground, never fully snuffed out. No matter how far down the movement retreated, this served as its fuel—the irrepressible anger of Peng Shuai, of the iron-chained woman, of the woman of Tangshan, of all the Chinese women saying to themselves, again and again: I will not take this anymore. It smolders below the surface, waiting for the right conditions to spark.

CHAPTER 17

Closed Loop

After the pandemic broke out in China in 2020, Eric Liu knew it was time to leave.

To quash the virus, the Chinese government instituted a mandatory tracking system, launched on WeChat and Alipay, Alibaba's mobile payment app, to monitor the health and location of its citizens. It assigned every smartphone user a QR code, linked to their name, travel history, identification, and phone number and correlated with their device's tracking data. The color of the code—green, yellow, or red—determined whether or not a person could move freely, enter buildings, or use public transportation. Within weeks of the outbreak, health code checkpoints appeared in front of every train station and storefront, requiring citizens to scan their phones to pass.

Eric's heart pounded each time he scanned his phone. To receive a red health code felt like being branded with a scarlet letter; a quarantine order resembled a temporary house arrest. What was to say that they wouldn't track other things besides your Covid-19 status? News broke that proactive government officials proposed to integrate the health code into daily life; in Suzhou, local officials introduced plans for a civility code that would apply to other activities, rewarding positive behavior like doing volunteer work and punishing the negative, like jaywalking. They retracted the plans in response to a public backlash, but the technology to implement such an intrusion was in place.

Eric had every reason to be paranoid. His smartphone contained his entire life—personal messages, VPN software, late-night searches, past deeds. Everything. He had quit his job at the streaming platform Leshi in 2017. Since then, he'd done contract work as an editor at various social media start-ups, all the while continuing to save censorship directives. What if someone scanned his phone, decided to dig a little deeper, saw everything he'd done? He became hypervigilant: Every time he left his apartment, he scanned his surroundings, double-checked his front-door lock, and avoided walking under construction scaffolding.

Leaving China meant leaving behind a comfortable life in Tianjin. He lived with his family in their own house, with his own car and a *hukou* residency permit—all the trappings of middle-class comfort most would consider absurd to give up. Tianjin was the only home he'd ever known, where three generations of his family had grown up and grown old, where he'd attended college, gotten his first job, met his wife and started a family.

But he had no space to dance anymore. The Firewall had hardened into a literal barrier, suppressing not only the free flow of information but the physical movement of people themselves. He'd already witnessed two man-made disasters over the past decade—the Wenzhou train crash in 2011 and the Tianjin explosions in 2015—and each jolted him into action. This last one, the Covid-19 pandemic of 2020, would only do the same. So, in March of that year, he packed up his belongings and, along with his wife and children, took a one-way flight out of the country for good.

. . .

I landed in China a few months after Eric left. After spending the first half of the year outside the mainland, at home in Hong Kong, I decided to return and, as mandated for all international travelers, undergo quarantine. For two weeks, I was an esteemed guest at the Blue Sky Hotel in Shanghai, isolated in my room and denied all human contact except for the hazmat-suited figure who dropped off a plastic-bagged meal outside my door three times a day. I was also permitted one delivery of groceries, but with a few exceptions: no alcohol, no glass (jars, bottles), and, inexplicably, no kiwis. There had been no cases of local transmission in months.

When I emerged after two weeks, I found the entire country's infrastructure rehauled in the service of zero-Covid. Walls were everywhere. Airport metal gates, concrete residential compound barriers, Plexiglas screens, temporary isolation panels, makeshift quarantine centers. In the city of Ruili, Yunnan, on the China–Myanmar border, which had been placed under lockdown seven times in one year, officials put up spans of sheet metal and fences with razor wire to prevent exit and entry. The local mayor proudly dubbed it the "Steel Great Wall." For a while, the policies seemed to be working, flattening infection curves and keeping death rates low.

But as the highly transmissible Omicron variant started to spread and the rest of the world began to experiment with living with the virus, China doubled down on zero-Covid. To host the Beijing Winter Olympics in January 2022, China kept its walls in place. The Games would be open only to a select group of guests and athletes. All participants lived inside what was called a "closed loop," a tightly managed bubble cut off from the rest of Beijing, from the moment they arrived until they departed. Inside the "closed loop," residents had their own designated hotels, venues, cafeterias, and taxi systems. Traffic authorities ordered Beijing residents to stay away from accidents involving vehicles from the closed loop; a special unit of ambulances would respond. An American TV producer who spent two months living in the bubble told me it was like "going on a weird vacation, going to school, and going to prison—all in one."

If the 2008 Beijing Summer Olympics marked China's "coming out to the world," the 2022 Winter Olympics signaled its turning inward. Tourist visas were restricted, educational exchanges were canceled, many international journalists were still barred from entering, and the number of foreign businesspeople and students entering the country plummeted. Instead of eagerly trying to impress the international community with its spirit of openness, as it did in 2008, the Party now adopted an attitude of assertive indifference. When the United States and its allies staged a diplomatic boycott to condemn China's treatment of Uyghurs, a spokesperson for the Chinese Foreign Ministry responded in a public briefing: "Nobody cares."

After the Games ended, zero-Covid policies remained, and closed-loop management was extended as an official pandemic-control measure for society at large. University students lived together on what were called "closed-loop campuses," unable to leave. To keep supply chains running, factory workers worked in a system of "closed-loop manufacturing," forced to work, sleep, and eat inside factory grounds for months on end. The closed loop embodied China's new posture toward the outside world: selectively allowing in people, ideas, and capital that aligned with its values while shutting everything else out.

In March 2022, when Shanghai went under lockdown, closed-loop management revealed itself to be a futile and farcical game of whack-a-mole. Residents were forced to stay in their apartments, and those who tested positive were hauled off to centralized quarantine centers. Because businesses and grocery stores were shut down, people struggled to get basic necessities, like food and medicine. Within two months, the nation's bustling cosmopolitan center transformed into a city crippled by health care crises, food insecurity, and soaring unemployment. When residents in a locked-down apartment complex started to sing from their balconies, local officials sent up a drone with a megaphone that repeated, "Please comply with Covid restrictions. Control your soul's thirst for freedom. Do not open the window or sing."

People suffered under the very policies created to protect them. To prevent infections, authorities separated babies from their parents, denied sick and elderly prompt medical treatment, and left workers stranded on construction sites. A woman, eight months pregnant, miscarried after she was forced to wait for hours at a hospital because she did not have a valid Covid-19 test. A nurse who suffered from an asthma attack died after being denied timely care because she did not have a recent PCR test. By May, at least 170 people died not from the virus but as a result of lockdown measures, according to the Chinese-language news outlet *Initium.*

The Shanghai lockdown was officially lifted in June. But Omicron continued to spread. By late August, at least seventy-four other cities, and almost a quarter of China's population, had been placed under similar lockdowns. One late night in September, in Guizhou Province, a bus carrying close contacts of Covid patients to a mandatory quarantine center flipped over on a mountain highway, killing twenty-seven people. In Guizhou, only two people had actually died of the virus. Inside the absurd parallel of the closed loop, numbers, not humans, were the central priority. The goal was to keep infection rates at zero while allowing capital to circulate, no matter the human cost.

. . .

In his 1970 treatise *Exit Voice, and Loyalty,* the German economist Albert O. Hirschman theorized that when members of an organization, be it a business or a nation or any form of human grouping, are unhappy with a deteriorating situation, there are two ways that they can create change. They can "voice"—attempt to fix the organization by communicating a complaint or proposal for change—or they can "exit," or withdraw from the group altogether. An employee in a bad work environment can either express concerns to their boss or quit their job. A spouse trapped in a toxic marriage can choose to discuss the problem with their partner or file for divorce. A citizen dissatisfied with their government can vote for another leadership or they can emigrate—vote with their feet.

Increasingly, Chinese citizens were choosing the second option: to exit. In the 2010s, as China's tech industries flowered, many overseas Chinese students and professionals returned home, lured by the wealth of new job opportunities. But in 2022, after crippling lockdowns, those who had the means were again looking for ways to leave. In the first days of April, during Shanghai's lockdowns, the number of WeChat searches of the word "immigration" spiked by over 400 percent.

One of the hottest topics on social media was how to 润—a Chinese character with the Pinyin romanization spelled like the English word "run"—or, in other words, how to escape the country. On GitHub, users even created a "Run Philosophy" page. According to creators, its central purpose "was to answer three major questions: why run, where to run, and how to run." Titles of popular entries included:

Why Run

Alibaba's Top Expert Shares Personal Experience: Comprehensive Guide to Applying for [US] EB1A Overseas

How People with No Money Can Emigrate to Australia

Methods for Obtaining Passports During the Pandemic Period

Run Methodology: How Humanities Majors and Female Job Seekers Can Run to the United States (Updated with Post-Marriage Green Card Issues)

The page reflected the opportunities available largely to an educated upper-middle class who had spending power and college degrees. Some pursued job opportunities and graduate programs in Europe and North America; others bought condos and sought long-term residence in Southeast Asian countries like Malaysia and Thailand. An influx of artists, media workers, and progressive parents seeking better education for their children moved to Chiang Mai, Thailand, drawn to the city's affordable, laid-back lifestyle. In Bangkok, demand from Chinese students to attend an international school soared, doubling within a year. Intellectuals and tech entrepreneurs alike flocked to Japan; so many have bought apartments in Tokyo's luxury high-rises that some areas have been dubbed Chinatowns.

The elite flocked to Singapore, drawn to its low wealth tax and large Chinese-speaking population, moving their assets via property and by setting up family offices. Requests for immigration services have skyrocketed. Henley & Partners, a London-based firm that offers services to people seeking to acquire residence or citizenship in countries around the world, reported a 134 percent increase in investment inquiries from Chinese nationals in the second quarter of 2022 over the first.

With fewer options, the poorer took the dangerous journey through Panama's Darién Gap: flying visa-free to Ecuador, traveling to Colombia's northern border, trekking through the jungle for three to ten days, and finally reaching the US–Mexican border to seek asylum. In 2023, more than fifteen thousand Chinese citizens crossed the Darién Gap, according to Panamanian authorities—the fourth-highest-ranked nationality after Venezuelans, Ecuadorans, and Haitians. The journey became so popular that it earned its own name in Chinese: *zouxian,* or "walk the line." On platforms like WeChat and Douyin, netizens provided detailed instructions on what to pack, how to find guides, which paths to take, and how to handle encounters with border officials and cartels. So many new migrants scattered across the globe that they spawned their own meme: 华润万家. The characters referred to China Resources Vanguard, a popular Chinese supermarket chain. But read literally, they translated roughly as "Chinese people are running away, to all ends of the world."

But running was an expensive path that required not only courage but resources and good fortune. For the many more who wished to exit but could not run, there was, of course, another way out: to "lie flat," as increasing numbers of young Chinese had already chosen to do. In 2022, as lockdowns intensified, Chinese embraced a new viral phrase that took lying flat a step further: to *bailan,* or "let it rot." The term was first used by Chinese sports commentators to describe a phenomenon they observed in NBA games, where teams performed poorly on purpose to try to score a higher draft pick in the future. Gamers started using the term to refer to deliberately losing in order to hasten the end of a hopeless game. "Letting it rot" took "lying flat" to its extreme: not only to accept failure but to revel in it, to actively embrace a deteriorating situation instead of trying to turn it around. Letting it rot was actively nihilistic. If entropy was inevitable, why not help speed up its progress?

The *bailan* attitude was crystallized in one moment, captured on a video during the Shanghai lockdown. In the video, cops clad in hazmat suits arrive at an apartment to take a young couple to a centralized quarantine spot. When the couple refuses, a cop scolds them, wagging his finger. "You'll be punished! And this will have bad consequences for your family for the next three generations," he says.

"Sorry," the response comes, abrupt and matter-of-fact. "But we are the last generation, thanks."

After the video went viral, the phrase "We Are the Last Generation" became a mantra of defiant despair as netizens jumped to express empathy for the young couple. The phrase was the strongest condemnation a young person could make of their era. To choose not to have children was to reject a system that no longer gave them space to dance—to refuse to bring life into a future that was no longer worth striving for. Or, as a Chinese user tweeted succinctly: "Those who can 'run' are voting with their feet; those who cannot 'run' are voting with their genitals."

. . .

On Sunday, October 23, 2022, during the 20th National Congress of the Communist Party of China, the last ember of hope that the situation would change was snuffed out. During the congress, held every five years, the Party announced new policies and unveiled the new seven-member Politburo Standing Committee. In the lead-up, despite Xi Jinping's intent to stay for a third term, observers watched closely for smaller shifts: appointments of technocrats, hints of reviving economic growth, and easing of zero-Covid rules.

Instead, Xi prioritized national security over economic growth and replaced technocrats like Premier Li Keqiang with loyalists like Li Qiang, the Shanghai Party official who botched the lockdown and declared that China would continue with its zero-Covid policy "without wavering." Covid controls would further suppress consumption, deter investors, and exacerbate unemployment. Doubling down on control would only stifle adaptability and entrepreneurialism, the dance that allowed its citizens to navigate challenges for so many years. "It's like riding a bike," a government official once told the professor Yuen Yuen Ang. "The tighter you grip the handles, the harder it is to balance."

In November, the zero-Covid deaths continued to add up. In Lanzhou, Gansu, a three-year-old boy died of carbon monoxide poisoning after pandemic restrictions delayed his hospital treatment. In Hohhot, Inner Mongolia, a woman in mental distress from lockdown fell to her death from the twelfth floor of her apartment building. In Zhengzhou, Henan, a four-month-old girl died in quarantine after emergency services sent her to a hospital over a hundred kilometers away. In Guangzhou, Guangdong, a middle-aged woman locked down in a quarantine center hanged herself in a toilet cubicle. She feared being shunned at home for testing positive.

On November 23, 2022, in Zhengzhou, desperate workers, locked down in a Foxconn iPhone factory for months, clashed violently with police. Cops fired tear gas and water cannons as thousands of workers scaled fences, smashed security cameras, and tore down barriers.

On November 24, at 7:49 p.m., in Urumqi, Xinjiang—one of the highest concentrations of Uyghur people and, due to long-standing surveillance and control targeting the ethnic minority, one of the most heavily policed regions in the world—a fire blazed through a residential building. On the fifteenth floor, a power strip sparked, and flames spread quickly to the rest of the floors, black smoke billowing. The blaze took three hours to extinguish. Ten people died in the flames. Most of the city had been locked down for over one hundred days.

The fire was the last straw. When the news broke, I watched my social media feeds light up with anger, kindling that had been smoldering for months, if not years. State media claimed that the fire had occurred in a "low risk" area where citizens could move about freely. But netizens shared footage of fire trucks blocked by pandemic roadblocks and screenshots between government officials and the neighborhood's residents suggesting strict lockdown measures that could have hampered rescue and escape. I frantically saved the posts, fearing they might at any moment fade into smoke.

The Path was Clear. They did not Run.

People have the power.

Clearly explain what happened in the fire in Urumqi!

How many more lives have to be lost before this ends?

Each time a post vanished, a new one appeared. The fire ignited a firestorm of grief, blazing too fast for censors to extinguish.

. . .

On Saturday afternoon, November 26, a college student stood in the center of the Communication University of China Nanjing's campus, wearing a black mask and cap. According to *The Wall Street Journal,* the student was a young man with long hair tied up in a ponytail. He stood silently, holding a blank sheet of A4 paper. When a faculty member seized his paper, he kept his hands outstretched like a mime. Soon, others joined him. As night fell, they held up phone flashlights, lighting up the campus courtyard like a field of fireflies.

By then, the students' silent protest had gone viral on Chinese social media, and Shanghai residents had started to gather at Urumqi Road to mourn the victims of the fire. At first, participants were silent and somber; they lit candles, laid down white chrysanthemums, and held up sheets of blank paper as police officers watched quietly. But as midnight struck, the crowd swelled from dozens to hundreds of people, and a quiet vigil exploded into a heated protest, not just demanding the end to Covid controls but demanding free speech and democracy as well.

On Sunday, the protesters returned—not only to Shanghai's Urumqi Road but to major cities nationwide, from Wuhan to Chengdu to Beijing, sweeping through twenty-one provinces and over two hundred university campuses and taking as their symbol a blank sheet of white paper. Some protesters told reporters that the white paper was inspired by a Soviet-era joke, when a dissident accosted by the police says he has no need for words because "everyone knows." Language was so suppressed that silence became the only way to dissent, but the reasons for dissent were so obvious and self-explanatory that no words were needed.

I watched the protests unfold entirely on the internet. I was stunned. For days, my once-apolitical WeChat feed overflowed with endless protest videos, memes, and euphemisms, all striving to express dissent while evading censorship. People shared clips of "Do You Hear the People Sing?" performances from *Les Misérables* and Patti Smith's "People Have the Power." When those got taken down, they commented "404 404 404" on official posts in reference to the error page to highlight relentless censorship, and "Long Live the Motherland," "good good good good," and "correct correct correct" to mock the Party's push to flood the web with positive energy.

Online irony and humor spilled into the streets. A trending photo on Twitter showed that in Shanghai, someone walked a real-life alpaca on Urumqi Road—in reference to the "Grass-Mud-Horse" meme popularized during the Weibo Spring. In Beijing, when police told protesters at Liangma River to stop chanting "No more Covid tests," they sarcastically switched to "We want Covid tests!" When a man with a megaphone warned protesters of "anti-Chinese foreign forces in our midst," they joked, "By foreign forces, do you mean Marx and Engels?" a nod to the Party's own ideological roots. "We can't even browse foreign websites. How can we have foreign forces?"

Eric Liu noted a spike in new Twitter users that November as Chinese netizens jumped the Firewall to access unfiltered information. By then, he and his family had started a new life in San Bernardino, California, where he took a job as an editor at *China Digital Times* (*CDT*), a US-based bilingual news site founded by the Chinese human rights activist Xiao Qiang. Xiao was completing his PhD in astrophysics in the United States in 1989 and decided to become a full-time human rights activist after the Tiananmen protests. He launched *CDT* in 2003 with the goal of documenting and analyzing information controls and online resistance in China, publishing, for example, the government censorship directives that

Eric had collected. The *CDT* team discovered Eric through an interview published by Voice of America shortly after he arrived in the States. They reached out to ask if he wanted to join them.

If his first job at Weibo was to delete sensitive keywords, his new job was to preserve them. Every day, after sending his children to school, he spent hours at his computer, scouring Chinese news and social media for neologisms, puns, and expressions of dissent, explaining them in blog posts on *CDT*'s website in hopes of capturing them before they vanished. He still sported the Harry Potter–style glasses that he'd bought over a decade ago, when he started working as a censor. "I don't make much money, but it's kind of my dream job—like doing what I'd spend all my time doing anyway but getting paid for it," he told me. "You know how professional gamers can't tell the difference between being on and off work? It's kind of like that." Once a builder of the Great Firewall, Eric was now its archaeologist, taking it apart to help others better understand the edifice.

Since he started working at Weibo a decade ago, the Firewall had become far more sophisticated. In 2011, Weibo, which at the time had one of the largest operations of all social media companies, employed a few hundred content moderators; Eric's previous Weibo colleagues now working at ByteDance told him that in 2020, Byte-Dance employed ten thousand in Tianjin alone. Eric said that one of his colleagues at Weibo would go on to manage a team of three thousand ByteDance censors on his own. When the protests broke out, Eric stayed up for four days straight, fueled by adrenaline, scouring social media to save as much as he could. "I was exhausted, but I stayed awake because I knew that I had to record it all or it would disappear within minutes, seconds," he told me. "I felt that phrase that everyone keeps saying: *It's my duty.*"

Eric was referring to a phrase uttered in the spring of 1989, when he was still a toddler. A BBC journalist had asked a student cycling through the streets of Beijing where he was going. To Tiananmen Square, the student responded.

"Why?" the journalist asked.

"Why?" the student repeated rhetorically, with a big grin on his face, as if the answer was painfully obvious. "Because it's my duty!"

It was startling to see this old phrase—and the lexicon and iconography of 1989, buried deep in the nation's subconscious—suddenly resurface everywhere, on flyers and Instagram posts. A student at Nanjing University, who went by the Telegram instant-messaging handle Shostakovich, snuck around campus at night posting flyers with the words "*This is our era. It is my duty.*" An anonymous group of young diaspora Chinese created a website called MyDuty.net to crowdsource protest art and information in an anonymous online database. The popular Instagram account @CitizensDailyCN, which published a slate of political memes and protest-witness accounts, posted a screenshot of a moving conversation between a person and a previous tenant. It read:

> The internet in the apartment I rent was set up by the previous tenant, so every year I transfer him the fee. I made the last payment at the beginning of the month, and we hadn't communicated since.
>
> Today, when I woke up, I saw an unfamiliar message pop up. When I opened it, I found that he had refunded me the entire year's worth of payments, captioned by "Hope you protect yourself." I was moved and excited and thanked him. I told him it is because of people like him that we feel like all the struggle is meaningful. He replied:
>
> "I was there in 1989, at the square."

. . .

Inevitably, the so-called White Paper protests of late 2022, the largest protests in China since 1989, revived memories of that spring. For over three decades in between, protests in China remained localized and issue-specific as the Party applied a key lesson from 1989: Divide and conquer. Fragmented social unrest could never gain enough momentum to threaten the government. As a result, different sectors of society harbored different grievances. Although state workers lost their jobs, private entrepreneurs were allowed to start new businesses. Farmers lost their land, but city dwellers could buy new high-rise apartments. Isolated protests occurred all the time but never amounted to nationwide collective action.

Covid controls united the Chinese people for the first time under a shared grievance. Like the Tiananmen protests, the White Paper protests united a broad sector of Chinese society, in particular those who took the biggest hit from Covid policies: migrant workers suffering from economic deprivation, middle-class urbanites locked down at home, and university students stuck in their dormitories during the years they expected to be the most promising of their lives.

Despite similarities of their actions and their coalitions, the White Paper protests broke out in a drastically different China than the 1989 Tiananmen protests. The latter unfolded during the most liberal and tolerant period in Chinese history, as the country opened up to the world. Protesters took advantage of the new reform policies and a split in the Party's leadership between the reformers, who favored dialogue with the students, and the hard-liners, who argued that concessions would endanger the regime. Over the entire spring, hundreds of thousands of protesters converged on Tiananmen Square, the symbolic center of the Party's power, to participate in a freewheeling carnival of freedom, rock music blasting on boomboxes, and wide-eyed students dancing around the statue of the goddess of democracy. The movement's student leaders graced magazine covers and stood on soapboxes, chanting slogans in front of roaring crowds. Back then, anything seemed possible.

The White Paper protests emerged during one of China's most repressive eras, as the country was turning inward. Taking place in 2022, the protests lasted under a week, with only a few thousand on-the-ground participants. It was impossible to know exact numbers: Public spaces were so closely monitored that even one lone dissenter would've failed to reach Tiananmen Square. Information was so siloed that in Shanghai, on the second day of protests, some clueless pedestrians asked if the crowds were filming a movie or waiting for a celebrity. In 1989, China had opened up so quickly that it became unstable, empowering young people to take to the streets to demand more; in 2022, the country closed up so tightly that it had ossified, driving people to the streets in despair.

Yet even under such difficult conditions, a movement burst forth. Unlike Tiananmen, this time it played out largely online. Protesters spread slogans through encrypted messaging apps, AirDropped posters in subway cars, and shared memes on WeChat feeds. Unlike Tiananmen, the movement was transnational, decentralized, and leaderless. Within days of the protests at Urumqi Road, hundreds of gatherings emerged worldwide, from Tokyo's Shinjuku Station to New York City's Washington Square Park. The movement's most famous mobilizer was a Chinese art student living in Milan, Teacher Li, known for his Twitter profile picture of a cartoon tabby cat. Within a week, Li gained six hundred thousand Twitter followers and turned into a one-man newsroom, crowdsourcing and posting protest coverage on his account. At the peak of the protests, he received dozens of submissions every second.

Such a brittle and repressive system as the closed loop directly contradicted one of the most basic human urges: to be connected to one another and to the world. Students at Beijing's Tsinghua University understood this. They gathered in front of their cafeteria, holding up sheets of white paper but with the Friedmann Equation written on it:

$$H^2 = \left(\frac{\dot{a}}{a}\right)^2 = \frac{8\pi G}{3}\rho - \frac{kc^2}{a^2} + \frac{\Lambda c^2}{3}$$

The basic reality of the universe, the equation states, is not of stasis but of constant expansion—of opening up.

.   .   .

The Party responded to the protests by reverting to their old playbook—a mix of freedom and control, concessions and repression. Days after the protests, Covid-19 policies were radically reversed: The government lifted test requirements, dismantled the closed-loop system, and no longer required mild or asymptomatic cases to quarantine. The entire experience underwent a dizzying reversal: lockdowns lifted, health code system gone, and Big Whites—the hazmat-suited workers who patrolled every city—no more. Government officials who once spoke of Covid-19 as a deadly virus now described it as a mild flu. By late December, the virus had surged through the population, infecting more than 250 million people and resulting in an estimated 1.4 million deaths.

At the same time, authorities arrested protesters using internet and surveillance tools, analyzing data from telecommunications centers and through facial recognition. For many, the protests were their first experience of civil disobedience in their own country, and they did not know to mask their faces or put their phones on Airplane mode to evade surveillance. Police conducted random phone checks on the streets, searching for keywords like "Urumqi" in WeChat logs and looking for Telegram and VPN accounts. A friend in Shanghai described to me the atmosphere of dread and paranoia during the week after the protests. One rainy night, while walking alone in the streets, he heard a woman call his name. "Delete all your social media. Tell everyone to delete it all," she warned him before running off. He later learned she had just been interrogated by the police.

But on the surface, most people seemed to simply move on with their lives. As the virus ran its course, once-empty streets teemed again with traffic and once-shuttered cafés filled with patrons. All that remained of the past three years were abandoned relics of the closed loop: discarded barricades, fraying QR code posters, and abandoned quarantine centers. Before long, those, too, were removed and scrubbed of their history. Thousands of vacant testing booths were repurposed as food stalls, lottery ticket booths, tourist counters for the Asian Games, and even a Hoegaarden beer kiosk. *Life is moving forward again!* a *People's Daily* editorial praised the new policies. "Covid controls vanished with a snap of Thanos's fingers," Li Houchen, a protestor in Shanghai, wrote in an account of his experience. "It felt like a war had ended, the army had retreated, and citizens had walked onto the streets, stunned by the devastation."

Nobody discussed the protests in public; perhaps vast swaths of the country were completely unaware of their existence. Many friends shared with me stories of visiting nearby relatives living in cities only an hour away from Beijing or Shanghai, to find they were unaware that the protests had happened. "Objectively, the White Paper revolution was like a forced restart of a system that had gotten stuck. It came back to life, lighter on its feet, and once again eliminated the threat of dissent," Lü Pin wrote in a reflection she posted online on March 7, 2023. But the protests also awakened her from her silence. "I reawakened to the basic fact that society never dies, that no one is one hundred percent submissive, and that people are always looking for a way to resist."

Before the White Paper protests, Lü wanted to give up. After the online harassment of Chinese feminists in 2021, she slowed down her organizing work and stopped discussing the feminist movement in public. She was pessimistic, fearing that the movement had no path forward. After the 20th National Congress, a dark feeling took hold of her: It seemed as if there was no space to dance anymore. But the protest movement she watched from afar rekindled her hope. Although short-lived and fragile, "it was like a bolt of lightning that split the darkness," she wrote. "I was grateful to bathe in its light, ashamed that I was neither part of it nor had paid the price for it."

She and many other feminist activists told me how they were heartened to see so many young women driving the protests forward. A young woman delivered an impassioned speech in front of her peers at a protest at Tsinghua University; a young woman spoke out at a vigil at Beijing's Liangma River, calling on the crowd to remember the whistleblower doctor, Li Wenliang, who died from coronavirus; a young woman walked down a busy street in a city in Zhejiang Province with chains around her hands and tape on her mouth while holding up a piece of blank paper. In Beijing, *The Wall Street Journal* reported, a majority of the more than twenty detained protestors were women. Young women dominated the White Paper gathering on Hong Kong's Shanghai Street. Even the cops who arrived on scene were shocked. *Wah, dou hai nu zai,* an officer was captured on video saying in Cantonese. "Wow, they are all girls."

Feng Yuan, the feminist activist and Lü's former colleague at *China Women's News,* suggested a few likely reasons for this. First, Chinese women suffered disproportionately during the pandemic and from Covid controls, such as the effects of job loss, economic deprivation, and anger over the high-profile cases of violence against women. But also, years of exposure to feminist activism, especially through the #MeToo movement, taught them to connect with one another, harness this collective anger, and channel it into action. "When so much of society has become atomized, the feminist movement remained resilient and gave young women the spiritual oxygen to speak out," Feng told me.

Just because people went underground, turned inward, or went overseas did not mean they were submissive. Silence did not necessarily mean obedience, apathy, or amnesia. "There is no shame in the fact that everyone has fear in their hearts, some lesson of a past repression. Yet there is still space in people's hearts that authority cannot get to, even if people outwardly submit, silence themselves," Lü wrote. "So when you do decide to speak out, trust that there are people who are silent and listening. And that eventually, you will hear an echo."

Epilogue

Writing this book was a race against disappearance. I clicked on broken links and returned to websites that I'd visited before only to find them vanished. Public records I'd relied on heavily in my research—news articles on the Wenzhou train crash, *Feminist Voices'* Weibo posts, an entire archive of Danlan's early blogs—dissipated into the ether. I began saving sites through the Wayback Machine, a digital archive tool created by a California-based nonprofit. Still, I often arrived too late, left with nothing but a blank page and that dreaded error message *404 not found.* When I plugged Lü Pin's name into Baidu's search engine for the date range of 1995 to 2005, the first decade of the Chinese internet, it yielded no relevant results. Nor did Ma Baoli's or Chen Qiufan's. Kafe Hu's listed a page of posts about coffeepots.

The Chinese internet is shrinking. In 2024, He Jiayan, a Chinese blogger, brought this to public attention in a WeChat post. He had discovered that if you enter the keywords "Jack Ma" into Baidu for a date range before 2005, the search yields no results, nothing on one of the biggest celebrities in recent Chinese history. It isn't just Ma; a search for Xiaomi founder Lei Jun yields nothing, and one for Tencent's Pony Ma yields three entries. In fact, almost all content from major internet portals during the first decade of the Chinese internet is gone. In 2017, there were 5.3 million websites in China; in 2023, that number decreased by a third to 3.9 million. The number of Chinese-language websites was half that of Italian-language sites and a quarter of those in Japanese. "It seems a monster is devouring web pages along the timeline of history, from the past to the present, taking small bites, then big bites, swallowing all online content in increments," He Jiayan wrote. Shortly after, his essay also disappeared.

In some ways, this trend was shaped by forces not unique to China—the rise of paywalls and the limiting of search engine access, the cost of storage and the subsuming of smaller platforms by large social media companies. But the shrinking of the Chinese internet stands out. Frequent online crackdowns have expunged politically sensitive content from the Chinese web. A large bureaucratic machine of moderators works alongside algorithms to erase an ever-growing list of censored keywords, from social trends (#MeToo, Rice Bunny) to news events ("Henan Floods," "Occupy Central") to global cultural content ("Chloe Zhao," "South Park"). Companies proactively self-censor to remove risks that might implicate them in the future. Netizens avoid detection by coming up with increasingly obscure euphemisms, but once the secret words are popularized, they, too, are banned and subtler forms are devised, "the literature becoming increasingly more obscure, eventually losing all traces of life," as the Polish novelist Tadeusz Konwicki said in the 1980s of writers who skirted the Soviet censor.

He Jiayan compared the collapse of the Chinese internet to a scene in *The Three-Body Problem*. An advanced alien civilization eradicates intelligent life in a solar system, flattening it to a two-dimensional plane—resembling Van Gogh's *Starry Night*. "If you can still see early information on the Chinese internet now," he wrote, "it is the last ray of the setting sun."

The contraction of the Chinese web reflected a broader contraction of Chinese society as a whole. Even after Covid policies were dismantled, economic growth did not rebound as expected but slowed to around 5 percent, nearly the slowest since the beginning of economic reforms. Youth unemployment soared to over 20 percent. Even the population shrunk: faced with bleak future prospects, many young people decided to forgo parenthood altogether. In 2023, the national birth rate dropped to its lowest since the People's Republic of China was first founded more than a half-century ago. By the end of the year, Chinese netizens began to refer to the current era as "the garbage time" of history, borrowing a sports term that describes the sluggish period at the end of a match when players run out the clock before an inevitable defeat.

Faced with a stagnant economy and a declining population, the Party has chosen to continue turning inward and tightening control. Scholars, faced with restrictions on attending foreign conferences, are increasingly isolated from the international community. Foreign businesses, spooked by arbitrary raids, are leaving the country in droves. Artists, wary of provoking authorities, choose to say nothing at all. In Beijing, the physical world, like the online realm, was marked by disappearance: Bookstores and clubs I once frequented have closed, close friends I once shared a neighborhood with have emigrated, NGOs whose work I once followed have shuttered. After fifteen years as a crucial hub for China's queer communities, the Beijing LGBT Center announced that they were shutting down, citing "forces outside their control." China had once again entered a closing cycle, but I saw no signs of reversal.

When I visited Ma Baoli in the fall of 2023, I found him doing what Chinese entrepreneurs did best: adapting to the times and starting over again. After he left Blued and lifted himself out of a depressive lull, he launched a new company—much smaller and more discreet. He reunited his former team, many left jobless and adrift after Ma's departure from Blued. He proposed to them: Why don't we start something new?

He had signed a noncompete clause with Blued's new owners, barring him from working on LGBTQ-related ventures for two years. So he opted for another business model: livestream e-commerce, where products are sold in real time via live video, which became a booming trend in China during the pandemic. As the economy declined, livestream sales had become one of the go-to paths for people hoping to make a quick buck. Ma's team rented out a small office, using one room as an ad-hoc recording studio, decked out with a green screen and floor lights. Five hours a day, Ma livestreamed on Douyin, selling items ranging from North Face fleeces to cup noodles, targeting an audience composed mostly of gay men and Blued users who had missed him and wanted to hang out online.

"Sorry it's kind of messy and embarrassing," Ma apologized as he led me through the new space, gesturing at the portable clothing racks and cardboard boxes strewn across the floor. I understood his embarrassment. His world had also shrunk. When we last met, in 2021, he was leading a team of eight hundred people out of a two-story glass-walled office, preparing to list the world's largest gay dating app on NASDAQ. Two years later, he was operating from a cluttered office the size of a two-bedroom apartment with a dozen friends, devising business strategies to sell jackets and snacks. It felt like time travel to two decades ago, except now they were world-weary middle-aged men, not wide-eyed twenty-somethings. A sign at the office entrance bore the company's new name: Blued Bros. "Because we're starting again with the same band of brothers we began with," Ma explained. Even his first collaborator, Shen Wenjie, who angrily left the company in 2022, vowing never to return, rejoined the team after spending a year studying Daoist texts in the mountains.

In an atomized society, where it's easy to simply withdraw and isolate oneself, the crucial challenge was to do just the opposite: to reach out, reconnect, and rebuild community. "I couldn't just abandon my friends to the tides of the era," Ma said. The new company was a way to bring his team back together, so they could heal together instead of apart, he told me.

Still, this was a temporary project, and he had bigger ambitions. When the noncompete agreement expired, he wanted to create a new app for the younger generation of queer people in China. After all, they were more out, more accepting, and more affirming of one another than their predecessors; they would have more sophisticated needs than a dating app. The new company's Chinese name reflected this forward-looking ethos: Qingchuyulan, or "Blue Comes from

Indigo," a proverb that describes how one generation surpasses the next in a state of endless evolution. "The story of Blued has come to an end," Ma said. "But my story is not over."

.   .   .

By the time I spoke with Ma in fall 2023, I no longer lived in Beijing. My departure had been unintentional and drawn out. At the peak of the pandemic lockdowns, I took a short trip home to Hong Kong for the Lunar New Year, which turned into a longer break, and then a yearlong hiatus. As with so many of my friends who left during this period, the decision was based on multiple factors: pragmatism (spending time with family and friends outside of China was impossible, given the endless uncertainty of quarantines and lockdowns), love (my partner was leaving the country for a new job), and fear.

After five years of living and working in Beijing, two of those during a global pandemic, anxiety had seeped into my everyday life. For a long time, this anxiety served as a welcome protection mechanism. It taught me when to hold my tongue and when to speak, how to approach certain topics in public conversation and steer away from others, whether to share or delete a post, trust a stranger or remain at a distance.

This self-censorship could only be intuitive, hazily delineated. After all, I had no guidebook of banned phrases or forbidden actions. Questions of risk were calculated in the recesses of each private mind. Real punishments dictated those calculations: the loss of a job, interrogation, detention, separation from loved ones. However, most censorship did not directly involve such punishments but, rather, a fear of them, as the scholar Perry Link wrote in a 2002 essay published in *The New York Review of Books*. By "fear," he did not mean "a clear and present sense of panic" but "a dull, well-entrenched leeriness that people . . . eventually accept as part of their natural landscape." He compared the threat, at once real and imagined, to a "giant anaconda coiled in an overhead chandelier." "Normally, the great snake doesn't move. It doesn't have to.

It feels no need to be clear about its prohibitions. Its constant silent message is 'You yourself decide,'" Link wrote. "After which, more often than not, everyone in its shadow makes his or her large and small adjustments—all quite 'naturally.'"

When I first arrived in Beijing, in 2017, the anaconda seemed to go for the boldest, most prominent voices: entrepreneurs, dissidents, activists. I read about their arrests in news headlines. But before long, the anaconda started coming for people I knew—first acquaintances, friends of friends, then friends themselves. I'd hear about them via word of mouth. Healthy caution morphed into hypervigilance. The checking and double-checking, evaluating and equivocating, devolved into an obsessive-compulsive disorder. Anxiety transformed from protection into pathology, and I was afraid that it would distort my ability to think clearly and independently. It was time to go.

I decided to stay in Hong Kong. Despite the rapid erosion of the city's freedoms in recent years, there was more space to dance there. While the Chinese web was tightly controlled and surveilled within the Firewall, Hong Kong still had a relatively free and open internet, where all websites could be accessed without the need of a VPN. While all the oxygen had been sucked out of Chinese civil society, Hong Kong still had pockets of fresh air: independent galleries exhibiting subtly provocative art, festivals celebrating the queer community, feminist workshops in bookstores.

I took on a job as the China editor of *Rest of World*, an international tech publication. Outside the country, as the influence of the Chinese internet expanded beyond its borders, I realized that the dance was only just beginning. Hawkish tech moguls and regulators called for AI labs to race against China to save democracy, while others pushed to engage with the country on AI safety to protect the future of humanity. In January 2025, when Chinese AI start-up DeepSeek shocked the world with its new R1 model—a development dubbed an "AI Sputnik moment" for matching the performance of OpenAI's top model at a much lower cost—some voices called for the United States and China to work together, but many more urged America to curtail China at all costs, dominate, and win. News headlines revolved around not our shared humanity but the hardware—the chip export controls and rival GPU clusters—that fractured the web into digital fortresses vying for dominance. But for all the rhetoric of "decoupling" and "cyber sovereignty," in today's interconnected world, working with China remains imperative in challenges that implicate us all, from pandemic preparedness to climate change. For better or worse, the continuation of this particular dance has become crucial to the planet's survival.

Stanley was keenly aware of this challenge. In 2023, he turned his attention to the climate crisis. He wrote a children's book about a boy who travels in time to 2060, the year by which China had pledged to go carbon neutral. He also started working on a dystopian novel set on an "eco-friendly" artificial island built by a tech giant that greenwashes its own image to exploit the indigenous ecosystem. At a moment when most global issues felt polarized and intractable, Stanley saw himself as a connector, he told me, looking for stories to encourage China and the world to work together instead of pushing them further apart.

He had never planned on leaving China but had spent the past two years on the road, living out of a suitcase. He left Shanghai for Los Angeles in February 2022, days before the lockdown, for a three-month artist's residency at the Southern California Institute of Architecture. As Shanghai struggled under lockdown, he chose not to return. Instead, he drifted to Europe for another residency, in Lavigny, a small Swiss village. There, he lived with other writers from around the world, including a Russian journalist seeking asylum in Berlin after persecution for her coverage of the Ukraine war and a Kurdish novelist who fled to Denmark in the nineties yet still received death threats for criticizing Islam. Like Stanley, they were uprooted from their homelands. But while they were political dissidents, permanently banished, Stanley was not in exile but a wandering nomad. He was still a dancer, tiptoeing between the cracks of multiple worlds, celebrated abroad and at home.

After Covid restrictions lifted, he briefly returned to China to bring Paxlovid to his parents before resuming his travels. In 2023, he went to Hawaii to research his novel, to the Caribbean to wait for his US visa, and then to New Haven, where he spent half a year as a research scholar at Yale. He circled the globe four times in 2023 alone, his journeys including Dubai for the COP 28 UN Climate Change Conference, Seoul for the Asia 21 Next Generation Fellows Summit, and Paris for the Paris Peace Forum. Having been nomadic for so long, he wasn't sure whether he'd return to live in China. Eventually, he would need to go home to care for his aging parents. He was an only child and their sole caretaker, as was common for his generation; who would look after them if he left the country for good? "As long as my parents are alive," Stanley said, quoting Confucius's *Analects,* "I cannot wander too far from home."

Stanley is but one of many Chinese nationals dispersed across all corners of the globe, from Chiang Mai to London to Ecuador, in a state of transient uncertainty, wondering if and when they would return. In China, authorities have restricted outbound travel through exit bans and by confiscating the passports of civil servants. Outside the country, governments around the world have tightened visa policies for Chinese nationals; Chinese students traveling to the United States are increasingly turned away at the border and face a climate of heightened fear and suspicion. Lived experience and human connection to China is perceived no longer as an asset but as a liability; many of my Chinese and non-Chinese friends have been turned down for jobs abroad because they lived in China previously or because they have a Chinese partner.

As an editor, I encountered many like-minded bridge builders and connectors in the Chinese diaspora and hoped to bring their voices to light: Tech workers who organized against Zhonguancun and Silicon Valley companies alike. #MiTu activists who drew and shared inspiration with #MeToo movements around the world. Ambitious, idealistic journalists forced to waltz through a minefield of risks in order to do the thankless yet crucial job of covering the country they once called their own. In a world of hardened walls and borders, this was perhaps the most difficult dance of all: figuring out where in the world they could call home.

. . .

When I spoke with Lü Pin on the phone in September 2023, she hadn't been back to China in more than eight years. She was starting her fourth year at Rutgers. She was noticeably more upbeat than the last time we'd spoken: energized and busy auditing classes, studying for exams, and serving as a TA for a class on American Law and Policy, a subject she knew nothing about but chose in order to challenge herself. She'd started researching her dissertation on the relationship between state repression and the feminist movement in China. She loved learning. "I've realized that when authorities have stripped everything from me, the one thing that they cannot take away is the knowledge that I've learned and generated," she told me. If one of the greatest threats of authoritarianism was its ability to make people dumb and thoughtlessly conforming, Lü believed that the most crucial place of resistance was one's own mind.

When I asked her if she was working on anything in China, her response was so vague that we both laughed. She had already assessed, in her head and in her heart, what she could and could not say, whom she needed to shield and protect. "I guess I can say that I am in touch with my friends in China every single day, even though some I haven't seen in years," she said. "They are working in very difficult conditions, without support. But they are improving, growing, and getting better at what they do, day by day."

A month later, I received a message on Signal from an unknown number. I often used Signal to conduct interviews with sources. But this time, the sender reached out because she wanted to interview me, and in person. She introduced herself as a feminist worker in China, writing an article on how journalists cover Chinese feminist issues from abroad. In a low-trust society, this was how common sense was nurtured: through encrypted messages, credible mutual acquaintances, an in-person meeting. We even exchanged pseudonyms: To her readers, I would be known by the name of a character from *One Hundred Years of Solitude*. To mine, she asked to be called Susan.

When we met for the first time, at a coworking space in Hong Kong, where she was visiting for the weekend, Susan arrived with her laptop in a tote bag, hair cut above her shoulder, wearing a simple cotton dress. She was soft-spoken and self-assured. We introduced ourselves, discussed our work and its challenges, and discovered several mutual friends. When we met again, at a café in Beijing's Andingmen neighborhood, we exchanged stories of our upbringings, our worldviews, and our journeys. She explained her tattoos: an iron chain on her right forearm, a cartoon bunny on her left. ("Today, I say it's for the iron-chained woman and the MeToo bunny, but I got them way before both," she said, laughing.) The words "404 not found" adorned the nape of her neck.

Susan was twenty-seven years old, a year younger than me. She grew up in Jiangsu Province, raised by her single mother and her grandmother after her father's death when she was ten. Although she was a quiet and diligent student, she dropped out of high school and spent a year working odd jobs, first at a beauty salon, then inspecting Nokia phones at a factory. During this time, she discovered feminism through the *Feminist Voices* Weibo account and volunteered handing out stickers raising awareness of sexual harassment during International Women's Day. She also realized that she was gay, became involved in local lesbian groups, and came out to her grandmother. In 2016, she moved to Shenzhen to take a job with a women's labor NGO, which she loved, and stayed for six years until it was forced to close, in 2021.

Since then, she has worked as what she called a "freelance worker," a deliberately ambiguous title that kept her unaffiliated and avoided unwanted attention. Although she found her job meaningful, she spoke about it vaguely, careful not to reveal details: what she works on, who she works with, how she is funded. All she could say on the record was that she worked with a small team on various community projects. This involved drafting blog posts, organizing discussions on feminism, connecting women with grassroots lawyers for legal issues like labor rights and sexual harassment.

"My work can often feel isolating," Susan said. She couldn't explicitly discuss her work with those she loved and trusted, including her family, who thought her job was dubious and unofficial. Each year during the Spring Festival, her grandmother would ask two questions: first, whether she was working on anything risky, and second, if she had found a boy to marry. Each time, Susan gave the same reply: No, don't worry, and no, because she was a lesbian. "We go through this ritual once a year," she told me.

Her work could feel at once uncertain and high-stakes, and like many of her feminist friends, she found ways to cope with the stress. One friend joined a local soccer team; another raised cats. Some have gone to therapy, but it was expensive. Susan, a self-declared introvert, decompresses by playing *Baldur's Gate*, a role-playing video game series set in the *Dungeons & Dragons* universe. Most important, they turned to each other, not only for practical advice but also for emotional support, meeting once a week to watch a film or eat hot pot, to stay connected and feel less alone.

Some of Susan's friends started discussing plans to go abroad—to "run." Many prominent feminist activists "ran" a while ago. Susan understood the appeal of emigration. A few months before we met, she visited New York for the first time, to reconnect with friends who had moved abroad. She visited an aunt who emigrated to the United States twelve years before and now lived in Queens.

New York was a breath of fresh air. During her visit, Susan attended a sold-out stand-up comedy show organized by Chinese-diaspora feminists. In a packed Midtown Manhattan basement bar, she glimpsed what a free and vibrant Chinese society might look like in an alternative world. On a stage in front of an audience of two hundred people, performers parodied Chinese state television, poked fun at Party leaders, and shared deeply personal stories about everything from their coming-out journeys to police detentions—words she would have only dared to whisper in private conversations back home.

But for now, Susan had no plans to leave China. In New York, she encountered many people who seemed incredulous about her decision. They believed that her work back home was a thankless self-sacrifice. "How have you not gone overseas yet?" they asked. This question annoyed her. First, going overseas was expensive. Those who "ran" often had resources and privileges—visas, education, finances—that she did not.

But most important, she disagreed with the assumption that her work was a form of brave self-sacrifice. In New York, she noticed that once her fellow feminists went abroad, they were often reduced by others into one of two simplistic identities: either opponent or victim of a totalitarian state. But she did not see herself as either. She saw her work not as sacrifice but as a source of strength, community, and purpose. Leaving China would cut her off from this work, from the local, grassroots networks that she dedicated most of her life to keeping alive—groundfire, smoldering below the surface, waiting for the right moment to spark.

"People outside China are more pessimistic," she said. "They think there is no more space left."

I asked if she still thought there was space left.

"Yes, of course," she replied without hesitation. "And I still have work to do."

Acknowledgments

This book would not have possible without the generosity of Ma Baoli, Chen Qiufan, Kafe Hu, Lü Pin, Liu Lipeng, and the many more individuals I met in China who have shared their experiences and insights with me. I am deeply grateful to them for entrusting me with their stories.

Emily Cunningham, my brilliant editor, was essential to shepherding this book into existence. Your dedication and care, your insightful edits, and your confidence in my vision, even when my own confidence was waning, carried me from the beginning to the finish line. Having the chance to work with you has been a true gift. I am also grateful to the excellent team at Knopf, including Tiara Sharma, Linda Huang, Andrea Monagle, and Candice Gianetti, who helped improve the manuscript and prepare it for publication. Many thanks to Wufei Yu for his meticulous and thorough fact-checking of the book.

Elias Altman, my agent, believed in this book when it was still a one-page blurb, brought its ideas to life, and found it a home. Thank you for being the best ally that I could ask for, and thanks to the team at the Massie McQuilkin & Altman Agency for supporting me through the whole process.

I started my career writing about China at the Associated Press, thanks to the support of the Overseas Press Club Foundation and to Gillian Wong, who guided me through my first job in journalism. My understanding of the Chinese internet was later enriched by my role as an editor at *Rest of World*, where I had the privilege of working with many talented colleagues, especially the stellar China reporters Viola Zhou and

Caiwei Chen. I'm grateful to them for all they have taught me, and to Anup Kaphle, Michael Zelenko, and Ravi Hiranand for bringing me onto the team.

My career as a freelance writer was made possible by several exceptional editors, including Rachel Poser at *Harper's Magazine,* Willy Staley at *The New York Times Magazine,* Michael Agger at *The New Yorker,* Jon Eilenberg at *WIRED,* Jessica Loudis and Sarah Hilton at *Rest of World,* Ratik Asokan and Max Nelson at *The New York Review of Books,* and Jennifer Gersten at *Guernica.* My writing was supported by the generosity of the Matthew Power Literary Reporting Award, as well as the New America Fellows Program, thanks to Awista Ayub and Sarah Baline. The Tarbell Center for AI Journalism, thanks to Cillian Crosson and Shakeel Hashim, provided me a professional home as I finished the book and focused my attention on the future of China and AI.

Fred Strebeigh, who has been an invaluable mentor ever since I visited his office hours during my sophomore year of college, taught me how to make a life out of writing narrative nonfiction. I am indebted to Fred for giving crucial feedback on the manuscript when I was feeling stuck and for connecting me with Sarah Esther Maslin, whose camaraderie sustained me as we embarked on our book-writing journeys together. We were lucky to meet Colleen Kinder, Anna Vodicka, and the wonderful group they brought together through the Nest, who showed me the power of writing in community. Many thanks to Deborah Davis, for her mentorship and for showing me what a career centered around meaningful inquiry into Chinese society could look like. Richard Deming inspired me to put my whole heart into grappling with a big idea and distilling it into words.

I am grateful to friends who offered feedback on the manuscript at various stages of the process. Kyle Hutzler's wise counsel and advice were essential, as they have always been over the past decade. Daniel Huang shared both moral support and his keen writer's eye. Kaitlin Chan helped me navigate not just the work of making art but also sustaining the life around it. Darius Longarino's expertise on queer life in China was indispensable, as was Feng Yuan's insights on the feminist movement. Fan Wenxin gave an incisive read for accuracy.

Krish Raghav and Tianyu Fang not only shared vital feedback on the draft, but they were also two of the several visionary minds behind Chaoyang Trap—a group chat, an experimental newsletter, a vibrant crew—

which energized me during my years in China and beyond. I'm grateful for the laughter and friendship shared by its members, especially Jaime Chu and Yan Cong.

I was inspired by the conversations and insights of fellow journalists covering China and its internet, both on the ground and from afar, especially from Mengwen Cao, Amy Cheng, Vincent Chow, Emily Feng, Zhaoyin Feng, Karen Hao, Mary Hui, Dake Kang, Tony Lin, Shen Lu, Louise Matsakis, Isabelle Qian, Matt Sheehan, Christian Shepherd, Alice Su, Meaghan Tobin, Afra Wang, Vivian Wang, Erin Wong, Sarah Wu, Xifan Yang, and Zeyi Yang.

Throughout the process of writing this book, I relied on the guidance and encouragement of many people. Big thanks to Jonathan Blitzer, Mayan Braude, Yanci Bukovec and Julia Plueckebaum, Stephanie Cheng, Tien Chong, Yifu Dong, Alexandra Esnouf, Jonathan Esty, Claire Goldsmith, Brian Goldstone, Rajiv Golla, Georgia Gray, Sophie Haigney, Peter Hamilton, Emmet Hedin, Alfonso Morgan Herrero, Casey Herrick, Lewis Ho, Sarah Holder, Jasmine Horsey, Sean Hyatt, Megan Jenkins, Stefani Kuo, Man-Chun Kung, Fil Lekkas, Vera Lummis, Cassidy McDonald, Shawn Moore, Fangdi Pan, Bohan Phoenix, David Rossler, Lucas Sin, Katie Stewart, Joyce Tang, Vincent Tang, Lucas Tse, and Emily Tsui.

I am deeply grateful for the unwavering support of my family: Thank you, Anna and Angela, for bringing light and joy into our lives; Wei and Meiz, for your good humor and lifelong friendship. Mom and Dad, thank you for your unconditional love, which has been everything to me. Miro, your wisdom, care, and love sustained me the whole way. Thank you for holding my hand and walking alongside me through every step of this journey.

Notes on Sources

This book is a result of eight years of writing and reporting about China and fifteen years engaging with its central questions. Crucial to the writing of it were the interviews that I conducted with its main subjects. I spent hours interviewing Ma Baoli, Lü Pin, Kafe Hu, Chen Qiufan (Stanley Chan), and Eric Liu about their lives over the course of several years. When possible, I corroborated their stories with social media posts, other people's accounts, and news stories.

In researching and writing the book, I consulted both Chinese and foreign scholarship and news sources. For Chinese sources, I relied especially on Caixin, *Caijing, Initium Media, The Paper, 36Kr,* and *Sixth Tone.* For English-language sources, I turned to *The New York Times, The Wall Street Journal, WIRED, Rest of World, The Guardian, The Wire China, The New Yorker,* and the Associated Press. My research drew from many Chinese social media platforms, including WeChat, Weibo, Douban, Douyin, Kuaishou, Toutiao, Xiaohongshu, Zhihu, and Blued. For translations and analyses of the Chinese internet, I depended on *China Digital Times, The China Project,* the *China Media Project,* and *Reading the China Dream.*

My experience in writing this book was informed by my work in China, as the China editor at the international tech news publication *Rest of World* in 2023, as an editor of the newsletter *Chaoyang Trap* from 2021 to 2022, as a reporting fellow at the Associated Press in 2017, and as an intern at the state-run English-language newspaper *China Daily* in 2010.

INTRODUCTION

I first came across the comparison of TikTok and Douyin as "twins separated at birth" in Chris Stokel-Walker, *TikTok Boom: China's Dynamite App and the Superpower Race for Social Media* (Canbury Press, 2021). Stokel-Walker's comparison came from D. Bondy Valdovinos Kaye, Xu Chen, and Jing Zeng, "The Co-Evolution of Two Chinese Mobile Short Video Apps: Parallel Platformization of Douyin and TikTok," *Mobile Media & Communication* 9, no. 2 (May 2021): 229–53.

For background on TikTok refugees on Xiaohongshu, I consulted a range of sources, especially Claire Fu and Meaghan Tobin, " 'Red Note,' a Chinese App, Is Dominating Downloads, Thanks to TikTok Users," *New York Times,* January 14, 2025, https://www.nytimes.com/2025/01/14/business/tiktok-rednote-xiaohongshu-app.html; Kinling Lo and Viola Zhou, "U.S. TikTokers Flock to Xiaohongshu, Baffling and Bonding with Chinese Users," *Rest of World,* January 14, 2025, https://restofworld.org/2025/tiktok-refugees-rednote-xiaohongshu-chinese-users/; and Lilian Kong and Shiqi Lin, " 'Hello My Chinese Spy, Take My Data': Welcome to the Playground of the Digital Cold War," *positions politics,* January 31, 2025, https://positionspolitics.org/lilian-kong-and-shiqi-lin-hello-my-chinese-spy-take-my-data-welcome-to-the-playground-of-the-digital-cold-war/.

For the promise of China's early internet and the image of the Chinese internet as "Rivers and Lakes," see Guobin Yang, *The Power of the Internet in China: Citizen Activism Online* (Columbia University Press, 2009). To understand the changing narrative of the Chinese internet, I consulted "Code Red," *Logic Magazine,* May 1, 2019, https://logicmag.io/china/code-red/; and Graham Webster, "A Brief History of the Chinese Internet," *Logic(s),* May 1, 2019, https://logicmag.io/china/a-brief-history-of-the-chinese-internet/.

John Perry Barlow popularized the term "electronic frontier" in "Crime and Puzzlement," Electronic Frontier Foundation, June 8, 1990, https://www.eff.org/pages/crime-and-puzzlement; and "A Declaration of the Independence of Cyberspace," Electronic Frontier Foundation, February 8, 1996, https://www.eff.org/cyberspace-independence.

Bill Clinton's quote comparing control of the Chinese internet to "nailing Jell-O to the wall" comes from "Full Text of Clinton's Speech on China Trade Bill," Institute for Agriculture and Trade Policy, March 9, 2000, https://www.iatp.org/sites/default/files/Full_Text_of_Clintons_Speech_on_China_Trade_Bi.htm.

The description of Weibo as a "maggot-infested pile of shit" comes from Guo

Yuhua, "Farewell Sina Weibo," trans. David Ownby, *Reading the China Dream,* June 8, 2020, https://www.readingthechinadream.com/guo-yuhua-farewell -sina-weibo.html. An archive of original posts can be found here: https:// drive.google.com/file/d/1VHAUB-u4lPNekJqfL3hNzQBSjbG4ptEQ/view.

The description of Twitter as a "throbbing networked intelligence" comes from David Carr, "Why Twitter Will Endure," *New York Times,* January 1, 2010, https://www.nytimes.com/2010/01/03/weekinreview/03carr.html.

For background on the term "boundary ball," see Rachel E. Stern and Kevin J. O'Brien, "Politics at the Boundary: Mixed Signals and the Chinese State," *Modern China* 38, no. 2 (March 2012): 174–98.

For background on the term "dance in shackles," see Susan L. Shirk, ed., "Changing Media, Changing China," in *Changing Media, Changing China* (Oxford University Press, 2010). Liu's quote on "invisible shackles" is published in Liu Cixin, *The Three-Body Problem,* trans. Ken Liu (Tor Books, 2014), p. 394. The viral post about Google's "dance" is archived here: https:// web.archive.org/web/20100118081600/http://www.donews.com/Content /201001/b264cb9d3fa44b5a93c468c1c6efcd66.shtm. For a shortened translation, see Evan Osnos, "After Google: 'Dance with Shackles On,'" *New Yorker,* January 19, 2010, https://www.newyorker.com/news/evan-osnos/after -google-dance-with-shackles-on.

For discussions of the *fang-shou* cycle of liberalization and repression, I consulted Richard Baum, *Burying Mao: Chinese Politics in the Age of Deng Xiaoping* (Princeton University Press, 2018).

The phrase "living in truth" comes from Václav Havel's essay "The Power of the Powerless," trans. Paul Wilson, in John Keane, ed., *The Power of the Powerless: Citizens Against the State in Central-Eastern Europe* (Routledge, 2016).

My account of my experiences attending the Hong Kong June 4th vigil draws from my article "Between Memory and Forgetting," *The Baffler,* June 17, 2020, https://thebaffler.com/latest/between-memory-and-forgetting -liu. The documentary that I watched on the Tiananmen Square protests was *The Gate of Heavenly Peace,* directed by Richard Gordon and Carma Hinton (1995).

For evidence of the Chinese internet's influence outside China, I turned to the "China Outside China" section of *Rest of World*'s website, https:// restofworld.org/series/china-outside-china/. For Xiaohongshu's influence abroad, I referred to Krish Raghav, Yan Cong, and Carwyn Morris, "How China's Hottest Social Media App Turned Düsseldorf into a Foodie Destination," *Rest of World,* April 4, 2023, https://restofworld.org/2023/xiaohongshu

-users-make-dusseldorf-destination/; and Zhaoyin Feng, "Xiaohongshu Has Revolutionized Chinese Tourism in Southeast Asia," *Rest of World*, October 3, 2024, https://restofworld.org/2024/xiaohongshu-southeast-asia-tourism.

Walter Russell Mead's article "China Is the Real Sick Man of Asia," published on February 3, 2020, can be found in *The Wall Street Journal*, https://www.wsj.com/articles/china-is-the-real-sick-man-of-asia-11580773677.

Mike Masnick's quote first appeared in "TikTok Users Gleefully Embrace Even More Chinese App to Spite US TikTok Ban," *Techdirt*, January 14, 2025, https://www.techdirt.com/2025/01/14/tiktok-users-gleefully-embrace-even-more-chinese-app-to-spite-us-tiktok-ban.

CHAPTER 1: Coming Out

I am grateful to Ma Baoli for sharing his recollections of his early life as a young gay man in Qinhuangdao, his experiences at the police academy and police bureau, and his decision to create the gay website Danlan. Insights from my previous writing on Ma's journey, for "How a Dating App Helped a Generation of Chinese Come Out of the Closet," *New York Times Magazine*, March 5, 2020, https://www.nytimes.com/2020/03/05/magazine/blued-china-gay-dating-app.html, were integral to shaping this narrative.

For a broader context on the development of queer life in China, I drew from two books by Hongwei Bao: *Queer China: Lesbian and Gay Literature and Visual Culture under Postsocialism* (Routledge, Taylor & Francis Group, 2020) and *Queer Comrades: Gay Identity and* Tongzhi *Activism in Postsocialist China* (Copenhagen: NIAS Press, 2018).

To understand the influence of economic reforms on sex and love in China, I read with Lisa Rofel, *Desiring China: Experiments in Neoliberalism, Sexuality, and Public Culture* (Duke University Press, 2007); and Richard Burger, *Behind the Red Door: Sex in China* (Hong Kong: Earnshaw Books, 2012). Lin Yinhe's statistics on premarital sex in China can be found in an interview of her in *China Daily*, "Expert: Sexual Revolution in Place in China," November 8, 2005.

For historical perspectives on queer China before Deng's economic reforms, I consulted Jing Wu, "From 'Long Yang' to 'Du Shi' to Tongzhi: Homosexuality in China," *Journal of Gay & Lesbian Psychotherapy* 7, no. 1–2 (February 2003): 117–43.

Accounts of queer communities and nightlife in the 1990s were informed by my interviews with Susie Jolly, as well as by "Queer Culture in 1990s Beijing: An Interview with Susie Jolly," Chinese Independent Film Archive, Octo-

ber 27, 2020, https://www.chinaindiefilm.org/queer-culture-in-1990s-beijing
-an-interview-with-susie-jolly. For other valuable perspectives, see Ting Lin
and Xuandi Wang, "Queer Memories in Beijing," *The Baffler*, September 2,
2021, https://thebaffler.com/latest/queer-memories-in-beijing-lin-wang.

To explore the influence and history of *Beijing Story*, the online novel
that inspired Ma Baoli during his time in an internet café, I consulted Bei
Tong, *Beijing Comrades*, trans. Scott E. Myers (Feminist Press, 2016). For
those interested in the film adaptation of *Beijing Story*, I recommend *Lan Yu*,
directed by Stanley Kwan (2001).

For insights into Beidaihe, I relied both on my visits to the area and
accounts from *The New York Times* and *The China Project*. The quote comparing Beidaihe to a "Chinese combination of Jersey Shore and Martha's
Vinyard" comes from Edward Wong and Jonathan Ansfield, "China's Communist Elders Take Backroom Intrigue Beachside," *New York Times*, July 21,
2012. For Deng Xiaoping's presence in Beidaihe, as well as his role in China's
Reform and Opening policy and his Southern Tour, I referred to Ezra F.
Vogel, *Deng Xiaoping and the Transformation of China* (Harvard University
Press, 2011). Deng's quote to "experiment and break a new path" can be
found in "Excerpts from Talks Given in Wuchang, Shenzhen, Zhuhai and
Shanghai (January 18 to February 21, 1992)," *The Selected Works of Deng
Xiaoping Vol. III* (People's Press, 1993), https://dengxiaopingworks.wordpress
.com/2013/03/18/excerpts-from-talks-given-in-wuchang-shenzhen-zhuhai
-and-shanghai.

My research on the Tiananmen Square protests and subsequent crackdowns primarily drew from Richard Baum, *Burying Mao: Chinese Politics in
the Age of Deng Xiaoping* (Princeton University Press, 2018), and the documentary *The Gate of Heavenly Peace*, directed by Richard Gordon and Carma
Hinton (1995).

CHAPTER 2: Speaking Out

I am indebted to Lü Pin for sharing with me accounts of her feminist awak-
ening, from her teenage years to her decision to become a freelance writer.
For detailed accounts of her early life, I also relied on "Feminism and Social
Change in China: An Interview with Lü Pin (Part One of Three)," *China
Change*, August 26, 2019, https://chinachange.org/2019/08/26/feminism
-and-social-change; and her essay 呂頻:見證中國女權二十年, 端傳媒 in
Initium Media, August 14, 2020, https://theinitium.com/article/20200814
-opinion-china-feminist-movement-20-years.

The quote from Li Xiaobo on Chinese writers comes from an interview with Liu in December 1986, translated in *Seeds of Fire: Chinese Voices of Conscience,* edited by Geremie Barmé and John Minford (Hill & Wang, 1988), p. 397.

David Ownby provided me with crucial context to understand Chinese establishment intellectuals in the 1990s. For a deeper understanding of China's intellectual landscape in the nineties, see Ownby's blog, *Reading the China Dream,* https://www.readingthechinadream.com; David Ownby, "Chinese Intellectual Ecology," *Palladium Magazine,* September 21, 2021; and Timothy Cheek, *The Intellectual in Modern Chinese History* (Cambridge University Press, 2015). To explain how Soviet intellectuals like Yuri Levada framed their regime's cycles between opening and restriction, I referred to Masha Gessen, *The Future Is History: How Totalitarianism Reclaimed Russia* (Riverhead Books, 2017).

For background on the career and ideas of Wang Huning, I referred to his *Meiguo Fandui Meiguo* 美国反对美国 (Shanghai Literature and Art Publishing House, 1991), and the English translation, *America Against America* (independently published, 1991). I also consulted analysis provided by the Center for Strategic Translation at https://www.strategictranslation.org/articles/america-against-america-2. His quote on "core values" comes from Wang's essay "The Structure of China's Changing Political Culture," translated here by David Ownby in *Reading the China Dream,* https://www.readingthechinadream.com/wang-huning-ldquothe-structure-of-chinarsquos-changing-political-culturerdquo.html. The quote from the former debate team member comes from Jeremy Page, "The Wonk with the Ear of the Chinese President Xi Jinping," *Wall Street Journal,* June 4, 2013, https://www.wsj.com/articles/SB10001424127887323728204578513422637924256. Further insights into Wang's influence on contemporary Chinese governance are drawn from N. S. Lyons, "The Triumph and Terror of Wang Huning," *Palladium Magazine*, October 11, 2021, https://www.palladiummag.com/2021/10/11/the-triumph-and-terror-of-wang-huning; and Haig Patapan and Yi Wang, "The Hidden Ruler: Wang Huning and the Making of Contemporary China," *Journal of Contemporary China* 27, no. 109 (January 2, 2018): 47–60.

I am indebted to Feng Yuan and Susie Jolly for helping me understand the significance to China's feminist awakening of the United Nations' Fourth World Conference on Women, held in Beijing in 1995. To understand the events and the historical impact of the conference, I also relied on a range of other sources, including the documentary *We Are Here,* directed by Zhao Jing and Shi Tou and produced by Wei Tingting (2015); Hongwei Bao, "'We

Are Here': The Politics of Memory in Narrating China's Queer Feminist History," *Continuum* 34, no. 4 (July 3, 2020): 514–29; and Ping-Chun Hsiung, Maria Jaschok, and Cecilia Milwertz, eds., *Chinese Women Organizing: Cadres, Feminists, Muslims, Queers* (Taylor & Francis Group, 2001).

Sebastien Veg helped me understand the rise of grassroots intellectuals in China. For an in-depth study, see his *Minjian: The Rise of China's Grassroots Intellectuals* (Columbia University Press, 2019).

For an account of the Sun Zhigang incident and the role of online public opinion, I consulted Xiao Qiang, "The Rising Tide of Internet Opinion in China," *Nieman Reports* (blog), June 15, 2004, https://niemanreports.org /the-rising-tide-of-internet-opinion-in-china; and David Bandurski, "How the Internet Has Changed China," *China Media Project,* October 25, 2010, https://chinamediaproject.org/2010/10/25/how-the-internet-has-changed -china.

For details on China's Great Firewall and early internet censorship, I relied on a range of sources, including James T. Griffiths, *The Great Firewall of China: How to Build and Control an Alternative Version of the Internet* (Zed Books, 2019); Jack L. Goldsmith and Tim Wu, *Who Controls the Internet?: Illusions of a Borderless World* (Oxford University Press, 2006); and Geremie Barmé and Sang Ye, "The Great Firewall of China," *WIRED,* June 1, 1997, https://www.wired.com/1997/06/china-3.

CHAPTER 3: Plunging into the Sea

For accounts of China's second Gay Website Conference, Danlan's early days in Qinhuangdao, and the team's move to Beijing, I am grateful to Ma Baoli, Shen Wenjie, and Yang Jiajiun for sharing their experiences with me. I also drew from Ma Baoli's public speeches and interviews.

For the history and background of Jack Ma and the founding of Alibaba, I relied on a range of sources, most crucially Duncan Clark, *Alibaba: The House That Jack Ma Built* (Ecco, 2016); and the documentary *Crocodile in the Yangtze: The Alibaba Story*, directed by Porter Erisman (2012). The quote comparing Jack Ma to Bill Gates comes from Michael Smith, *The Last Correspondent: Dispatches from the Frontline of Xi's New China* (Ultimo Press, 2021). Jack Ma's comments on "following the law" comes from a transcript of a televised interview between Ma and Kristie Lu Stout on CNN, October 26, 2005, https://edition.cnn.com/2005/TECH/10/19/spark.jack.ma /index.html. Video footage of the interview can be found in *Crocodile in the Yangtze.*

Details on the 2008 Beijing Summer Olympics were drawn from news stories published by Reuters, *The Economist,* and *The Guardian.* Ai Weiwei's quote comes from his essay "Why I'll Stay Away from the Opening Ceremony of the Olympics," *The Guardian,* August 7, 2008, https://www.theguardian.com/commentisfree/2008/aug/07/olympics2008.china. Hu Zhijun provided me with important information on the significance of the 2008 Beijing Olympics in shaping queer life in China.

For an account and analysis of the same-sex wedding staged by Common Language, I referred to Hongwei Bao, *Queer China: Lesbian and Gay Literature and Visual Culture under Postsocialism* (Routledge, Taylor & Francis Group, 2020), pp. 110–11.

On the Deng Yujiao incident, I turned to news reports, including those from sources published in *Southern Metropolis Daily,* translated by *East South West North,* http://zonaeuropa.com/200905c.brief.htm#011.

Lü Pin's experience covering the Deng Yujiao incident was detailed in her essay 呂頻:見證中國女權二十年, 端傳媒 in *Initium Media,* August 14, 2020, https://theinitium.com/article/20200814-opinion-china-feminist-movement-20-years.

Lü Pin shared with me an account of why and how she decided to found *Feminist Voices.* I also drew from "Feminism and Social Change in China: An Interview with Lü Pin (Part 2 of 3)," *China Change,* September 16, 2019, https://chinachange.org/2019/09/16/feminism-and-social-change-in-china-an-interview-with-lu-pin-part-2-of-3; and Lü Pin's essay "Finding a Voice," *Logic(s),* May 1, 2019, https://logicmag.io/china/finding-a-voice.

CHAPTER 4: American Dreams

I am thankful to Kafe Hu for sharing his story with me and showing me around his homes in Jiangyou and Chengdu. Charlie Moseley provided detailed accounts of their lives in the city, their friendship, and their musical collaborations.

For an understanding of China's musical landscape in the 1980s and 1990s, *dakou* tapes, and the rise of the *dakou* generation, I relied on a range of sources, especially Jeroen de Kloet's *China with a Cut: Globalisation, Urban Youth and Popular Music* (Amsterdam University Press, 2010), and "Popular Music and Youth in Urban China: The *Dakou* Generation," *China Quarterly* 183 (September 2005): 609–26; Nathanael Amar, "The Lives of Dakou in China: From Waste to Nostalgia," *Études chinoises* 38, no. 2 (2018): 35–60.

For a narrative account of this period, I recommend *Radiolab*'s podcast "Mixtape: Dakou," October 22, 2021, https://radiolab.org/podcast/mixtape -dakou.

Shuhong Fan, J-Fever, and Wes Chen were crucial in explaining to me the evolution of Chinese hip-hop from the late 1990s to the 2000s and what it felt like to be a hip-hop listener and musician during that era. Shuhong Fan's thorough, chronological account of "The History of Rap in China" was published on the media platform *RADII* on February 1, 2019, https:// radii.co/article/the-history-of-rap-in-china-part-1-early-roots-and-iron-mics -1993-2009.

Descriptions and impressions of Chengdu were drawn from my article "Chengdu Cool: The Rise of Sichuan's Homegrown Hip Hop," *Guernica,* August 29, 2018, https://www.guernicamag.com/chengdu-cool-the-rise-of -sichuans-homegrown-hip-hop.

Krish Raghav provided valuable insights into the atmosphere of Beijing's underground music scene in the late 2000s. Descriptions of the punk club D-22 were drawn from Anthony Kuhn, "As China Cracks Down on Cultural Fringe, Indie Rock Finds a Home in Beijing," NPR, October 18, 2015, https://www.npr.org/sections/parallels/2015/10/18/449160304/as -china-cracks-down-on-cultural-fringe-indie-rock-finds-a-home-in -beijing.

Passages on Rao Jin, the Anti-CNN movement, and the song "Don't Be Like CNN" were drawn from news sources including *China Daily* and NPR, as well as Jiang Ying's *Cyber-Nationalism in China: Challenging Western Media Portrayals of Internet Censorship in China* (University of Adelaide Press, 2012).

For background on the rise of nationalism in contemporary China, I relied on Jude D. Blanchette, *China's New Red Guards: The Return of Radicalism and the Rebirth of Mao Zedong* (Oxford University Press, 2022); Song Qiang, Huang Jisu, Song Xiaojun, Wang Xiaodong, and Liu Yang, *Unhappy China: The Great Time, Grand Vision and Our Challenges* (Jiangsu People's Publishing House, 2009); Evan Osnos, "Angry Youth," *New Yorker,* July 21, 2008, https://www.newyorker.com/magazine/2008/07/28/angry-youth; and Alec Ash, "China's New Nationalism," *Wire China,* August 8, 2021, https:// www.thewirechina.com/2021/08/08/chinas-new-nationalism.

Hank Paulson's exchange with Wang Qishan comes from his memoir, Henry M. Paulson Jr., *Dealing with China: An Insider Unmasks the New Economic Superpower* (Twelve, 2015).

CHAPTER 5: I'm Feeling Lucky

I am grateful to Chen Qiufan for sharing recollections of his childhood growing up in Shantou, his experiences as a student at Peking University, and his later work in the tech industry. Also appearing in this chapter are insights from my previous writing and reporting on Chen, published in "Sci-Fi Writer or Prophet?: The Hyperreal Life," *WIRED*, March 9, 2021, https://www.wired.com/story/science-fiction-writer-china-chen-qiufan.

I learned about the themes, characters, and style of Chen's early work from his short stories, both in the original Chinese and the English translations, including "The Fish of Lijiang" 丽江的鱼儿们, trans. Ken Liu, *Clarkesworld*, August 2011, https://clarkesworldmagazine.com/chen_08_11; "The Smog Society" 霾, trans. Ken Liu and Carmen Yiling Yan, *Lightspeed Magazine*, August 2015, https://www.lightspeedmagazine.com/fiction/the-smog-society; "The Year of the Rat" 鼠年, in Ken Liu, ed. and trans., *Invisible Planets: An Anthology of Contemporary Chinese Science Fiction in Translation* (Tor Books, 2016).

Ken Liu was also integral in sharing his early impressions of Chen, their friendship, and their literary collaborations.

For the history of Zhongguancun, I referred to Ning Ken, *Zhong Guan Village: Tales from the Heart of China's Silicon Valley*, trans. James Trapp (Hong Kong: ACA Publishing, 2019). Additional insights on the district's transformation into China's tech hub were drawn from Chang Che, "China's Innovation Renovation," *Wire China*, May 22, 2022, https://www.thewirechina .com/2022/05/22/chinas-innovation-renovation; Sarah Shafer, "The World's New Culture Meccas," *Newsweek*, September 1, 2002, https://www.newsweek .com/worlds-new-culture-meccas-144621; as well as reports from *The New York Times* and *WIRED*. To understand the influence of Alvin Toffler and futurism on the Chinese Communist Party's vision of technological progress, I consulted Julian Gewirtz, "The Futurists of Beijing: Alvin Toffler, Zhao Ziyang, and China's 'New Technological Revolution,' 1979–1991," *The Journal of Asian Studies* 78, no. 1 (2019): 115–40.

For an account of Google's presence in and departure from China, I referred to James T. Griffiths, *The Great Firewall of China: How to Build and Control an Alternative Version of the Internet* (Zed Books, 2019); Clive Thompson, "Google's China Problem (and China's Google Problem)," *New York Times Magazine*, April 23, 2006, https://www.nytimes.com/2006 /04/23/magazine/googles-china-problem-and-chinas-google-problem.html; Matt Sheehan, "How Google Took on China—and Lost," *MIT Technol-*

ogy Review, December 19, 2018, https://www.technologyreview.com/2018/12/19/138307/how-google-took-on-china-and-lost; and Evan Osnos, "After Google: 'Dance with Shackles On,'" *New Yorker,* January 2010, https://www.newyorker.com/news/evan-osnos/after-google-dance-with-shackles-on. Sergey Brin's quote comes from Jessica E. Vascellaro, "Brin Drove Google to Pull Back in China," *Wall Street Journal,* March 24, 2010, https://www.wsj.com/articles/SB10001424052748704266504575141064259998090. Eric Schmidt's quote comes from Josh Rogin, "Eric Schmidt: The Great Firewall of China Will Fall," *Foreign Policy,* July 9, 2012, https://foreignpolicy.com/2012/07/09/eric-schmidt-the-great-firewall-of-china-will-fall.

The text of Hillary Clinton's 2010 speech on internet freedom is archived on *Foreign Policy,* January 21, 2010, https://foreignpolicy.com/2010/01/21/internet-freedom.

A post by Baidu's chief product designer on Google and the need to "dance in shackles" is archived in the Wayback Machine, https://web.archive.org/web/20100118081600/http://www.donews.com/Content/201001/b264cb9d3fa44b5a93c468c1c6efcd66.shtm.

CHAPTER 6: Weibo Spring

I am indebted to Eric Liu for sharing accounts of his early life growing up in Tianjin and his experience working as a censor at Weibo.

I first learned of Liu through an article detailing his findings on Weibo censorship without giving his name: Yaqiu Wang, "The Business of Censorship: Documents Show How Weibo Filters Sensitive News in China," Committee to Protect Journalists, March 3, 2016, https://cpj.org/2016/03/the-business-of-censorship-documents-show-how-weib. His identity was later revealed in an interview: "Former Chinese Censor Calls on Social Media Users to Stand Up for Free Speech," *Radio Free Asia,* September 2, 2020, https://www.rfa.org/english/news/china/censor-09022020095239.html. My understanding of the working conditions of Weibo censors was supplemented by a Reuters report by Li Hui and Megha Rajagopalan, "At Sina Weibo's Censorship Hub, China's Little Brothers Cleanse Online Chatter," September 11, 2013, https://www.reuters.com/article/idUSDEE98A0GT.

China Digital Times was crucial in archiving and providing me with censorship directives, online slang, and news reports that informed much of this chapter. For examples of censorship directives, see https://chinadigitaltimes.net/chinese/137265.html. For examples of online slang, see https://chinadigitaltimes.net/space/China_Central_Adult_Video_(CCAV).

The original job posting for a Weibo censor position is archived at https://chinadigitaltimes.net/space/%E6%96%87%E4%BB%B6:2010%E5%B9%B4%E6%96%B0%E6%B5%AA%E5%AE%A1%E6%9F%A5%E5%91%98%E6%8B%9B%E8%81%98.jpg.

Murong Xuecun provided valuable insights into his early experiences on Weibo, his impressions of the internet in the early 2010s, and his rise to prominence as a Weibo "Big V." His acceptance speech for the People's Literature Prize Ceremony in 2010, which went undelivered there but was later given at the Hong Kong Foreign Correspondents' Club, was translated and published in *The New York Times* on November 6, 2011: https://www.nytimes.com/2011/11/06/world/asia/murong-xuecuns-acceptance-speech-for-the-2010-peoples-literature-prize.html.

Descriptions of *China Daily* draw primarily from my experience working as an intern at the paper in 2010. The article I wrote on Hong Kong literary journals is available at https://www.chinadaily.com.cn/life/2010-11/12/content_11540047.htm.

For the evolution and influence of Weibo on Chinese society, I consulted Shaohua Guo, *The Evolution of the Chinese Internet: Creative Visibility in the Digital Public* (Stanford University Press, 2020); Liz Carter, *Let 100 Voices Speak: How the Internet Is Transforming China and Changing Everything* (Bloomsbury Publishing, 2015); Jason Q. Ng, *Blocked on Weibo: What Gets Suppressed on China's Version of Twitter (and Why)* (New Press, 2013); Jian Xu, "Online Weiguan in Web 2.0 China: Historical Origins, Characteristics, Platforms, and Consequences," in Guobin Yang, ed., *China's Contested Internet* (Nias Press of the University of Copenhagen, 2015).

For background on China's censorship apparatus, I consulted PEN America's report *Forbidden Feeds: Government Controls on Social Media in China*, March 15, 2018; Margaret E. Roberts, *Censored: Distraction and Diversion Inside China's Great Firewall* (Princeton University Press, 2018); Gary King, Jennifer Pan, and Margaret E. Roberts, "How Censorship in China Allows Government Criticism but Silences Collective Expression," *American Political Science Review* 107, no. 2 (May 2013). The statistic on VPN usage came from Hal Roberts, Ethan Zuckerman, Jillian York, Robert Faris, and John Palfrey, "2010 Circumvention Tool Usage Report," Berkman Center for Internet & Society, October 2010, https://cyber.harvard.edu/sites/cyber.law.harvard.edu/files/2010_Circumvention_Tool_Usage_Report.pdf.

For an account of the Wenzhou train crash, I referred to the official investigation report published by the Ministry of Emergency Management, titled "July 23rd Yongwen Line Particularly Major Railway Traffic

Accident Investigation Report" (7·23甬温线特别重大铁路交通事故调查报告), December 28, 2011, https://www.mem.gov.cn/gk/sgcc/tbzdsgdcbg /2011/201112/t20111228_245242.shtml. I also consulted Yan Wu, "Micro-blogging as a Rapid Response News Service in Crisis Reporting: The 2011 Wenzhou Train Crash," *JOMEC Journal* 1 (June 1, 2012). *Southern Metropolis Daily*'s response to the crash is documented by Anne Henochowicz in *China Digital Times,* "Word of the Week: WTF?!," https://chinadigitaltimes.net /2012/07/word-week-wtf.

Social media responses referenced in this chapter are archived by the Wayback Machine at https://web.archive.org/web/20121103141857/https:// news.qq.com/a/20110724/000489.htm.

CHAPTER 7: Unbound

To reconstruct the Bloody Brides protest, I referred to "Feminism and Social Change in China: An Interview with Lü Pin (Part 2 of 3)," *China Change,* September 16, 2019, https://chinachange.org/2019/09/16/feminism-and -social-change-in-china-an-interview-with-lu-pin-part-2-of-3. Video footage, posted by Lü Pin on YouTube, is available here: https://www.youtube .com/watch?v=Tzz140ZjSIo.

Lü Pin, Feng Yuan, and Xiao Meili shared with me their experiences of the One Yuan Commune and the early feminist movement in 2012–2013.

I also consulted Qi Wang, "Young Feminist Activists in Present-Day China: A New Feminist Generation?," *China Perspectives* 2018/3 (September 1, 2018): 59–68; video, "Interview with Wei Tingting," University of Michigan Global Feminisms Project, May 2019; Zi, interviewer, "Li Maizi's Honest Spoken Account: 'I Have Not Committed a Crime. Feminism Is Innocent,'" *Wainao,* March 28, 2021, https://www.wainao.me/wainao-reads /li-maizis-honest-spoken-account-i-have-not-committed-crime-feminism -innocent-03282021; Eric Fish, "The Education of Detained Chinese Feminist Li Tingting," *ChinaFile,* March 16, 2015, https://www.chinafile.com /library/excerpts/education-detained-chinese-feminist-li-tingting; Lü Pin's essay 吕频:見證中國女權二十年, 端傳媒 in *Initium Media,* August 14, 2020, https://theinitium.com/article/20200814-opinion-china-feminist -movement-20-years; and Lü Pin, "Finding a Voice," *Logic(s),* May 1, 2019, https://logicmag.io/china/finding-a-voice/.

For an account of the feminist movement's broader impact in 2012, see Shen Lu, "Thwarted at Home, Can China's Feminists Rebuild a Movement Abroad?," *ChinaFile,* August 28, 2019, https://www.chinafile.com/reporting

-opinion/postcard/thwarted-home-can-chinas-feminists-rebuild-movement -abroad. Lü's thoughts on individuals needing a flag first appeared there.

For background on "Weibo feminism" and the online feminist movement, see Aviva Wei Xue and Kate Rose, *Weibo Feminism: Expression, Activism, and Social Media in China* (Bloomsbury Publishing, 2022).

Ma Baoli, Chen Zihuang, Shen Wenjie, and Yang Jiajun described for me their experiences working at Danlan's first Beijing office (2009–2012). A now-removed Sohu documentary on this period was privately provided to me by Ma Baoli. For Ma's negotiations with the government on HIV/AIDS initiatives, I relied on Shuaishuai Wang, "Living with Censorship: The Political Economy and Cultural Politics of Chinese Gay Dating Apps" (PhD diss., University of Amsterdam, 2019).

To understand the challenges faced by the Communist Party during the Hu–Wen era, I consulted Jude Howell and Jane Duckett, "Reassessing the Hu–Wen Era: A Golden Age or Lost Decade for Social Policy in China?," *China Quarterly* 237 (March 2019): 1–14. For analysis of Xi Jinping's Chinese Dream and the implications of his leadership, I relied on Elizabeth C. Economy, *The Third Revolution: Xi Jinping and the New Chinese State* (Oxford University Press, 2018).

The quote from Nicholas Kristof comes from his op-ed "Looking for a Jump-Start in China," *New York Times,* January 5, 2013, https://www .nytimes.com/2013/01/06/opinion/sunday/kristof-looking-for-a-jump-start -in-china.html.

The quote from Annie Zhang Jieping, who interviewed Chinese Party princelings about Xi's potential as a reformer, comes from Yuan Li's *Bumingbai Podcast* 不明白播客, EP-019 江雪/张洁平:中国媒体过去10年发生了什么?, October 2, 2022, https://www.bumingbai.net/2022/10/ep-019-jiang -xue-zhang-jieping.

CHAPTER 8: Going Public

Ma Baoli, Shen Wenjie, Calvin Liu, and other Blued employees and users shared their experiences of working at and using Blued, as well as of the company's transformation into China's largest gay dating app. Descriptions of Blued's office are based on my own visits and reporting in "How a Dating App Helped a Generation of Chinese Come Out of the Closet," *New York Times Magazine,* March 5, 2020, https://www.nytimes.com/2020/03/05 /magazine/blued-china-gay-dating-app.html.

I am grateful to Darius Longarino for his insights into LGBTQ rights and activism in China. Dan Zhou and Shuaishuai Wang also provided crucial perspectives on LGBTQ legal activism. On public attitudes toward LGBTQ people in China in the mid-2010s, see *Being LGBTI in China: A National Survey on Social Attitudes Towards Sexual Orientation, Gender Identity and Gender Expression* (United Nations Development Programme, 2016), https://www.undp.org/china/publications/being-lgbti-china.

David Chao shared with me his decision to invest in Blued, and Charles Fournier explained its international expansion. Ma Baoli's remarks about regretting the acquisition of Grindr are quoted in Shuaishuai Wang, *Living with Censorship: The Political Economy and Cultural Politics of Chinese Gay Dating Apps* (PhD diss., University of Amsterdam, 2019).

Descriptions of the film *American Dreams in China* 中国合伙人, directed by Peter Chan (2013), are drawn from my analysis in "The Larger Meaning of China's Crackdown on School Tutoring," *New Yorker,* May 16, 2022, https://www.newyorker.com/culture/culture-desk/the-larger-meaning-of-chinas-crackdown-on-school-tutoring.

For background on China's tech innovation, I relied on Matt Sheehan, "The Chinese Way of Innovation," *Foreign Affairs,* April 21, 2022, https://www.foreignaffairs.com/articles/china/2022-04-21/chinese-way-innovation; and Michael Schuman, "Venture Communism: How China Is Building a Start-Up Boom," *New York Times,* September 3, 2016. For early Western skepticism of Chinese innovation, see Regina M. Abrami, William C. Kirby, and F. Warren McFarlan, "Why China Can't Innovate," *Harvard Business Review,* March 2014, https://hbr.org/2014/03/why-china-cant-innovate.

For background on Zhang Yiming, ByteDance, and the rise of TikTok, I consulted Matthew Brennan, *Attention Factory: The Story of TikTok & China's ByteDance* (independently published, 2020); Alex W. Palmer, "How TikTok Became a Diplomatic Crisis," *New York Times Magazine,* December 20, 2022, https://www.nytimes.com/2022/12/20/magazine/tiktok-us-china-diplomacy.html; and an English translation of a March 20, 2018, interview with Zhang Yiming: Rui Ma, ed., "Bytedance CEO Zhang Yiming at Tsinghua University: Part 1," *Tech Buzz China,* June 3, 2020, https://www.techbuzzchina.com/index.php/2020/06/03/bytedance-ceo-zhang-yiming-at-tsinghua-university-part-1. Zhang's comparison of ByteDance to Facebook and Uber can be found in an interview with Zhang, "Three Things from My Time at Nankai: Patience, Knowledge, and Companionship," *PingWest,* November 17, 2015, https://www.pingwest.com/a/61954. Some of this analysis appeared in my article "Planet TikTok," *New York Review of Books,* July 9, 2024.

CHAPTER 9: Walled Garden

Eric Liu shared his experiences working at Weibo, providing crucial insight into how the company's censorship capacity expanded. For a public account of his observations, see his interview with the Committee to Protect Journalists, Yaqiu Wang, "Read and Delete: How Weibo's Censors Tackle Dissent and Free Speech," March 3, 2016, https://cpj.org/2016/03/read-and-delete -how-weibos-censors-tackle-dissent.

For an account of the *Southern Weekly* incident in 2013, I drew from a range of sources, including David Bandurski, "Inside the Southern Weekly Incident," *China Media Project,* January 7, 2015, https://chinamediaproject .org/2013/01/07/inside-the-southern-weekly-incident; Maria Repnikova and Kecheng Fang, "Behind the Fall of China's Greatest Newspaper," *Foreign Policy,* January 29, 2015, https://foreignpolicy.com/2015/01/29/southern -weekly-china-media-censorship; and Freedom House, "Special Feature: The 'Southern Weekly' Controversy," January 2013, https://freedomhouse.org /report/china-media-bulletin/special-feature-southern-weekly-controversy.

I am thankful to Murong Xuecun for sharing with me his experience of being shut down on Weibo and across multiple Chinese social media platforms. For a public account of his experience, see his essay "Chinese Internet: 'A New Censorship Campaign Has Commenced,'" trans. Helen Gao, *The Guardian,* May 15, 2013, https://www.theguardian.com/world/2013/may /15/chinese-internet-censorship-campaign.

A translation of Document No. 9, formally known as "The Communiqué on the Current State of the Ideological Sphere," can be found in *ChinaFile* at https://www.chinafile.com/document-9-chinafile-translation.

I quote from Perry Link's essay "China: The Anaconda in the Chandelier," *New York Review of Books,* April 11, 2002, https://www.nybooks.com/articles /2002/04/11/china-the-anaconda-in-the-chandelier.

To understand the impact of Edward Snowden's revelations of NSA surveillance on Chinese internet controls, I relied on the analysis by Eli Binder and Katrina Northrop, "The Snowden Effect," *The Wire China,* December 6, 2020, https://www.thewirechina.com/2020/12/06/the-snowden-effect. I also turned to news accounts of the incident published in Reuters, *The Washington Post,* and *South China Morning Post.*

Xi's description of the internet as a "main battlefield" comes from a translation of his August 19, 2013, speech, in *China Copyright and Media,* https:// chinacopyrightandmedia.wordpress.com/2013/11/12/xi-jinpings-19-august

-speech-revealed-translation. The Chinese version can be found in *China Digital Times,* https://chinadigitaltimes.net/chinese/321001.html.

For background on the Cyberspace Administration of China and China's Cybersecurity Law, I consulted PEN America's report *Forbidden Feeds: Government Controls on Social Media in China,* March 15, 2018. Kaiser Kuo's quote on China's regulatory agencies first appeared in that report.

For details on Lu Wei, see Paul Mozur and Jane Perlez, "Gregarious and Direct: China's Web Doorkeeper," *New York Times,* December 1, 2014, https://www.nytimes.com/2014/12/02/world/asia/gregarious-and-direct-chinas-web-doorkeeper.html. Lu Wei's description of the "spiritual garden" can be found in an English translation of his speech "Concentrate Positive Energy Online, Build the Chinese Dream Together," given at the Thirteenth Chinese Online Media Forum on October 30, 2013, and is available via Stanford University's DigiChina Project as "Lu Wei: Concentrate Positive Energy Online, Build the Chinese Dream Together" at https://digichina.stanford.edu/work/lu-wei-concentrate-positive-energy-online-build-the-chinese-dream-together.

To describe the Tianjin factory explosions in 2015, I relied on a firsthand account of the experience from Eric Liu, supplemented by a range of news sources, primarily *The Guardian,* the Associated Press, and the BBC. *China Media Project* and *China Digital Times* provided insights into how the media and censors responded to the incident.

CHAPTER 10: Positive Energy

The term "positive energy" was popularized by Richard Wiseman, *Rip It Up: The Radically New Approach to Changing Your Life* (Macmillan, 2013). To understand its adoption in China, I consulted Zifeng Chen and Clyde Yicheng Wang, "The Discipline of Happiness: The Foucauldian Use of the 'Positive Energy' Discourse in China's Ideological Works," *Journal of Current Chinese Affairs* 48, no. 2 (August 2019): 201–25; and Yang Peidong and Tang Lijun, " 'Positive Energy': Hegemonic Intervention and Online Media Discourse in China's Xi Jinping Era," *China: An International Journal* 16, no. 1 (February 2018): 1–22.

An English translation of Lu Wei's speech "Concentrate Positive Energy Online, Build the Chinese Dream Together," given at the Thirteenth Chinese Online Media Forum on October 30, 2013, is available via Stanford University's DigiChina Project as "Lu Wei: Concentrate Positive Energy Online, Build the Chinese Dream Together" at https://digichina.stanford

.edu/work/lu-wei-concentrate-positive-energy-online-build-the-chinese
-dream-together.

For Papi Jiang's post on positive energy, I referred to Zheping Huang, "China's Satirical Internet Queen Just Sold Her First Video Ad for $3.4 Million," *Quartz*, April 21, 2016, https://qz.com/666657/chinas-satirical -internet-queen-just-sold-her-first-video-ad-for-3-million; Beijing's call for the United States to show more positive energy in the South China Sea comes from Zhang Zhihao, "Beijing Seeks 'Positive Energy' in the South China Sea," *China Daily*, February 24, 2017, https://www.chinadaily.com .cn/china/2017-02/24/content_28328927.htm.

Kafe Hu provided observations and accounts of his life as a hip-hop art- ist in Chengdu from 2012 to 2018. His music from this period includes *The Guy* (independently released, 2014), *27: The Code of Lucifer* (27 路西法密碼) (Mintone Records, 2016), and *Kafreeman* (Modern Sky, 2017).

I am grateful to Bohan Phoenix and Allyson Toy for their perspectives on Chengdu's hip-hop scene from 2015 to 2019. Allyson also helped explain China's digital music landscape. ATM, Young13DBaby, and Hustar shared their experiences as Chengdu-based hip-hop artists. Shuhong Fan, Jake Newby, Wes Chen, and Krish Raghav provided key insights into the rise of Chinese hip-hop and *The Rap of China*'s impact.

Descriptions of Poly Center and Chengdu's nightlife draw from my own reporting and my article "Chengdu Cool: The Rise of Sichuan's Home- grown Hip Hop," *Guernica*, August 29, 2018, https://www.guernicamag .com/chengdu-cool-the-rise-of-sichuans-homegrown-hip-hop.

A video of Fat Shady performing "Daddy Don't Want to Go to Work Tomorrow" 老明天不上班 is available on CCTV's YouTube channel, https:// www.youtube.com/watch?v=KugiopC40ac.

For the rise of *danmei* (Boys' Love) in China, I relied on Sheng Zou, "When a Subculture Goes Pop: Platforms, Mavericks, and Capital in the Production of 'Boys' Love' Web Series in China," *Media Industries* 9, no. 1 (2022).

Descriptions of Kuaishou draw from my article "The Chinese Farmer Who Live-Streamed Her Life and Made a Fortune," *New Yorker*, October 29, 2018, https://www.newyorker.com/culture/culture-desk/the-chinese-farmer -who-live-streamed-her-life-and-made-a-fortune. For the fast-paced nature of online life in China, I consulted Christina Xu, "Bullet Time," *Logic(s)*, May 1, 2019, https://logicmag.io/china/bullet-time.

For the controversy surrounding *The Founding of an Army*, see my reporting in "Chinese Propaganda Faces Stiff Competition from Celebrities," Associated Press, October 22, 2017, https://apnews.com/article /1616c60ab01d43caae024d34cb98d532; and Amy Qin, "China's Pretty Boys Find a New Gig: Propaganda Films," *New York Times,* August 8, 2017, https://www.nytimes.com/2017/08/08/world/asia/china-founding-army -xiao-xian-rou-oho-ou-lu-han.html.

The term "the Streisand Effect" was coined by Mike Masnick in his blog post "Since When Is It Illegal to Just Mention a Trademark Online?," *Techdirt,* January 5, 2005.

The Higher Brothers' music video of "Made in China" is available at https://www.youtube.com/watch?v=rILKm-DC06A. GAI's tryout performance for the CCTV Spring Festival Gala is posted at https://www.youtube .com/watch?v=wTezYyU_zbU&t=2301s.

The list of banned topics by the China Netcasting Services Association from July 1, 2017, is available at http://www.xinhuanet.com//zgjx/2017-07 /01/c_136409024.htm. For analysis, see Steven Lee Myers and Amy Cheng, "68 Things You Cannot Say on China's Internet," *New York Times,* September 24, 2017, https://www.nytimes.com/2017/09/24/world/asia/china -internet-censorship.html.

For the origins and evolution of the Little Pinks, I relied on Kecheng Fang and Maria Repnikova, "Demystifying 'Little Pink': The Creation and Evolution of a Gendered Label for Nationalistic Activists in China," *New Media & Society* 20, no. 6 (June 2018): 2162–85; and Freya Ge and David Ownby's translation of Yu Liang's "The Genealogy and Ecology of the Little Pinks, and the Future of Chinese Youth" (*Beijing Cultural Review,* May 2021) in "Yu Liang on 'Little Pinks,' " *Reading the China Dream,* no date, https:// www.readingthechinadream.com/yu-liang-on-little-pinks.html.

For background on and the quote from Eric Li, I turned to Han Zhang, "An International Spokesman for Chinese Nationalism," *Dissent Magazine,* Spring 2022.

CHAPTER 11: Burning Out

Chen Qiufan (Stanley Chan) generously shared his observations on the rise of Chinese science fiction from 2012 to 2019. Some passages appeared in my article "Sci-Fi Writer or Prophet?: The Hyperreal Life," *WIRED,* March 9, 2021, https://www.wired.com/story/science-fiction-writer-china -chen-qiufan. Descriptions of the 2016 Science Fiction Conference draw from 科普大视野, 2016中国科幻大会在京召开, https://mp.weixin.qq.com /s/fktRRQkNiqxmcRpCVC7eGg.

To understand Stanley's writing during this period, I consulted Chen Qiufan's *The Waste Tide* in the original, 荒潮, 陈楸帆 (Shanghai Literature & Art Publishing House, 2013); Chen Qiufan, *The Waste Tide,* trans. Ken Liu (Tor Books, 2019); and Ken Liu, ed. and trans., *Invisible Planets: An Anthology of Contemporary Chinese Science Fiction in Translation* (Tor Books, 2016).

For details on Li Yuanchao's speech at the 2016 Science Fiction convention, I consulted "李源潮勉励科普科幻工作者 为建设世界科技强国播撒科学种" (Li Yuanchao Encourages Popular Science and Science-Fiction Workers to Sow the Seeds of Science for Building a World-Leading Science and Technology Power,) *Xinhua News Agency,* September 8, 2016, http://www.xinhuanet.com/politics/2016-09/08/c_1119534479.htm.

I am grateful to Ken Liu, Emily Jin, Jing Tsu, and Kai-Fu Lee for sharing their insights on Chinese science fiction and Chen's career. For additional perspectives on Stanley's work, I consulted Ken Liu, "Staying Sensitive in the Crowd: A Conversation with Chen Qiufan," *Clarkesworld,* March 2015, https://clarkesworldmagazine.com/chen_interview; and Cara Healey, "Estranging Realism in Chinese Science Fiction: Hybridity and Environmentalism in Chen Qiufan's *The Waste Tide,*" *Modern Chinese Literature and Culture* 29, no. 2 (2017): 1–33.

Liu Cixin's comparison of China to the United States during sci-fi's golden age comes from his essay "The Worst of All Possible Universes and the Best of All Possible Earths: Three Body and Chinese Science Fiction," *Reactor,* May 7, 2014, https://reactormag.com/the-worst-of-all-possible-universes-and-the-best-of-all-possible-earths-three-body-and-chinese-science-fiction. I also consulted his novel *The Three-Body Problem,* trans. Ken Liu (Tor Books, 2014).

For background on Hao Jingfang, I read her short story "Folding Beijing," trans. Ken Liu, in *Uncanny Magazine,* January/February 2015, https://uncannymagazine.com/article/folding-beijing; and her novel *Vagabonds,* trans. Ken Liu (Gallery/Saga Press, 2020). I also consulted Deborah Stanish, "Interview: Hao Jingfang," *Uncanny Magazine,* January/February 2015, https://www.uncannymagazine.com/article/interview-hao-jingfang; and "三体2" 无缘本届雨果奖. . . . . . 别失落,我们还有她, 不存在日报, archived here: https://web.archive.org/web/20170613021754/http://www.guokr.com/post/730262.

To understand China's rural-urban divide and its impact on the migrant workforce, I relied on Scott Rozelle and Natalie Hell, *Invisible China: How the Urban-Rural Divide Threatens China's Rise* (University of Chicago Press, 2020).

Descriptions of the Daxing migrant evictions and the RYB kindergarten scandal draw from my 2017 reporting for the Associated Press, as well as coverage in Caixin Global, *The Guardian, The New York Times,* and *China Digital Times.*

Chen Qiufan's experience at Burning Man is detailed in his essay "The Chinese Burner," *Logic(s),* May 1, 2019, https://logicmag.io/china/the-chinese-burner. Kai-Fu Lee's insights on Chinese tech companies are from his *AI Superpowers: China, Silicon Valley, and the New World Order* (Houghton Mifflin Harcourt, 2018).

For the background and transnational influence of the 996.ICU movement, I consulted Jek Tan and Moira Weigel, "Organizing in (and Against) a New Cold War: The Case of 996.ICU," in Mark Graham and Fabian Ferrari, eds., *Digital Work in the Planetary Market* (MIT Press, 2022). Descriptions of GitHub's role in Chinese activism draw from my article "In China, GitHub Is a Free Speech Zone for Covid Information," *WIRED,* September 9, 2020, https://www.wired.com/story/china-github-free-speech-covid-information.

CHAPTER 12: Going Underground

Lü Pin generously shared with me an account of her life in the United States after the detention of the Feminist Five from 2015 to 2019. Descriptions of her experience during this time also draw from "Feminism and Social Change in China: An Interview with Lü Pin (Part 3 of 3)," *China Change,* October 1, 2019, https://chinachange.org/2019/10/01/feminism-and-social-change-in-china-an-interview-with-lu-pin-part-3-of-3; Lü Pin, "Finding a Voice," *Logic(s),* May 1, 2019, https://logicmag.io/china/finding-a-voice; and her essay 呂頻:見證中國女權二十年, 端傳媒 in *Initium Media,* August 14, 2020, https://theinitium.com/article/20200814-opinion-china-feminist-movement-20-years.

For an account of the detention of the Feminist Five, I relied on Leta Hong Fincher, *Betraying Big Brother: The Feminist Awakening in China* (Verso Books, 2018). Wei Tingting's account drew from the video "Interview with Wei Tingting," University of Michigan Global Feminisms Project, May 2019, https://deepblue.lib.umich.edu/handle/2027.42/171770. I refer to reports on the detention by Tania Branigan, "Five Chinese Feminists Held over International Women's Day Plans," *Guardian,* March 12, 2015, https://www.theguardian.com/world/2015/mar/12/five-chinese-feminists-held-international-womens-day; and by Emily Rauhala, "Five Feminists Remain Jailed in China for Activities the Government Supports," *TIME,* March 19,

2015, https://time.com/3750389/china-feminists-international-womens-day
-wu-rongrong-wei-tingting-wang-man-zheng-churan-li-tingting.

Xiao Meili and Guo Jing shared with me their observations and experiences of China's feminist movement after the detentions, from 2016 to 2019. Zheng Churan's open letter to Donald Trump is archived at https://web.archive.org/web/20170913200736/https://mp.weixin.qq.com/s/_MQmJ55cy3QlE5i1tPDTOQ. On morality schools, see my story "Rise of 'Morality Schools' for Chinese Women Sparks Outcry," Associated Press, February 1, 2018, https://apnews.com/article/877193b3121c4c4a988ba7aad66f8283.

To understand China's feminist movement in the Chinese diaspora, I turned to Shen Lu, "Thwarted at Home, Can China's Feminists Rebuild a Movement Abroad?," *ChinaFile*, August 28, 2019, https://www.chinafile.com/reporting-opinion/postcard/thwarted-home-can-chinas-feminists-rebuild-movement-abroad. Xiao Meili's quote was from this article.

For background on Xi's extension of constitutional term limits, I consulted Susan L. Shirk, "China in Xi's New Era: The Return to Personalistic Rule," *Journal of Democracy* 29, no. 2 (April 2018): 22–36. For the broader implications of Xi's leadership, I consulted Yuen Yuen Ang, "How Resilient Is the CCP?," *Journal of Democracy* 33, no. 3 (2022): 77–91.

For discussions of the *fang-shou* cycle of liberalization and repression, I consulted Richard Baum, *Burying Mao: Chinese Politics in the Age of Deng Xiaoping* (Princeton University Press, 2018); David Shambaugh, *China's Future* (Polity Press, 2016); an interview with Shambaugh on the War on the Rocks website's podcast *Jaw-Jaw*, "Vicious Cycle: The Opening and Closing of Chinese Politics," December 11, 2018, https://warontherocks.com/2018/12/jaw-jaw-vicious-cycle-the-opening-and-closing-of-chinese-politics; and Sungmin Cho, "The Fang-Shou Cycle in Chinese Politics," in Alexander L. Vuving, ed., *Hindsight, Insight, Foresight: Thinking About Security in the Indo-Pacific* (Daniel K. Inouye Asia-Pacific Center for Security Studies, 2020), pp. 269–82.

Perry Link's quote appears in his essay "Why We Remember June Fourth," *ChinaFile*, May 28, 2019, https://www.chinafile.com/reporting-opinion/viewpoint/why-we-remember-june-fourth.

CHAPTER 13: Speech Tax

Kafe Hu generously shared an account of his personal life and hip-hop career from 2019 to 2022. He also showed me around his childhood home in

Jiangyou. I reference several of his songs, including "Far" (远), *27: The Code of Lucifer* (27 路西法密碼) (Mintone Records, 2016), https://music.apple .com/tw/song/%E9%81%81%A0/1578282819; and "Hope and Reality" (所希 望和实际上), *The Guy* (independent release, 2014), https://www.youtube .com/watch?v=IGZDD8HppkE. His performance of "Economy Class" 经 济舱 on *The Rap of China* is available here: https://www.youtube.com/watch ?v=X8COjmk4Jkg.

Bohan Phoenix and J-Fever provided valuable accounts of their experience making music and performing during the pandemic. Krish Raghav, Jake Newby, Wes Chen, and Shuhong Fan provided crucial insights into how the music scene has evolved in recent years.

Descriptions of the Hong Kong protests, in particular the quote from the local activist about speaking Putonghua, drew from my reporting in "Dream State: The Radical Imagination of the Hong Kong Protest Movement," *Harper's Magazine,* April 30, 2020, https://harpers.org/archive/2020 /05/dream-state-hong-kong-protests.

For incidents of Chinese celebrities and rappers speaking in support of the government, I consulted a range of sources, including Echo Huang, "After a Chinese Flag Was Thrown into the Sea, Hong Kong Celebrities Flex Their Patriotic Muscles," *Quartz,* August 7, 2019, https://qz.com/1682950/hong -kong-celebrities-vow-to-protect-chinese-flag-on-weibo; and *RADII* Staff, "China's Biggest Rappers Are Posting an Anti–Hong Kong Protest Meme," *RADII,* August 15, 2019, https://radii.co/article/china-rappers-hong-kong -protest-meme. The rap song "Hong Kong's Fall" was posted on YouTube by China Global Television Network, no date, https://www.youtube.com/watch ?v=D0Ck3XcrrtM. Descriptions draw from my reporting in "Why Chinese Rappers Don't Fight the Power," BBC, November 6, 2019, https://www.bbc .com/culture/article/20191106-why-chinese-rappers-dont-fight-the-power.

For background on Wang Xiaobo, I relied on Wang's "The Silent Majority," trans. Eric Abrahamsen, in Wang Xiaobo, *Pleasure of Thinking: Essays* (Penguin Classics, 2023), pp. 195–224; and Sebastien Veg, *Minjian: The Rise of China's Grassroots Intellectuals* (Columbia University Press, 2019). I compare Wang's ideas to those in Václav Havel's essay "The Power of the Powerless," in *The Power of the Powerless: Citizens Against the State in Central-Eastern Europe,* trans. Paul Wilson (Routledge, 2016).

For the controversy around Fang Fang, see Fang Fang, *Wuhan Diary: Dispatches from a Quarantined City,* trans. Michael Berry (HarperVia, 2020).

The poll on Chinese citizens' trust of their government references Cary Wu, Zhilei Shi, Rima Wilkes, Jiaji Wu, Zhiwen Gong, Nengkun He et al.,

"Chinese Citizen Satisfaction with Government Performance During COVID-19," *Journal of Contemporary China* 30, no. 132 (2021): 930–44.

To understand the ideas of Ren Yi, I read his blogs under the alias "Chairman Rabbit," especially 美国的革命、制度陷阱与中国要汲取的教训, available at https://web.archive.org/web/20201030055546/https:/mp.weixin.qq.com/s/5wQzdfCYdQ3InHfHhMt2VA. I also relied on the insights and translations of Tianyi Xu, "Chairman Rabbit: China's 'Cosmopolitan Patriot,'" *ChinaTalk*, February 27, 2021, https://www.chinatalk.media/p/chairman-rabbit-chinas-cosmopolitan.

To understand the evolution of Chinese nationalist sentiment, I consulted Alec Ash, "China's New Nationalism," *Wire China*, August 8, 2021, https://www.thewirechina.com/2021/08/08/chinas-new-nationalism. The paper I reference that discusses Chinese students' supporting their government after experiencing discrimination is by Yingjie Fan, Jennifer Pan, Zijie Shao, and Yiqing Xu, "How Discrimination Increases Chinese Overseas Students' Support for Authoritarian Rule," 21st Century China Center Research Paper No. 2020-05, June 29, 2020, https://ssrn.com/abstract=3637710.

For background on Chinese dissidents and intellectuals supporting Trump, I relied on Yao Lin, "Beaconism and the Trumpian Metamorphosis of Chinese Liberal Intellectuals," *Journal of Contemporary China* 30, no. 127 (2021): 85–101; and Ian Johnson, "Why Do Chinese Liberals Embrace American Conservatives?," *New York Times*, November 18, 2020, https://www.nytimes.com/2020/11/18/opinion/trump-chinese-liberals-biden.html.

Sun Liping's quote comes from "整个世界可能都忽视了这个信号:谈特朗普对政治正确的冲击" (The Whole World May Have Missed This Signal: On Trump's Attack on Political Correctness), *Liping Guancha*, February 17, 2019, https://2newcenturynet.blogspot.com/2019/02/blog-post_407.html.

CHAPTER 14: Swimming Against the Current

Chen Qiufan shared with me an account of his experiences and his writing life during the pandemic. Some passages in this book have previously appeared in my article "Sci-Fi Writer or Prophet?: The Hyperreal Life," *WIRED,* March 9, 2021, https://www.wired.com/story/science-fiction-writer-china-chen-qiufan. I also reference several of his works, including: "The Year of the Rat" 鼠年, in Ken Liu, ed. and trans., *Invisible Planets: An Anthology of Contemporary Chinese Science Fiction in Translation* (Tor Books, 2016); "The Fish of Lijiang" (丽江的鱼儿们), trans. Ken Liu, *Clarkesworld*, August 2011, https://clarkesworldmagazine.com/chen_08_11; and Kai-Fu Lee and Chen Qiufan, *AI 2041: Ten Visions for Our Future* (Currency, 2021).

Ken Liu, Jing Tsu, Emily Jin, and Kai-Fu Lee shared invaluable insights into Chen's writing life and the evolution of Chinese science fiction in recent years. "We do the works a disservice . . ." was quoted from the introduction of Ken Liu, ed. and trans., *Invisible Planets: Contemporary Chinese Science Fiction in Translation* (Tor Books, 2016).

Xiang Biao explained the term "involution" to me. I first learned of it from an interview with Biao by *The Paper,* October 22, 2020, 人类学家项飙谈内卷:一种不允许失败和退出的竞争, 澎湃新闻, https://www.thepaper.cn/newsDetail_forward_9648585. Analysis of the term draws from my article "China's 'Involuted' Generation," *New Yorker,* May 14, 2021, https://www.newyorker.com/culture/cultural-comment/chinas-involuted-generation.

The 2021 survey of 1,500 Americans comes from Kristy Threlkeld, "Employee Burnout Report: COVID-19's Impact and 3 Strategies to Curb It," Indeed, March 10, 2021, https://www.indeed.com/lead/preventing-employee-burnout-report.

Descriptions of Li Ziqi draw from my article "She Drew Millions of TikTok Followers by Selling a Fantasy of Rural China. Then Politics Intervened," *Rest of World,* November 1, 2021, https://restofworld.org/2021/tiktok-china-influencer-liziqi.

For background on "lying flat," I consulted a range of sources, especially J. S. Tan, "Tech Workers Lie Flat," *Dissent,* Spring 2022, https://www.dissentmagazine.org/article/tech-workers-lie-flat; Elsie Chen, "躺平学大师":一个好的社会是可上可下的, 纽约时报中文网, https://cn.nytimes.com/china/20210714/lying-flat-in-china); Elsie Chen, "These Chinese Millennials Are 'Chilling,' and Beijing Isn't Happy," *New York Times,* July 3, 2021, https://www.nytimes.com/2021/07/03/world/asia/china-slackers-tangping.html; and Anonymous, "Tangpingist Manifesto," The Anarchist Library, 2021, https://theanarchistlibrary.org/library/anonymous-tangpingist-manifesto. An archived screenshot of the "Lying Flat Is Justice" post is available here: https://web.archive.org/web/20210807101130/https://gnews.org/zh-hant/1275088.

CHAPTER 15: Retreating Ashore

Ma Baoli and Shen Wenjie shared their accounts of Blued's IPO party. I am grateful to Ma for inviting me to the company's twentieth-anniversary gathering for insight into the company and its employees.

Darius Longarino, Zhijun Hu, and Yanzi Peng shared valuable insights on the future of LGBTQ advocacy in China. For background on how the space for LGBTQ advocacy has evolved from 2019 onward, I relied on Darius's "Precarious Progress: Advocacy for the Human Rights of LGBT People in China," Outright International, December 16, 2020, https://outrightinternational.org/our-work/human-rights-research/precarious-progress-advocacy-human-rights-lgbt-people-china; and the Outright International report "Fading Rainbow: A Q&A on LGBTQ Equality in China," February 7, 2022, https://outrightinternational.org/our-work/human-rights-research/fading-rainbow-qa-lgbtq-equality-china.

Descriptions of Hupan University are drawn from my visit to the campus with Ma Baoli and his cohort. They also draw from reporting I conducted for "Why the Chinese Government Turned on Jack Ma's 'Harvard for China,'" *Rest of World,* June 28, 2021, https://restofworld.org/2021/why-the-chinese-government-turned-on-jack-mas-harvard-for-china. For background on Hupan, see Jill Shen, "Jack Ma's Hupan University Kicks Off New Class, Includes Horizon Robotics CEO," *TechNode,* March 26, 2019, https://technode.com/2019/03/26/jack-ma-hupan-new-students; and Biyi and Yan, "Jack Ma and Hupan University: Cultivating the Next Generation of Chinese Entrepreneurs Through Failure Education," *Elephant Room,* April 12, 2017, http://elephant-room.com/2017/04/12/hupan.

Passages on the crackdown on Big Tech and the common prosperity campaigns previously appeared in my article "The Larger Meaning of China's Crackdown on School Tutoring," *New Yorker,* May 16, 2022, https://www.newyorker.com/culture/culture-desk/the-larger-meaning-of-chinas-crackdown-on-school-tutoring.

Dan Wang shared valuable insights on the Party's common prosperity drive; his quote "make babies, make steel, and make semiconductors" was first published in his blog's 2021 annual letter, https://danwang.co/2021-letter. For background on common prosperity, I also turned to Kaiser Kuo, Jeremy Goldkorn, Lizzi Lee, and Jude Blanchette's *Sinica Podcast* "What's the Deal with the Red New Deal," *The China Project,* https://thechinaproject.com/podcast/whats-the-deal-with-the-red-new-deal.

A translation of Li Guangman's August 2021 essay on the second cultural revolution, "Everyone Can Sense That a Profound Transformation Is Underway!," is available through *China Digital Times,* https://chinadigitaltimes.net/2021/08/translation-everyone-can-sense-that-a-profound-transformation-is-underway. For a translation of Xi Jinping's common prosperity speech, see "Full Text: Xi Jinping's Speech on Boosting Common Prosperity," Caixin

Global, October 19, 2021, https://www.caixinglobal.com/2021-10-19/full
-text-xi-jinpings-speech-on-boosting-common-prosperity-101788302.html.

For background on Wang Huning, I relied on the English translation
of his *America Against America* (independently published, 2022); and N. S.
Lyons, "The Triumph and Terror of Wang Huning," *Palladium Magazine,*
October 11, 2021, https://www.palladiummag.com/2021/10/11/the-triumph
-and-terror-of-wang-huning.

I am grateful to Guo Jing for sharing her experience as a feminist activist and her life in Wuhan during the lockdown. For Guo's own written
account of this period, see Guo Jing, 武漢封城日記 (*Diary of the Wuhan
Lockdown*) (Taipei: Linking Publishing, 2020). Passages about Guo and the
feminist movement during the pandemic appeared in my article "Solidarity
Now, Solidarity Through Screens," *Rest of World,* January 24, 2021, https://
restofworld.org/2021/solidarity-now-solidarity-through-screens.

Lü Pin, Xiao Meili, and Feng Yuan shared crucial observations and
accounts of how the feminist movement evolved from 2018 to 2022.

For background on China's #MeToo movement, I relied on a range of
academic and news sources, especially Jing Zeng, "You Say #MeToo, I Say
#MiTu: China's Online Campaigns Against Sexual Abuse," in Bianca File-
born and Rachel Loney-Howes, eds., *#MeToo and the Politics of Social Change*
(Palgrave Macmillan, 2019), pp. 71–83; Han Zhang, "One Year of #MeToo:
How the Movement Eludes Government Surveillance in China," *New Yorker,*
October 10, 2018, https://www.newyorker.com/news/news-desk/one-year
-of-metoo-how-the-movement-eludes-government-surveillance-in-china;
Shen Lu, "Thwarted at Home, Can China's Feminists Rebuild a Movement
Abroad?," *ChinaFile,* August 28, 2019, https://www.chinafile.com/reporting
-opinion/postcard/thwarted-home-can-chinas-feminists-rebuild-movement
-abroad.

Xianzi's Weibo post about her experience with sexual harassment is
archived and translated in "Weibo Exposed CCTV Host Zhu Jun to Sexually
Harass Interns," *China Digital Times,* July 25, 2018, https://chinadigitaltimes
.net/chinese/590459.html.

To understand how China's feminist movement mobilized online, I consulted Aviva Wei Xue and Kate Rose, *Weibo Feminism: Expression, Activism,
and Social Media in China* (Bloomsbury Publishing, 2022); Hongwei Bao,
"'Anti–Domestic Violence Little Vaccine': A Wuhan-Based Feminist Activ-

ist Campaign During COVID-19," *Interface* 12, no. 1 (July 2020): 53–63; Wanqing Zhang, "Heavily Persecuted, Highly Influential: China's Online Feminist Revolution," *Rest of World,* September 26, 2023, https://restofworld .org/2023/china-online-feminist-movement.

Guo Yuhua's farewell letter can be found at Guo Yuhua, "Farewell Sina Weibo," trans. David Ownby, *Reading the China Dream,* June 8, 2020, https://www.readingthechinadream.com/guo-yuhua-farewell-sina-weibo .html.

For background on Xiao Meili's experience with online harassment, I read Yifan Yu, "Xiao Meili Asked a Man to Stop Smoking—China's Right Wing Went Berserk," *Nikkei Asia,* May 15, 2021, https://asia.nikkei.com/Life-Arts /Life/Xiao-Meili-asked-a-man-to-stop-smoking-China-s-right-wing-went -berserk; and "Weibo Is 'Treating the Incels Like the Royal Family,'" *Protocol,* April 15, 2021, https://web.archive.org/web/20240205044727/https://www .protocol.com/china/weibo-incels. Zheng Churan's public response to the incident, archived and translated by *China Digital Times* as "You Only Live Once: We're Scared, We're Brave, We'll Keep on Trying," is available here: https://chinadigitaltimes.net/2021/05/translation-were-scared-were-brave -well-keep-on-trying-by-zheng-churan.

On censorship of Peng Shuai, see Alexander Boyd and Alex Yu, "Inside Peng Shuai's Accusation Against Former Top Leader: #MeToo, Censorship, and Resistance Discourse," *China Digital Times,* November 4, 2021, https:// chinadigitaltimes.net/2021/11/inside-peng-shuais-accusation-against-former -top-leader-metoo-censorship-and-resistance-discourse.

CHAPTER 17: Closed Loop

Eric Liu shared with me his experience leaving China at the start of the pandemic, details of his life in California, and his observations on Chinese censorship while working as an editor at *China Digital Times.*

For background on the closed-loop system, I consulted Eli Friedman, "Escape from the Closed Loop," *Boston Review,* November 28, 2022, https:// www.bostonreview.net/articles/escape-from-the-closed-loop.

For the Shanghai lockdown, I drew from a range of news sources, interviews, personal accounts, and social media posts, particularly the Chinese English-language online publication *Sixth Tone*'s interactive feature "Memory Project: The Shanghai Lockdown," June 22, 2022, https://interaction .sixthtone.com/feature/2022/Memory-Project-The-Shanghai-Lockdown; the viral video *Shanghai Voices of April* 上海四月之声, YouTube, April 23,

2022, https://www.youtube.com/watch?v=UtJzvJBZZ4M; Dan Wang and Silvia Lindtner, "Locked Down in Shanghai," *New York,* April 13, 2022, https://nymag.com/intelligencer/2022/04/locked-down-in-shanghai.html.

The statistic that at least 170 people died not from the virus but as a result of lockdown measures comes from *Initium Media,* 上海疫情線上紀念館:人們因什麼而逝去? (Shanghai Pandemic Online Memorial: What Are People Dying For?), https://theinitium.com/project/20220506-mainland-covid-shanghai-lockdown.

I consulted Albert O. Hirschman's *Exit, Voice, and Loyalty: Responses to Decline in Firms, Organizations, and States* (Harvard University Press, 1970). I first encountered this framework as a way to understand Chinese people's predicament under zero-Covid policies through Yuan Li's conversation with Wu Guoguang in the *Bumingbai* podcast 不明白播客, "EP-021 吴国光:极权时代反抗的可能性," (EP-021 Wu Guoguang: The Possibility of Resistance in the Totalitarian Era), October 14, 2022, https://www.bumingbai.net/2022/10/ep-021-wu-guoguang-text.

To understand the "run philosophy" phenomenon, I consulted the Git-Hub page The Run Philosophy Organization, https://github.com/The-Run-Philosophy-Organization/run; "China's Young Elite Are Considering Moving Abroad," *The Economist*, May 5, 2022, https://www.economist.com/china/2022/05/05/chinas-young-elite-are-considering-moving-abroad; Wenxin Fan and Shen Lu, "Determined to Flee China, Thousands Take a Long, Dangerous Route to the Southern U.S. Border," *Wall Street Journal,* April 16, 2023, https://www.wsj.com/articles/determined-to-flee-china-thousands-take-a-long-dangerous-route-to-the-southern-u-s-border-73acfbe9; Yoojung Lee and Anuchit Nguyen, "International School Worth Close to $1 Billion Turns CEO into Multimillionare," *Bloomberg News,* https://www.bloomberg.com/news/articles/2023-07-05/international-school-worth-close-to-1-billion-becomes-magnet-for-china-s-rich; and Dake Kang, Yuri Kageyama, Caterina Morbiato, and Huizhong Wu, "China's New Migrants," AP News, https://apnews.com/projects/china-migration-thailand-mexico-japan-map.

The statistic from Henley and Partners comes from Denise Ng, *East Asia: Q3 2022 Investment Migration Insights,* Henley & Partners, 2022, https://www.henleyglobal.com/publications/henley-global-citizens-report/2022-q3/regional-insights/east-asia-q3-2022-investment-migration-insights.

For the *bailan* meme, see Vincent Ni, "The Rise of 'Bai Lan': Why China's Frustrated Youth Are Ready to 'Let It Rot,'" *The Guardian,* May 25, 2022, https://www.theguardian.com/world/2022/may/26/the-rise-of-bai-lan

-why-chinas-frustrated-youth-are-ready-to-let-it-rot. The "We Are the Last Generation" video, archived by *China Digital Times*, is available at https://chinadigitaltimes.net/2022/05/were-the-last-generation-becomes-a-slogan-for-chinas-disenchanted.

For discussion of the Party's 20th National Congress, I relied on Yuen Yuen Ang, "An Era Just Ended in China," *New York Times,* October 26, 2022, https://www.nytimes.com/2022/10/26/opinion/china-communist-xi-economy.html. The quote from the government official comes from Yuen Yuen Ang, "The Robber Barons of Beijing," *Foreign Affairs,* June 22, 2021, https://www.foreignaffairs.com/articles/asia/2021-06-22/robber-barons-beijing.

For the first viral article on my social media feeds about the Urumqi fires, see 桃花潭李白, 路是通的,他们不跑, archived by *China Digital Times,* November 25, 2022, https://chinadigitaltimes.net/chinese/690102.html.

For a description of the protester at the Communication University of China Nanjing, see Wenxin Fan, "China Protesters Face Possible Criminal Charges," *Wall Street Journal,* December 14, 2022, https://www.wsj.com/articles/in-chinese-protests-aftermath-some-people-could-face-criminal-charges-11671022802.

To reconstruct the White Paper protests, I relied on numerous social media posts, interviews, and personal accounts, particularly the Twitter account of Teacher Li 李老师不是你老师 @whyyoutouzhele; Yuan Li's *Bumingbai* podcast, "EP-027 那些年轻的抗议者:我们为什么要上街," November 2022, https://www.bumingbai.net/2022/11/ep-027-china-protestors-text; and Li Houchen's book 疫年紀事:2022上海封城到白紙革命 (*Chronicle of the Plague Year: From the 2022 Shanghai Lockdown to the White Paper Revolution*) (independently published, 2023).

For further accounts of the White Paper protests, I drew from Vivian Wang, "A Protest? A Vigil? In Beijing, Anxious Crowds Are Unsure How Far to Go," *New York Times,* November 28, 2022, https://www.nytimes.com/2022/11/28/world/asia/china-protests-covid-beijing.html; Chang Che and Amy Chang Chien, "Memes, Puns and Blank Sheets of Paper: China's Creative Acts of Protest," *New York Times,* November 28, 2022, https://www.nytimes.com/2022/11/28/world/asia/china-protests-blank-sheets.html; Agnes Chang and Chang Che, "What China's Protesters Are Calling For," *New York Times,* November 29, 2022, https://www.nytimes.com/interactive/2022/11/29/world/asia/china-protests-demands.html; and Viola Zhou and Meaghan Tobin, "Graffiti, Flyers, Word of Mouth: China's Protesters Embrace Low-Tech Organizing to Escape Surveillance," *Rest of*

World, December 1, 2022, https://restofworld.org/2022/china-covid-protests -surveillance.

For online actions by the Chinese diaspora, I relied on Instagram accounts @CitizenDailyCN, @Northern_Square, and @whatsup_beijing. The "I was there in 1989" Instagram post is available at https://www.instagram.com /p/Clly4Gjrwlf/?hl=en&img_index=1. For an analysis of Instagram's role in Chinese-diaspora protests, see Caiwei Chen, "Instagram Is a Site of Protest for the Chinese Diaspora," *WIRED,* December 16, 2022, https://www.wired .com/story/china-protests-a4-memes-instagram.

For analysis of the White Paper protests, comparisons to the Tiananmen Square movement, and the Party's "divide and conquer" strategy, I consulted Yasheng Huang, "Xi Broke the Social Contract That Helped China Prosper," *New York Times,* December 1, 2022, https://www.nytimes.com/2022/12/01 /opinion/china-covid-protests.html; and Yuen Yuen Ang, "The Problem with Zero: How Xi's Pandemic Policy Created a Crisis for the Regime," *Foreign Affairs,* December 2, 2022, https://www.foreignaffairs.com/china/problem -zero-xi-pandemic-policy-crisis.

Feng Yuan provided key insights into the role of women in the White Paper protests. I also consulted Shen Lu and Liyan Qi, "In China, Young Women Become Accidental Symbols of Defiance," *Wall Street Journal,* January 25, 2023, https://www.wsj.com/articles/in-china-young-women-become -accidental-symbols-of-defiance-11674667983.

Lü Pin's quotations were drawn from her essay 吕频:被挫败的女权运 动如何催生出新一代'白纸革命'者, *Wainao,* March 7, 2023, https://www .wainao.me/wainao-reads/thwarted-feminist-movement-spawned-white -paper-revolutionaries-03072023; an English translation by David Ownby, *Lü Pin on Feminism and the Blank Paper Revolution,* is available at *Reading the China Dream,* https://www.readingthechinadream.com/luuml-pin-on -feminism-and-the-blank-paper-revolution.html.

EPILOGUE

To understand the "shrinking" of the Chinese internet, I referred to He Jiayan's essay 中文互联网正在加速崩, archived here: https://web.archive.org/web /20240523001943/https:/mp.weixin.qq.com/s/afg3zHPpEyRzSfOR1Aeh3w. I also consulted David Bandurki's analysis in "Goldfish Memories," *China Media Project,* May 27, 2024, https://chinamediaproject.org/2024/05/27 /goldfish-memories; and statistics on the shrinking number of Chinese web-sites come from Yuan Li, "As China's Internet Disappears, 'We Lose Parts

of Our Collective Memory,'" *New York Times,* June 4, 2024, https://www
.nytimes.com/2024/06/04/business/china-internet-censorship.html.

I turned to *China Digital Times* as a crucial archive of sensitive words
banned on the Chinese internet. I also referred to its eBook by Alexander
Boyd, Cindy Carter, Arthur Kaufman, Josh Rudolph, Samual Wade, Xiao
Qiang, and Alex Yu, *China Digital Times Lexicon, 20th Anniversary Edition*
(China Digital Times, 2023).

Tadeusz Konwicki's quote "the literature becomes increasingly more
obscure" is noted in J. M. Coetzee, *Giving Offense: Essays on Censorship* (University of Chicago Press, 1996), p. 149.

I quote from Perry Link's essay "China: The Anaconda in the Chandelier,"
New York Review of Books, April 11, 2002, https://www.nybooks.com/articles
/2002/04/11/china-the-anaconda-in-the-chandelier.

I am grateful to Susan for sharing her perspective and experience with me.

Index

About the Author

Yi-Ling Liu's work has been published in *The New York Times Magazine, The New Yorker, Harper's Magazine, WIRED,* and *The New York Review of Books.* She has been a New America Fellow, a recipient of the Matthew Power Literary Reporting Award, and an Overseas Press Club Foundation Scholar. Born and raised in Hong Kong and a graduate of Yale University, she now lives in London.

A Note on the Text

This book was set in Adobe Garamond. Designed for the Adobe Corporation by Robert Slimbach, the fonts are based on types first cut by Claude Garamond (ca. 1480–1561). It is to Slimbach that we owe the letter we now know as "old style." He gave to his letters an elegance and feeling of movement that won him an immediate reputation and the patronage of Francis I of France.

Typeset by Scribe, Philadelphia, PA

Designed by Betty Lew